The Empty Sleeve

The story of The West India Regiments of the British Army

Brian Dyde

First published in 1997 by Hansib Caribbean
PO Box 2773, St John's, Antigua WI
Distributed in the United Kingdom by Readers Book Club
Tower House, 141-149 Fonthill Road, London N4 3HF
Printed in the United Kingdom by Hillman Printers, Frome

British Library Cataloguing in Publication Data.
A Catalogue record for this book is available from the British Library

ISBN 976-8163-09-7

BY THE SAME AUTHOR

Antigua and Barbuda: Heart of the Caribbean

Islands to the Windward: Five Gems of the Caribbean

St Kitts: Cradle of the Caribbean

Caribbean Companion: The A-Z Reference

This book is dedicated to
my beloved wife and best friend
Veronica

In the small coffin of his house, the pensioner,
A veteran of the African campaign,
Bends, as if threading an eternal needle:
One-eyed as any grave, his skull, cropped wool,
Or lifts his desert squint to hear
The children singing, "Rule, Britannia, rule,"
As if they needed practise to play dead.
Boys will still pour their blood out for a sieve
Despite his balsam eye and doddering jaw;
And if one eye should weep, would they believe
In such a poor flag as an empty sleeve?

Derek Walcott

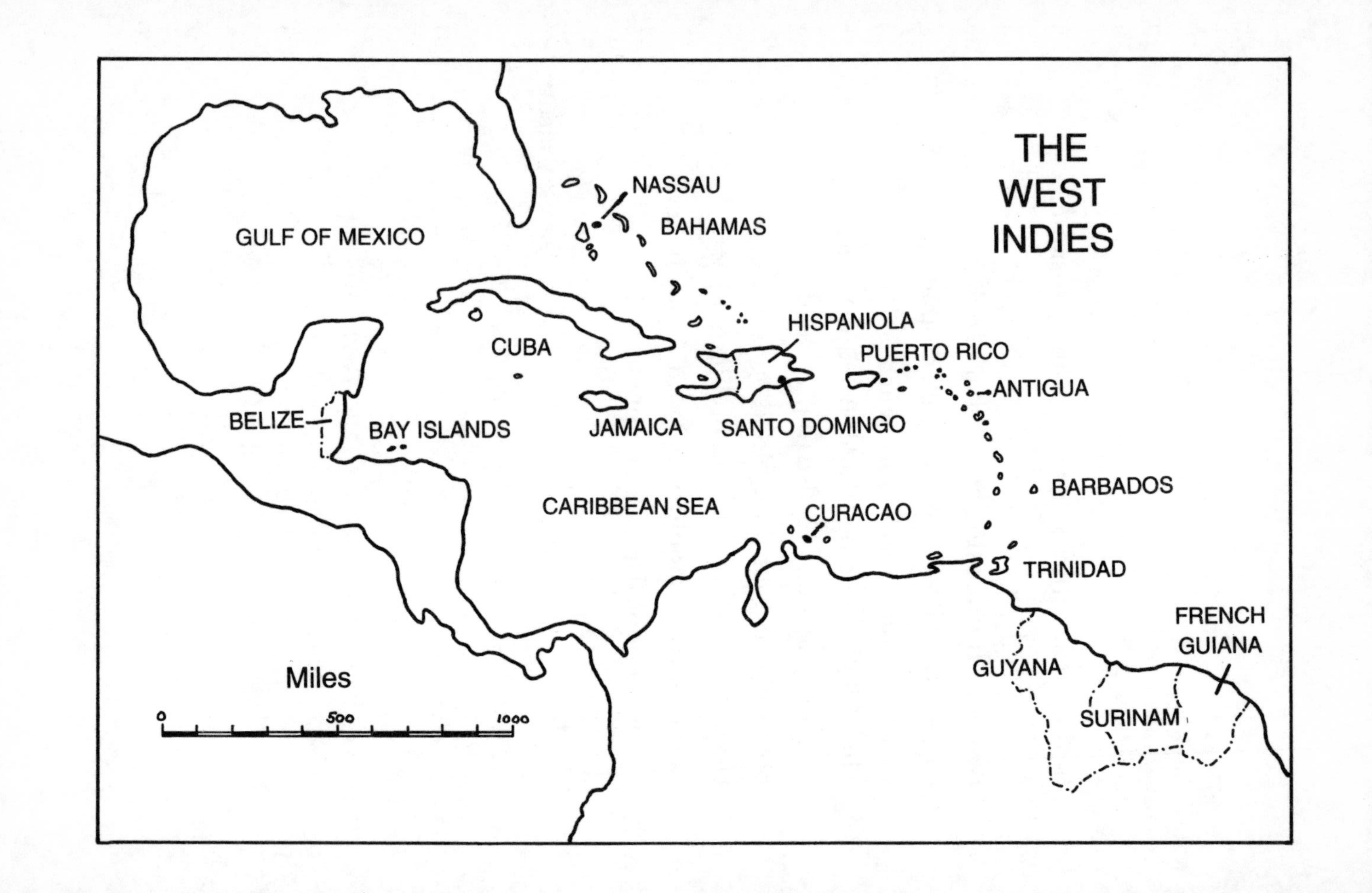
THE WEST INDIES
GULF OF MEXICO
NASSAU
BAHAMAS
CUBA
HISPANIOLA
PUERTO RICO
ANTIGUA
BELIZE
BAY ISLANDS
JAMAICA
SANTO DOMINGO
BARBADOS
CARIBBEAN SEA
CURACAO
TRINIDAD
FRENCH GUIANA
GUYANA
SURINAM
Miles
0
500
1000

CONTENTS

LIST OF MAPS

Maps drawn by the author

LIST OF ILLUSTRATIONS

AUTHOR'S NOTE AND ACKNOWLEDGEMENTS

This is a book about black soldiers in a white man's army, and the part played by men of African descent, as colonial subjects, in preserving and enlarging Britain's colonial empire in the Westindies and West Africa. It is intended for the general reader not the student of military history, although I hope it will be of use to the latter - even if only to awaken interest in the part played by Westindian soldiers in the British Army. I should also like to think the book will be of interest to Westindian students of Westindian history, by whom the existence of black soldiers in the service of the British has been almost totally ignored up to now. If it does nothing else, it may help them to see that military prowess and mastery of the art of war, as well as such intangibles as loyalty and devotion to duty, are attributes quite unconnected with a man's race or the colour of his skin. The life, exploits and achievements of Westindian soldiers are worthy of proper academic study by both military and Westindian historians.

That the West India regiments and Westindian soldiers have received little attention from either so far is reflected in the age, origin and authorship of most of the contents of the bibliography. I have found very little of any consequence about them in modern books concerned with the Great War with France from 1793 to 1815, with the military history of the British West African colonies during the nineteenth century, or with the First World War in Africa. From the works consulted I have taken as much curious, illuminating, humorous and little-known detail as I could find, but no references to sources are indicated in the text. For readers who might be interested, fully annotated copies of the book have been deposited in the library of the National Army Museum in London, and in the West India Reference Library in Kingston, Jamaica.

For finding much of this material in the first place I am indebted to the staff of both of these institutions, as well as to those of the Royal Commonwealth Society, the Institute of Commonwealth Studies at the University of London, the Royal Geographical Society, the Imperial War Museum, the University of Aberdeen, the Haverfordwest Public Library, the Barnet Public Library, the Bahamas Department of Archives, the Bermuda Archives, and the Royal Archives at Windsor. I also wish to thank Bob Marrion, Jeffrey Green, Jane Grell, Trevor Hearl, Captain Geoffrey

Hope RN, John Oakes, Victor Sutcliffe, Shamus Wade and Val Wilmer for their interest and assistance, and Miss Bridget Craig-Brown for permission to quote from her father's letters.

The quotations from *Two Poems on the Passing of an Empire, Homage to Gregorias,* and *The Estranging Sea* by Derek Walcott are taken from the author's *Collected Poems 1948-1984* and are used with the permission of Faber & Faber Ltd. The quotation from Derek Walcott's *Parades, Parades* is taken from *Hinterland* by E A Markham (Bloodaxe Books 1989) and is reproduced by permission of the publisher. The quotation from Papa-T by Fred D'Aguiar appears in *Mama Dot* and is used with the permission of Random House UK Ltd. The quotation from *Breaklight* by Knolly S La Fortune is taken from the anthology Breaklight edited by Andrew Salkey (Hamish Hamilton 1973), and is reproduced with the permission of the publisher.

Finally, I need to express my deepest gratitude to Don Cribbs and René Chartrand for all their help and encouragement, and for their generous provision of much hard-to-come-by material and many of the illustrations. I can only hope that what follows does not fall too far below their expectations.

PROLOGUE

On 20th October 1933 a small stone monument was unveiled in Waima, a village in eastern Sierra Leone. It commemorated the British losses in a brief but bloody skirmish with French troops which had taken place there nearly forty years earlier. The combined casualties reached nearly thirty killed and as many more wounded. Among the names recorded on the simple stone column, which still stands, are those of Privates Carter, Grant, Marsden, Pickering, Skilner, Small, White and Wilkinson, and a Drummer Browne. These were all buried close to the site of the monument on Christmas Eve, 1893. Within less than six months their graves had been obliterated and the ground dug up for cultivation. By the time the memorial was erected their remains had disappeared for ever. Apart from the manner of their deaths and the desecration of their remains, the one thing these nine had in common was that they were all Jamaicans.

Waima is about 170 miles east of Freetown, the capital of Sierra Leone, and close to the border with Guinea. It is no different from any number of small, rural communities in that part of West Africa. A hundred years ago it was even smaller and more remote than it is today. The border between the British colony of Sierra Leone and what had recently been termed French Guinea was more or less agreed, but had still to be firmly established. The village appeared on no map of the region, as the work necessary to produce such a document had hardly begun. The inhabitants, although only too well aware of the presence and power of the British colonial administration, still recognized only tribal loyalties. But Waima was to have its day. For a few hours in December 1893, in the closing years of the 'scramble for Africa' - that form of collective madness which overtook Europe in the last quarter of the nineteenth century - the village was the scene of one of the international incidents which characterized the era. It involved a shooting match, mostly in darkness, between forces representing Britain and France, lasting for no more than a couple of hours.

The British troops involved were in the vicinity of Waima for exactly the same reason as their French counterparts; to suppress an uprising among tribesmen known as Sofas. The Malinké leader of the Sofas was a passionate, proselytizing Muslim named Samori, who during the previous decade had created a large Muslim enclave in the region of the Upper Niger. He and his Sofa warriors were now fighting to maintain its integrity, and to prevent it being incorporated into either Sierra Leone or French Guinea. A column of British troops occupied the village on 21st December and fortified it against attack. The following day an approaching French column was warned of the presence of armed men in Waima, but deliberately misled into believing they were part of Samori's forces.

The subsequent attack by the French during the pre-dawn hours of 23rd December was then assumed by the British defenders to be a surprise raid by Sofas, and the battle was joined in mutual ignorance. The type of fire and accuracy of the shooting soon made each side aware of something odd, but by the time those in command had grasped the truth it was too late. By dawn, when the shooting ended, the defenders had three officers and fourteen men killed, and a similar number wounded. As the sun rose a party was sent out to clear the surrounding bush, and soon discovered equal devastation among the attackers, who were now recognised as belonging to the French Army. The lieutenant who had led the attack was found with a fatal wound, from which he died within an hour. Twenty-seven of his men had been wounded and another ten killed outright.

Although the 'Waima Incident' caused alarm and anger in London and Paris it was immediately recognised for what it was, an accident, and the only long-term result was a protracted contest to apportion blame and agree compensation. The legal battle rumbled on for a number of years before it was decided to refer the matter to arbitration, and was not settled until July 1902 when the Belgian Foreign Secretary found the French offer to pay slightly less than £4,000 was too small, and fixed the indemnity at £9,000.

The French troops involved belonged to a colonial regiment called the *Tirailleurs sénégalais*, which had been raised in 1857. They were African soldiers led by white officers seconded from regular units of the French Army. The British troops also belonged to units in which the other ranks were black and the officers were white. A few were from the Sierra Leone Frontier Police, formed two years earlier and still far from being a fully trained and properly disciplined military body. The bulk of the defenders of Waima though were men who, while just as African in appearance, were not from the region or indeed any other part of the continent. They belonged to the West India Regiment, a regular unit with its own corps of (albeit always white) officers which, by this time, had seen more years of service in West Africa than any other regiment in the British Army.

Those who took part in the defence of Waima, men of the 1st Battalion, were the colonial descendants of West African slaves. Those who died did so fighting West Africans on behalf of Great Britain, the nation which had enslaved their forefathers and was now intent on colonizing what they and the survivors must have considered their ancestral homeland. The remains of the dead were ploughed into the African soil, joining the bones of the many other Westindian soldiers killed over the years throughout West Africa from the Gambia to the Niger. The little monument put up in 1933 hardly did them justice; out of the nine Jamaican names inscribed, four were misspelled and six consisted of surnames only. But by then the service of the Westindian soldiers in Sierra Leone, which had lasted for the best part of the century, was only a distant memory, and the regiment itself had gone out of existence seven years earlier.

To understand how all these things came about it is necessary to look at events which took place in the Westindies at the end of the eighteenth century. Only then can the deaths of the men it is now possible to identify correctly as Privates C Carter, C Grant, W Marston, J Pickron, S Skinner, S Small, M White and J Wilkinson, and Drummer J Bourne be put into their true perspective.

PART ONE

RAISING THE REGIMENTS

I am of opinion that a Corps of one thousand men composed of blacks and Mulattoes, and commanded by British Officers would render more essential service in the Country, than treble this number of Europeans who are unaccustomed to the climate. And as the Enemy have adopted this measure to recruit their armies, I think we should pursue a similar plan to meet them on equal terms.

Lieutenant-General Sir John Vaughan,
in a letter to the Home Secretary of 22nd December 1794.

CHAPTER 1
SLAVES IN RED COATS

...the Soldiers of the West-India Regiments are amenable to the Slave Laws, and therefore subject to every degradation, that the unfortunate and wretched Slave is doomed to endure.

Brigadier-General Thomas Hislop (1801)

War between Britain and the recently created French Republic was declared on 1st February 1793. Within two years the 'Batavian Republic' established by the French in Holland had joined in on the side of France, and a year later Spain too declared war on Britain. This had an enormous effect on the Westindies. Between April 1793 and the signing of the Treaty of Amiens in March 1802 fighting took place in nearly every island between Hispaniola and Trinidad, and in places as far apart as Surinam in South America and the settlement of Belize in Central America. Even though the engagements were so widespread, and many of the battles extremely hard-fought, the British forces suffered casualties out of all proportion to the overall scale of the fighting. During the first five years alone at least 40,000 troops died, and a similar number were permanently disabled. The great majority were killed or invalided not as a result of encountering enemy forces, but through contracting a disease such as malaria or yellow fever, the two most common. In St Domingue (that part of Hispaniola which subsequently became the Republic of Haiti) which the British occupied from 1793 to 1798, the 96th Regiment was wiped out entirely by yellow fever, while the 23rd Regiment lost twelve officers and some six hundred men from the same cause in less than a year. In St Lucia in 1797 the 31st Regiment buried twenty-two officers and over eight hundred men as a result of disease. More than fifty regiments served in the Westindies during the war, but few escaped what amounted to their destruction.

The prospects for British soldiers sent to the Caribbean were not improved by the conditions under which they made the long passage across the Atlantic, packed sometimes for months on end into old and insanitary transport ships. From these they would move on arrival into camps or barracks which, if not equally insanitary, were usually sited in low-lying places close to swamps or salt-ponds. Such sites were particularly ill-chosen as at the time, and for the next hundred years, no-one had any idea of just how scourges like malaria and yellow fever were transmitted. Generally it was assumed that such diseases were associated with miasmas or impure air arising from marshes or other damp, low-lying regions. But even if a regiment was fortunate enough to be quartered well away from such places, the soldiers' uniform and diet offered few concessions to their health.

A uniform suitable for parade-ground work at Chelmsford in March, say, or for guard duties at Stirling in November, was hardly ideal for similar activities in places like Kingston or Port of Spain at any time of the year. Comments made in a history of Trinidad, published in 1838, would have been just as relevant forty years earlier, and equally applicable to any other part of the Caribbean:

> In the first place, the diet of the soldiers is unsuitable to the climate ... Secondly, they are clad and accoutred too heavily for the latitude of Trinidad: they wear the same dress and appointments that soldiers use in Canada, although the latter is colder than Russia. Let anyone look at the soldier's blanket of a coat with its heavy trimmings, his "portable pillory" of a stock, and his apoplexy-causing helmet with its brass weights, and say if these be fit for a British soldier in an Island where the mercury rises to 90 in the shade.

With regard to their standard diet, with its emphasis on salted meat, flour and rice, the soldiers were equally badly treated. The absence of any regulation issue of fresh vegetables or fruit did little to increase resistance to disease. The constant provision of salted beef or pork only added to thirsts already greatly increased by climatic conditions. This in turn further encouraged widespread addiction to a substance known as 'new rum', the consumption of which was tolerated as it was thought to have some antiscorbutic properties. In fact it was a killer, readily leading to chronic alcoholism and a sordid death. Not infrequently, as it often contained fusel oil and was normally distilled through equipment containing a great deal of lead, it was literally poisonous.

When the Commander-in-Chief of the British forces in the Westindies, Lieutenant-General Vaughan, wrote to the Home Secretary, the Duke of Portland, advocating the formation of 'a Corps of ... blacks and Mulattoes', it was as a result of seeing not only how well small bodies of such men had performed as irregular soldiers, but also how much healthier they remained in comparison with regular British troops. That the black man had a generally stronger constitution and a higher resistance to the various fever diseases than the white man, had long been apparent. That the black soldier enjoyed better health than his white confrËre because he had a better understanding of what in the Westindies he should, and should not, eat and drink was probably not so apparent.

Black soldiers had started to play an active part in Westindian history some years before Vaughan sat down to write his letter to the Duke of Portland. In 1789 the Declaration of the Rights of Man in the National Assembly in Paris had thrown the French Caribbean possessions into turmoil. During the period before the outbreak of war with Britain much fighting took place between Royalist forces and factions supporting the Revolution. There were in addition slave revolts in St Domingue and Martinique. That in Martinique was followed by a rebellion among the 'free coloured' population, and everywhere there was general unrest among the black population, whether free or bonded. It was during this time that the first black soldiers made their appearance, when Royalist officers in St Domingue, Guadeloupe and Martinique raised armed bodies from among the slaves.

War with Britain, and the subsequent capture and recapture of the islands in the eastern Caribbean, brought about yet more social upheavals. Some Royalists joined the British forces, bringing their armed slaves with them. Many free blacks, disappointed by the vacillation of the National Assembly in issuing and then revoking decrees which granted them equality with the whites, took the opportunity to emigrate to British islands and were then willing to take up arms. In addition, as the war continued, more and more slaves were seized as spoils of war by the British forces, and among the males there were many who were only too willing to be armed and trained to fight against their former owners. An army surgeon, writing from Barbados in February 1796, provides some idea of the numbers involved:

> We have an encampment of negroes formed near to Bridge-Town, upon a spot called Constitution-hill. They are a fine body of men, who have been enlisted from the revolted French islands, or brought away on the evacuation of them by our troops. They are active and expert, and are training into a formidable corps to assist in our intended operations. About sixteen hundred of them bear arms, besides whom there are twelve hundred to be employed as pioneers. They have all the vivacity and levity of the French character about them; and it occasionally, affords us amusement to observe the Barbados negroes regard them with evident amusement, gaping with wonder at their volatility and alertness.

These troops, including the pioneers (men who did not usually bear arms, but who did manual work connected with the preparation of defences, road clearance, and the provision of camp services) were later to provide the core of three British regiments.

The 41st Regiment arrived in the Caribbean at the end of 1793 and took part in the capture of Martinique in February of the following year. One of the officers left behind as part of the garrison was a young Scotsman, Captain Robert Malcolm. Soon after taking over as Town Major of St Pierre, in the north of the island, he set about recruiting a small force of irregular troops from among the free black population. This unit then supplemented the small number of regular troops under his command, and was used mainly in hunting down the many slaves who had escaped during the fighting and taken to the mountains. Known variously as Malcolm's Corps, Malcolm's Rangers, or the Royal Rangers they subsequently fought alongside British troops in St Lucia and St Vincent, before they too were assimilated into a British regiment. It is possible that Malcolm was inspired to raise his Rangers from seeing how well another unit of black troops performed during the invasion of Martinique. Since 1783 various small bodies of such troops which were raised in America and used during the American War of Independence had been stationed in the eastern Caribbean, where they were known collectively as the Black Corps of Dragoons, Pioneers and Artificers. Soon after the war with France began the name was changed to the Black Carolina Corps (Carolina being the state in which they were recruited) and later to just the Carolina Corps. After taking part in the capture of Martinique, they too fought in St Lucia.

The regular soldiers of the British Army with whom the Carolina Corps and Malcolm's Rangers served were trained to fight in a certain way - based on the much-practised and inviolable movements of close-ordered ranks, and firing by numbers - and in that way only. Independence of action was considered a recipe for disaster and almost unheard of: independence of thought was stifled by a harsh and unremitting disciplinary code. Black soldiers were unencumbered by any of the conventional doctrine. Nor were they hampered by the unsuitable uniforms and heavy equipment of the regular troops. In the heavily wooded, mountainous islands of the eastern Caribbean they proved ideal as skirmishers, perfectly suited to the small-scale, independent operations dictated by the conditions in which the fighting took place, and engaged in a different type of warfare altogether. By October 1794 there were well over three thousand black irregulars employed in this way.

By the end of the same year, as disease continued to overwhelm regiment after regiment of British troops, there was more than a note of urgency in a request sent by General Vaughan to the Secretary of War, Henry Dundas, for permission to enlist more blacks and put them on a more regular footing. He outlined a plan under which the bulk of the one thousand-strong corps he envisaged could be obtained, by requiring each island to provide a quota of slaves as a contribution to its defence. The numbers could then be made up by enlisting free blacks 'at a modest Bounty' or, if this failed, by buying potential recruits direct from slave dealers.

Once word of this proposal reached the ears of the local white proprietors they were enraged, and immediately began to put pressure on the British Parliament not to sanction it, using the powerful lobby of the London-based West India Committee. The prospect of arming slaves, or any black man for that matter, was bad enough: that implementation of Vaughan's plan would lead to interference by the British Government in each island's affairs was even worse, and something no local Assembly could bear to contemplate. The West India Committee, which even as late as 1906 the historian of the British Army, Sir John Fortescue, felt compelled to call "that blind, selfish, and rapacious body which ... has for two centuries and a half been the curse of the West Indies", represented some 1800 planters, of whom two-thirds lived in Britain. Using the corrupt election procedures of the time it had bought up various boroughs and had control of the votes of perhaps seventy Members of Parliament. Their influence on the government was brought to bear, and in April 1795 Vaughan was informed that no black corps or regiment would be authorized.

The General was infuriated and remonstrated immediately:

> I cannot but reflect with great regret that a set of self-interested merchants, who will not give a small part to save the whole, should be attended to in conducting operations in these countries instead of the Commander-in-Chief, who can have no motive, but his own credit and the success of His Majesty's arms. I hope that the Ministry will yet weigh this important point ... I do not hesitate to say that unless my advice be taken, these Colonies will very soon be wrested from us. The French blacks will invade us and gain ours by the promise of freedom.

His anger was fuelled by events which had taken place a month earlier while his proposal was still being considered by Dundas. A new kind of war had broken out in St Vincent and Grenada, islands which each had a large population of Caribs, the original pre-Colombian inhabitants. Stirred up in Grenada by disaffected French planters, and under a strong and determined leader in St Vincent, the Caribs now rose up against the British in a last attempt to retain control of their own affairs. News of the start of what came to be called the 'Brigands' War' reached London a day or two after the letter denying Vaughan his black corps had been dispatched. A second letter was hurriedly concocted, rescinding the first and recognizing that the new situation facing the Commander-in-Chief warranted overriding the views of the West India Committee and the island Assemblies. This reached Vaughan, no doubt to his great satisfaction, after he had sent off his diatribe about the 'set of self-interested merchants' and it was beyond recall. His new instructions from Dundas authorized the raising of two new regiments of black troops. A month later he was given permission to create another four. In September, by which time the general, like so many of his men, had succumbed to the Westindian climate, the total was raised to eight.

The first two, entitled Whyte's Regiment of Foot and Myers' Regiment of Foot, came into being on 24th April 1795. Each was named after the officer appointed as its Colonel and titular commanding officer: Major-General John Whyte from the 6th Regiment and Brigadier-General William Myers from the 15th Regiment. This followed the practice of the day, in awarding the colonelcy of a regiment to a senior officer in recognition of some particular service to the army, or to the government of the day, or perhaps even to the monarch. It entitled him not only to the pay of a colonel, but also because he enjoyed nominal command of one of the regiment's constituent companies, to that of a captain as well. In some cases the colonel was given full responsibility for outfitting his regiment with its uniforms, for which he was given a sizeable cash sum. For the less scrupulous officer, in an age when many expected to make a fortune out of military service, this was an invitation to peculation and a quick profit. To add cream to the multi-layered cake of his appointment, the colonel took no part in any fighting which came the way of his regiment: a lieutenant-colonel was appointed as the actual commanding officer, and it was he who led the troops in action. There is no evidence of any of the officers, Whyte and Myers amongst them, who raised the first eight regiments of black soldiers engaging in any corrupt practices. But neither is there any record of them taking much interest in how such troops were enlisted, trained and used in the field. By the time they were appointed the Colonel of a regiment was already a rather shadowy figure. Within a few years he was to lose the privileges of dual pay and the provision of uniforms, and assume an even more nominal status. In 1795 eight officers gave their names to the original eight regiments of black troops, drew the appropriate pay, and that was about all.

Each regiment was given an authorized establishment of about eleven hundred all ranks, with the men divided into ten infantry companies and two troops of dragoons or mounted infantry. Finding such numbers was no easy matter and it was quickly realised that such a large establishment was completely unrealistic. The concept of combining light dragoons with infantrymen was abandoned and the rank and file reduced to six hundred spread between eight companies. This produced a total requirement of almost five thousand men, of which the only ones immediately available consisted of irregular units such as the Carolina Corps and Malcolm's Rangers, perhaps a thousand captured or defected French blacks, and a much smaller number of British slaves. The remainder, according to the army's plan, would be recruited by four of the regiments among the islands of the eastern Caribbean, by two more in Jamaica, and by the remaining two in that part of St Domingue still under British control. Once this recruitment was underway, and with a cadre of British officers, non-commissioned officers, and even a few privates, each regiment it was hoped would quickly reach its full establishment. Ideally each company would then be made up of equal numbers of free blacks or 'coloureds' and slaves bought from willing, patriotic plantation owners, with any deficiency being made up by Africans purchased from slave dealers.

This policy, all very neat and simple on paper, was just as unrealistic as the original establishment devised for each regiment, and incapable of being implemented. The various island authorities, not wishing to see slaves armed and perturbed by the prospect of what might happen when such men were no longer needed by the army, refused to help. Few free blacks were willing to surrender any part of their freedom. Even fewer proprietors were ready to part with their strongest, healthiest and most reliable slaves - the only ones the army was interested in - for the price which had been set. The figure of £70 a head was considered too low and one which would only serve to depress the market. The only option left was to buy slaves at source. In October 1796 Lieutenant-General Sir Ralph Abercromby, who had taken over as C-in-C on Vaughan's death, was informed by the Secretary of War that:

> As it appears impossible to procure Negroes for these ... Corps except by purchasing them for Government, I am to signify to you His Majesty's pleasure that you are to authorize the officer commanding His Majesty's Forces in the Leeward Islands to procure in this manner the number that may be necessary for this purpose.

Similar instructions were also sent to the officer commanding the British forces in Jamaica.

From the time this policy was implemented until 1st January 1808, when the Abolition Act caused all trading in slaves to be 'utterly abolished, prohibited and declared to be unlawful', the British Army became the biggest single purchaser of African slaves anywhere in the Westindies, and quite possibly anywhere throughout the Americas. At least thirteen thousand were bought during this period, from selected merchants who dealt direct with the owners and masters of slave ships. They were obtained with a great deal of discretion, at a cost of over £900,000, using funds which Parliament voted annually to meet unforeseen wartime expenses. As the House of Commons did not scrutinize the way these funds were spent, the use to which they were put in this case never became the subject of debate or criticism. The policy also involved a fair degree of hypocrisy on the part of the government, several members of which - including William Pitt the Prime Minister for most of the period - were keen to be identified publicly with the Abolition movement. At the same time, and in trying to look at the matter dispassionately, the policy said something for the value now being placed on the black soldier; the army being prepared to pay £70 or so for a completely uneducated black recruit who, before anything else, had to be taught English, when an equally uneducated white recruit from any part of the British Isles could be obtained for a bounty worth less than a fifth of this amount.

In the middle of 1798, with Britain now at war with Spain and the 'Batavian Republic' as well as France, and with no abatement in the number of white troops being lost to disease, four more black regiments were authorized. By now the existing eight had lost their individual 'Regiment of Foot' names, and had been taken onto the army establishment as numbered West India regiments. Three of the new ones originated in irregular units raised four years previously in islands which were then under French control. Drualt's Rangers, de Soter's Royal Island Rangers, and O'Meara's Rangers were taken onto the strength as the 9th, 10th and 12th West India regiments in September, with the French officers among them being given temporary commissions in the British Army. The 11th West India Regiment was also formed from an existing unit - the South American Rangers, raised in Demerara in 1796. The officer responsible for their formation was Colonel Thomas Hislop who, as the commanding officer of the 39th Regiment, had taken part in the seizure of the Dutch colonies in South America, and then been made military commander.

Hislop was appointed Colonel of the 11th WIR and retained the post throughout the time he spent in the Westindies, which did not end until 1812. He was another officer, like Robert Malcolm in his own service, and French officers such as Drualt and de Soter, who was able to break with convention, subdue prejudice, and see black men not just as barely human possessions fit only for brutish labour, but as individuals well suited physically and mentally to undertake the unconventional type of soldiering demanded by the Westindian climate and conditions. He recorded his views in a long memorandum for the C-in-C in 1801.

Much of what he wrote, concerning the training of black soldiers and how they could be used in the field, was very practical and relevant to the conditions under which they could expect to fight. Future army policy towards the West India regiments was based largely on his recommendations, his memorandum having been forwarded to London by the C-in-C. He had strong views about the soldiers' continuing status as slaves and argued that they should be emancipated. He was equally strongly in favour of the army going direct to West Africa for recruits, and finding men...

> wholly unacquainted with and uncontaminated by the Vices which prevail among the slaves in the Towns and Plantations, having no acquaintance or connection of any sort, but such as they form in the Regiment. I have invariably found them to make the most orderly, clean and attentive Soldiers. Out of Two hundred and upwards, which have been received into the Regiment in the course of Five years and a half, there are not above three or four instances of any of them being punished, and not for any serious offence...

He proposed that 'Cargoes as they may be wanted, be purchased on account of Government, on the [West African] Coast, under the eye of a Governor or Superior there, and to be composed of a particular Class or Nation.' He then went on to suggest that 'In order to have the Recruiting service conducted with the greatest regularity, an Island might be fix'd on for the Depot, whither the Regiments should send for the proportion of Recruits they are to receive.'

It took a long time for the Army to recognize the merits of his last proposal and it was not until 1812 that a West African recruiting depot was established. By then black soldiers were no longer slaves, and it was needed to find *volunteers* for the West India regiments.

CHAPTER 2
SOLDIERS NOT SLAVES

> Abouberika Torre commonly called Joseph Samson.
> Hammadi Torrouke commonly called Louis Modeste.
> Mandingo sergeants offered Africa back,
> the boring process of repatriation ...
>
> **Derek Walcott**

The army's intentions with regard to the future recruitment for the West India regiments, and plans for dispersing the regiments throughout the Caribbean, were made known to the island authorities in January 1797. This created an immediate uproar and they all voiced misgivings and objections. The legislatures in Jamaica and Barbados were particularly incensed. Barbados refused to even consider letting a regiment near its shores, the House of Assembly possibly still recovering from the shock which must have been occasioned the year before by the sight of nearly three thousand blacks being trained 'near to Bridge-Town'. The Jamaican Assembly found it equally impossible to contemplate armed black troops being stationed in the island. The security of Jamaica stood for nothing in comparison with the damage the presence of armed slaves would inflict on society. It would be too much even to recruit free coloureds, as these

> whilst they remain enrolled in the militia, preserve the ideas of coloured subordination ... whereas, if they should be embodied as regulars, they would entertain notions of equality, and acquire habits pernicious to the welfare of the country.

In neither island were the proprietors (who of course can be considered as one with the legislators) prepared to see slaves 'distracted from the task of making money for their owners to so trivial an employment as defence of the country'. At the same time they were equally unwilling to raise regular troops from among themselves, or even to think of bearing the full cost of defending their islands. All they were prepared to do was to make a contribution towards the cost of providing a garrison of British troops in each island. Although their objections carried some weight and they managed to delay the deployment of the regiments sought by the army, by the seventh year of the war the British Government had had enough. Military considerations were now paramount and in 1800 the governors of Jamaica and Barbados were informed that, like it or not, from then on their garrisons would contain a proportion of black troops.

By this time there were twelve West India regiments in existence, with a total strength of perhaps ten thousand men. A policy for their recruitment, training and deployment had now been worked out, but one matter which still had not been resolved was that of the black soldier's legal status. To the army he was no different from a white soldier. Both wore the same uniform, drew the same rations, received the same punishments, were treated when sick in the same hospital, and enjoyed the same pay. But this equality ceased once they left the confines of their shared barracks. Outside the white soldier had the same freedom and rights as his civilian contemporaries; the black soldier was immediately 'amenable to the Slave Laws'. Even in carrying out his lawful military duties in a civilian setting the black soldier risked running into trouble. An observer of life in Jamaica, writing in 1823 of events perhaps twenty years earlier, illustrates what must have been the prevalent attitude:

> When a detachment of black soldiers was seen guarding and conveying some white deserters, pinioned and in a miserable plight, to headquarters, it was regarded by inhabitants as a novel and revolting sight; though, if white soldiers had guarded the delinquents, it would have excited no sensation.

The black soldier also ran into problems when he came to the end of his period of service. Although in theory he was enrolled for life, it was obvious that a time would come when he would be too old or too infirm to remain in uniform. What was to happen then? Where was he to go? How was he to support himself? Under what laws and conditions could he expect to live the remainder of his life?

These were all questions which, to give them their due, the army authorities had had in mind from the beginning. As early as 1797 General Abercromby, the C-in-C in the West Indies, had attempted to solve the problems of the discharged soldier by edict. He issued a decree which stated that any black soldier found permanently unfit for duty was to be discharged as a free man, entitled to a pension of one shilling a day. Unfortunately the British Government refused to endorse the measure, and the island authorities ignored it. Two years later, with the problem now even more acute due to the increased presence of the West India regiments, and more and more disabled or unfit men being discharged into the local societies, the Home Secretary took up the matter with the Law Officers of the Crown.

These worthies, the Attorney-General and the Solicitor-General, were asked to give opinions on two questions. They were to determine whether military service in the West India regiments made the soldiers exempt from colonial slave laws, and then to decide - if they found the troops were not exempt from these laws - whether they could be enfranchised by the King or by an Act of Parliament. Their reply was unequivocal: service in the British Army did not free black soldiers from the operations of the slave laws, and neither the King, nor the House of Commons, had powers of manumission. In their opinion a black soldier serving in one of the regiments could only be freed under the laws applying in the island in which he was stationed, and he would then still be subject to whatever restrictions the island authorities placed on free blacks.

This was a decided set-back, affecting all the men of the West India regiments whether or not they were still serving. As part of their indoctrination into army life all had been encouraged to believe they were superior to the slaves they saw all around them, in every island in which they were stationed. As they were treated in the same way as white soldiers, and paid for what they did, this attitude was easy to foster. Again, this was all very well inside the barracks, but anywhere else a display of anything but subservience could lead to all kinds of trouble. Amongst civilians black soldiers were viewed with distrust and suspicion. The owners of plantations adjoining forts or other military installations frequently accused soldiers of stirring up unrest among their slaves, when usually all they were doing was seeking the solace of female company. White soldiers who committed petty offences in civilian society almost invariably were turned over to the military authorities for punishment; black soldiers were treated as miscreant slaves and hauled away to be punished under the relevant slave laws.

This was clearly unacceptable to the army, particularly in wartime, and so in 1801 the Law Officers were asked once again to rule on the legal position of the soldiers of the West India regiments. At the end of December the Secretary of War was told that in their opinion the soldiers

> .... do not in consequence of their being employed by His Majesty in military service become soldiers within the Mutiny Act; and we think they remain to all intents and purposes slaves, and that their condition as slaves is in no

> respect altered in consequence of their being engaged in military service, but they remain precisely subject to the same laws as they would have been subject to had they been the property of His Majesty and employed in agriculture or public works or in any other species of civil service .... and must be subject to every species of personal incapacity which attaches upon the slaves of any other proprietor.

However, this time they went on to qualify this statement by observing that the men serving in the regiments

> ....can only be made soldiers by an effectual manumission and a voluntary enlisting or receipt of pay subsequent to such manumission under circumstances in which they were free to elect whether they would enlist and receive pay or not ...

but warned that, although 'such manumission His Majesty might clearly grant of His own Act alone', this would be at the same time 'an interference with the legislature of the colonies' in a matter about which they would be extremely jealous. They ended their opinion by stating that while the problem could be solved by an Act of Parliament as well this was a question of expediency and not law, and as such it was something about which they did not feel themselves competent to decide.

And there the matter rested for another six years. The British Government was unwilling to further antagonize the island legislatures and the white proprietors, already greatly agitated by the mounting campaign for the abolition of the slave trade, and nothing was done before 1807. By then the number of regiments had been reduced to eight and the existence of black soldiers in the West Indies was not quite such a sensitive issue. In that year the British Government, emboldened by its success in passing the Abolition Act in March and taking into account the growing movement for parliamentary reform in Britain, took the opportunity to impose its will even more firmly on the island Assemblies. It was done through the Mutiny Act.

Discipline in the Army was governed by the provisions of this Act, first passed in 1689 and then renewed and amended at intervals to meet changing conditions. In the middle of 1807 it was renewed once again, this time with the addition of a clause stating that

> all Negros purchased by or on account of His Majesty, His Heirs, and Successors, and serving in any of His Majesty's Forces, shall be, and deemed and taken to be free, to all Intents and for all purposes whatever, in like

> manner in every respect as if such Negro had been born Free in any part of His Majesty's Dominions, and that such Negros shall also to all Intents and purposes whatever be considered as Soldiers, having voluntary enlisted in His Majesty's service.

In consequence probably close to ten thousand men were immediately enfranchised, by far the largest number of slaves set free in one go anywhere in the Americas up until this time. Nothing like this was to happen again until August 1834, when slavery was abolished altogether throughout the British colonies. At the time both the Abolition Act of 1807 and the amended Mutiny Act were rightly seen as very creditable moves on the part of the British Government. Both however contained provisions which ruled out true equality between black and white soldiers.

Up until 1806 all British soldiers were taken to have enlisted for life, but in that year changes were made to allow a recruit to sign on for a period of seven years only. On completion of this he could take his discharge or re-enlist for another seven years. When that period expired he could either leave with a small pension, or sign on again for a final stretch of seven years. After that he was discharged on full pension. These options were denied the men of the West India regiments; the 1807 Mutiny Act specified that no restriction was placed on the period they were to serve, and in effect they were enlisted for life.

To enable the army to still find black recruits after the Abolition Act came into force a clause in the Act permitted the involuntary enlistment of any suitable slaves captured from an enemy or taken as prizes of war. Soon after the Act came into effect it was seen that its enforcement opened up another, potentially much larger, source of recruits. In March 1808 an Order in Council specified what was to happen to the slaves taken from any ship seized under the provisions of the Act. In each colony the Collector of Customs was made responsible for 'all Negroes who have been condemned to the crown, until they can be disposed of according to the acts of parliament'. He was 'to keep an exact list and description of every such Negro, and if the African name is not sufficiently clear, he is to substitute some other, by which such Negro shall afterwards be called, until sufficiently instructed for baptism, when the same shall become the surname; the name of baptism being prefixed thereto'. Then came the crux of his instructions. After having found out if any of his charges were related to each other he was to inform

> the chief officer of His Majesty's land forces in the colony, of the number of male Negroes fit for military service so received, that such officer may take

any number of them as recruits for West Indian or African regiments, or to form new corps, or as pioneers.

After that the local senior naval officer could take his pick, and the remainder were then to be apprenticed 'to prudent and humane masters and mistresses, to learn such trades, etc. as they may seem most fit for.'

Recruits from this source began to be supplied straight away. To enforce the Abolition Act the Royal Navy established patrols off West Africa, but any British warship could stop and board a ship suspected of being a slaver. Not only vessels flying the British flag could be stopped, but also of course any belonging to a country with which Britain was at war. In spite of the Act some British shipowners continued to trade, encouraged by the profits to be made, but were eventually driven out of business with the introduction of ever-harsher penalties, ending with terms of transportation in 1811. Depending on where a ship was seized her master was brought before the nearest Vice-Admiralty Court and the cargo of what were now normally referred to as 'recaptives' were given into the charge of the local Collector of Customs. These officials were certainly kept busy as in spite of the naval blockade the slave trade continued throughout the war years.

In March 1811 a Spanish ship escorted into St John's, Antigua, had on board 130 male slaves of whom nearly half were 'enlisted into 3d West India regiment'. Although earlier the army had specified that black recruits must be at least sixteen years old, with a minimum height of five feet, three inches, such details seem to have been largely ignored; a third of these recruits were judged to be aged 15 or less. Another Spanish ship, brought into St John's in April 1814, was was packed with more than 400 slaves. Out of the 308 males 200 were 'selected for the Army by order of The Commander of the Forces', even though many were considered to be under 16 years of age and some were less than five foot tall. The recruits which these two vessels provided were only a few of the total taken from all the slave ships seized during the war in or near the Caribbean Sea. Even more were obtained from ships taken off West Africa.

The Vice-Admiralty Court in Freetown, Sierra Leone, dealt with nearly 7800 liberated slaves between when it was set up in 1808 and the end of the war seven years later. Out of 5600 male 'recaptives' more than 2000 'Entered His Majesty's Land Service as Soldiers', although not all were taken for the West India regiments. In 1800 a regiment called the African Corps (later the Royal African Corps) had been raised for service in West Africa, and about 400 were enlisted in this unit. They were the more fortunate, as at least they remained in Africa. The other 1600 or so, having been saved from crossing the Atlantic to end up as Westindian slaves, were now obliged to cross it as Westindian soldiers.

This means of obtaining recruits, which continued long after the end of the war in 1815, while very convenient was obviously not a satisfactory or enlightened way of keeping the regiments up to strength. The more regular and conventional, not to mention more humane, method of recruiting needed was introduced in 1811. In November of that year Major R J Wingfield of the 8th WIR, who was at that time in England, received instructions from Horse Guards, the army's headquarters in London, informing him that he was being appointed to a new post. This was to be in West Africa where 'His Royal Highness the Prince Regent has ... been pleased to approve of a Recruiting Depot being formed either at Sierra Leone or Goree'. Wingfield's orders explained that, while 'it has been judged expedient, that such eligible Negroes as may be found amongst the cargoes captured under the Slave Abolition Act, should be appropriated to this service', it would soon 'be highly necessary to bring the military service into repute by the encouragement of voluntary enlistment'. To this end they continued, 'the Prince Regent has approved of a bounty of eight guineas being given for each recruit, under such regulations as may leave at least three guineas for his equipment in necessaries.'

The deduction of part of the enlistment bounty for 'necessaries' was normal throughout the Army, but the sum offered to a volunteer in the British Isles was nearly twice as much. That the reduced figure reflected official determination not to consider black and white soldiers as equals is surely borne out by the tone of the next part of Wingfield's orders:

> The usual full bounty of fifteen guineas is not proposed, in the hope that the sum of eight guineas will answer the purpose; under the idea, that such trifling articles of inducement, more acceptable to the Negroes than money, may be furnished by a portion of the latter sum.

Goree, a small island off Cape Verde in Senegal which had been captured from the French earlier in the war, was rejected as a possible site for the recruiting station in favour of an equally small island in Sierra Leone. Bance (Bunce or Bence) is an island in the Sierra Leone River, about fifteen miles from Freetown, at the entrance to the Rokel tributary. It had been used as a slave trading station for generations until the introduction of the Abolition Act, and was well supplied with buildings which could be made into barracks at no great expense. Its main advantage was that 'the recruits could be confined during training'. Major

Wingfield arrived there in April 1812, accompanied by seven other officers, a white sergeant-major, and '1 Sergeant, and 2 Corporals, from every Black Regiment in the West Indies'. These last had been provided by Lieutenant-General Sir George Beckwith, the C-in-C in the Westindies, who had had his 'special attention' drawn

> to the necessity of selecting for this service, the most trustworthy black non-commissioned officers, who speak the African language [sic]; the success of the measure depending in a great degree, upon the explanation of the advantages attending the situation of a British soldier; and which such persons will be enabled to give their countrymen.

The recruiting team were accompanied by a sizeable load of equipment, made up of not only 'Presents to the Kings and Chiefs', a selection of musical instruments 'For the Use of the Party', but also the 'trifling articles of inducement' intended for the recruits. These included 'Barley Corn Beads assorted', amber, coral, 'Agate Stones', 'Mock Turtle', bar iron and tobacco, as well as '1000 Snuff Boxes, with a painted portrait of a Black Soldier under arms'.

The recruiting station was operational before the middle of 1812, and within three years there were over seven hundred recruits under training. Whether Wingfield's success was due to the snuff boxes, or to the fluency of some of his staff in *the* African language, it is now of course impossible to say. What it is possible to state is that the depot was established not before time had largely discredited the previous means of finding recruits. After the Abolition Act came into force it was greatly to the credit of the British Government that, in a time of all-out warfare, a sizeable proportion of the country's naval resources was diverted to the suppression of the West African slave trade. At the same time it is possible to argue that, in carrying out this task, all the Navy was doing was helping to provide a ready supply of black soldiers to fight for British interests in the Caribbean, under conditions in which white troops were at a severe disadvantage. In its simplest terms, before 1808 the majority of recruits for the West India regiments were bought from slave ships; afterwards they came free of charge from the same source. The Bance Island recruiting depot was established not a moment too soon.

If anything it was established too late. The Napoleonic Wars ended in 1815, and peace soon brought with it the inevitable cuts in military spending. The number of West India regiments was reduced to six in the middle of 1816, at much the same time as Bance Island was closed down. Two more went the following year. By 1819 only the 1st WIR and 2nd WIR remained in being, each with a peacetime establishment of 650 rank and file, together with half of the 3rd WIR retained as part of the Trinidad garrison. Recruitment at this stage had ceased to be a problem: there were plenty of discharged soldiers around, keen to re-enlist if given the chance; and in any case the army still had first call on the male 'recaptives' mustered by a Collector of Customs from time to time.

When peace returned to the Westindies the regiments had been in existence for twenty years. During that time they had served in all parts of the Caribbean, fighting French and Dutch troops as well as Carib warriors, as the occasion demanded. Towards the end they also fought against Americans in Louisiana. In addition to being awarded three highly-prized Battle Honours, 'Dominica 1805', 'Martinique 1809' and 'Guadeloupe 1810':

> These negro West India troops won the highest encomiums from every British commander under whom they served. Sir Ralph Abercromby in 1796, Sir John Moore in 1797, Lieutenant-General Trigge in 1801, Sir George Prevost in 1805, Lieutenant-General Beckwith and Major-General Maitland in 1809 and 1810, all testified to the gallantry, steadiness, and discipline of the negro soldiers.

Major Alfred Ellis, from whose late nineteenth century *History of the First West India Regiment* these words are taken, may not have been a completely disinterested commentator, but there is no doubt that the senior officers he cites were impressed by the quality of black troops they used in their campaigns. That their 'encomiums' were not misplaced will be seen as these various campaigns are examined, but first it is necessary to look more closely at the soldiers themselves, and also at the officers who led, and not infrequently misled, them.

CHAPTER 3
THE QUEEN'S GENTLEMEN

> The soldiers are all black ...most of them having been enlisted at the English recruiting stations in Africa. Tall and athletic, with red coats, and, on a line, bristling with steel, their ebony faces gave them a peculiarly warlike appearance. They carry themselves proudly, call themselves the 'Queen's Gentlemen,' and look down with contempt upon the 'niggers'.
>
> **John L Stephens (1841)**

From the beginning, whether their soldiers were from West Africa or the Caribbean, slaves or freeman, the West India regiments were official, regular units of the British Army. In theory this should have entitled them to be considered the equals of any of the other infantry regiments, but in practice this was never the case; never more so than during the early years. None of the West India regiments had existed before 1795, whereas the army they became part of dated its origins to 1661 and a great many of its constituent units had been raised before the end of the seventeenth century. By the end of the eighteenth century most of the hundred or more 'Regiments of Foot' already had well-established traditions, and each was very conscious of its status. Many had fighting records of which they were justifiably proud; one or two with perhaps less glorious records were understandably tetchy. Few wanted much to do with, or had anything good to say about, any other regiment - least of all the Johnny-come-lately outfits with which many of them now came into contact in the Caribbean. The hundred and fifty years which had gone by since the founding of a standing army had allowed plenty of time for the development of reactionary attitudes along with regimental traditions, and a hidebound outlook dominated virtually all aspects of military life.

Nowhere was this more evident than in the conditions under which the private soldier was expected to serve, and in the way he was trained to fight. Regardless of the prestige enjoyed by a particular regiment, or of its standing in the army hierarchy, or of such things as the background of its officers or its recruitment area, the sort of men it could attract into the ranks were no different from those found by any other regiment. The concept of a standing army was generally unpopular in the community at large: the wealthy objected to being taxed to pay for its upkeep, and the less well-off - who usually only had dealings with soldiers acting as policemen - saw it as an oppressive arm of government. Army life was not attractive to a young man with a trade or with anything more than the most basic aspirations. The vast majority of recruits came from the lowest orders of society and until well into the nineteenth century most regiments were made up of rough countrymen, uneducated labourers, town idlers, petty criminals and general misfits.

In 1809, while in command of the British forces in the Peninsular War, Lieutenant-General Sir Arthur Wellesley commented on the sort of troops he had at his disposal:

> People talk of their enlisting for their fine military feeling - all stuff - no such thing. Some of our men enlist for having got bastard children - some for minor offences - many more for drink; but you can hardly conceive such a set brought together, and it really is wonderful that we should have made them the fine fellows they are.

Four years later, in a letter to the Secretary of War, he condemned them even more forcibly, using the phrase which, as the Duke of Wellington, he used on occasion for the rest of his life:

> It is quite impossible for me or any other man to command a British army under the existing system. We have in the service the scum of the earth as common soldiers ...

However objectionable such a remark may sound to modern ears, at the time it contained more than a grain of truth. The rank and file of many a regiment, composed of lumpish, unlettered youths and a core of foul-mouthed, alcoholic old sweats, probably well-earned such vilification. The sort of life the army offered to such men had been evolved accordingly. If only brutish, insensitive or maladjusted men could be persuaded to join, then it followed that the conditions under which they would then live need be no more than basic, their training would have to be beaten into them, and discipline would only be maintained with the application of a harsh and relentless code of punishment.

Up until the end of the eighteenth century many soldiers spent much of their service when not in action roughing it in temporary huts, ale-houses or even livery stables. The first programme for the construction of permanent barracks in the British Isles was not put into effect until 1792.

Even then the buildings erected were of the most utilitarian design, with no proper heating or ventilation, and often without ablution or cooking facilities. The training of recruits consisted of endless parade-ground drill and constant practice in handling their weapons. As the movements and drills learned and repeatedly rehearsed on the barrack square were precisely those used on the battlefield, it was essential that each man not only understood each word of command, but that he obeyed it instantly and without question. This form of blind, unthinking obedience was enforced by a pitiless code of discipline based on corporal punishment. By the beginning of the nineteenth century flogging with a cat-o'-nine-tails was the accepted punishment for every type of military offence, with the number of lashes ranging from a minimum of twenty-five to several thousand. No maximum number was laid down until 1807, but even then a man could still be sentenced to an inhuman one thousand lashes.

These then were the conditions of service which faced any young man volunteering to become a soldier in the final years of the eighteenth century. They had changed hardly at all since the 1660s, and were not to change very much before the 1860s, when the Army was transformed by the experiences of the Crimean War. It followed that these were also the conditions which awaited the first recruits of the West India regiments, men for the most part already traumatized from being taken into slavery, and who were now forced into taking part in someone else's wars. It says a great deal for resilience and aptitude of such men that they accepted the military life and became useful soldiers so quickly. Life in the army for such men began not with being issued with official numbers (regimental numbers were not introduced in the British Army until 1829) but with being given completely new identities:

> On arrival of negroes, as recruits for the black regiments, a piece of paper is suspended round their necks, with the name that has been given to them by the captain of the company to which they are appointed; this they are taught to understand; also the different words of command as they are drilled.

The sort of names they were given varied enormously. The more fortunate, particularly 'recaptives' named under the provisions of the Abolition Act when it came into force, ended up with common, unobjectionable names such as Abbott, Gibbs, Robinson or Williams. Many, perhaps the majority, ran up against the coarser side of the British Army. An English officer watching men being mustered for one of the West India regiments in Barbados in the early 1800s recorded in his journal:

> On being appointed to companies, the new recruits had a label hanging by a little brass chain round their necks, on which was engraved the names they were respectively to bear in the Regiment. These names were taken from celebrated Mountains, Rivers, Cities, or Fortresses, and when this source of nomenclature was exhausted, the numbers, first, second, third, etc, were had recourse to. Thus in calling over the roll of a black Company, I have heard men answer to the names of, Gibraltar 1st, Gibraltar 2nd, London 1st, London 2nd etc.

To indulge in crude, often insensitive and occasionally sadistic humour at the expense of the new recruit has always been a feature of service life. Few servicemen can have escaped some form of it, and many through the years have served their time stuck with some ribald nickname earned during basic training. But to be given some tasteless nickname for a period of years is one thing; to be given a name such as 'Plague', 'Coward', 'Duke of Manchester', 'Vesuvius the First' or 'Edinburgh the Third' to hold for life is something entirely different. Unfortunately, service humour - like that of the planters who gave their slaves names such as 'Monkey', 'Trouble' and 'Hard Times' - was frequently lacking in subtlety.

Basic training began as soon as the new recruits had been named and assigned to companies. In the beginning it had been assumed that the majority would be English-speaking slaves or freemen, and that all the NCOs who would be responsible for most of their training would be drawn from British regiments. In the event of course the majority of recruits came straight from Africa and knew no English, and not too many white NCOs could be found who were willing to transfer. Those who did volunteer were often of poor quality and, nor surprisingly, men their parent regiments were only too keen to be rid of. This meant that black sergeants and corporals made their appearance very early on in the history of the West India regiments, although some of them too were not always of the highest quality. Because the prime requirement of such men was the ability to understand English anyone who could do this, and also converse with at least some of the recruits in their own tongue, could hardly fail to earn a stripe or two.

The methods then used by such men in introducing recruits to the military life were observed by an army surgeon in Demerara in 1796. George Pinckard, who served throughout the early campaigns in the Westindies under Abercromby, watched men of the South American Rangers (who later became the 11th WIR) being drilled, and was struck by 'the very rough treatment exhibited towards them, by despotic sergeants and corporals of their own colour':

> Often when stepping forward to the words "left, right, left, right," a stout black serjeant suddenly seizes the leg of some one who does not put it forth to his mind, and jerks it on with a force that endangers the dislocation of his hip; when the poor fellow, forgetting that his body must maintain the military square, whatever becomes of his limbs, looks down to see that he steps out better next time; but another serjeant instantly lodges his coarse fist under his chin, and throws back his head with such violence as almost to break his neck ... Then, by some mistake, the right leg advances instead of the left, or the left instead of the right, the remedy for which is a hard kick, or a rough blow upon the shin ... thus the poor black is beset on all quarters and at all points, and, whether standing or moving, feels the weight of the cane, the fist, or some other weapon, upon either his head or his shoulders, his back, knees, shins, or naked toes.

The problems associated with training men who did not, when they joined, speak English remained with the regiments as long as Africans were recruited; scenes not too different from that described by Pinckard could still be seen thirty or forty years later. The regiments which survived into the post-war era, and then spent as much time in West Africa as the Caribbean, continued to recruit Africans up until 1855.

But, however harsh and humiliating the treatment of a recruit in the early days, it was still better than that afforded a slave being broken in as a plantation worker, and it did have its rewards. Not only did the former, as he acquired the soldier's skills acquire some status at the same time, but he also had the consolation of knowing he was being paid to have his shins kicked and his head punched by some 'despotic serjeant'. The basic pay for a private in the infantry had been raised to one shilling a day in 1794. Not that he ever received the full amount, due to the number of deductions which were made. Half was taken for food, together with small amounts to pay for laundry, shoe-repairs and cleaning materials for his uniform. As he also had to pay for any item of clothing or equipment lost or damaged by neglect he could never count on more than a few pence a day in his pocket. The sum of a shilling a day before stoppages remained his basic pay for most of the nineteenth century; the first increase, of twopence, being made in 1890. If today it is hard to imagine what could possibly have attracted a Westindian estate worker in, say, 1850 or even 1880, to enlist for seven shillings a week, it is as well to recall what conditions were like for such workers in the second half of the nineteenth century. Many earned much less than one shilling a day, and only got that on days when work was available.

In return for the deduction of half his day's pay each soldier was given a ration of, at best, one pound of flour, one pound of meat, three-quarters a pint of rice, with small quantities of peas and butter. Fresh vegetables or anything else which might alter or improve his diet had to be bought or obtained by bartering:

> We sold all our butter, rice, pease and beef and part of our pork and brought green plantains, vegetables and roast coffee and treacle and made a shift to have a jug of coffee and a piece of bread for breakfast and an ounce or two of pork for dinner with a plate of tolerable good broth made from the salt port, thickened with pum[pkin] and ... killaloo, well heated with Cayenne pepper. Any supper or third meal we had was a little pork brine, Cayenne pepper and the remainder of our bread and as much water as we could drink...

James Aytoun, recording his time in Dominica as a private in the 30th Regiment, seems to have been one British soldier who was both literate and able to resist the temptations of 'new rum'. Although he was writing about conditions in 1788, nothing much concerning the quality or quantity of the daily rations had changed by the time the West India regiments were raised; nor were many changes to take place for a long time to come. Meals similar to those described by Aytoun remained the basic fare of soldiers in the Caribbean long after he had returned to Scotland, and were probably not much different when he was writing his memoirs in 1829.

The men of the West India regiments drew the same rations as white troops, but from the beginning preferred to sell or barter as much as they could, in order to provide themselves with a more suitable diet. This became the established practice and, as army rations remained very much the same anywhere in the world, continued in West Africa as much as in the Westindies. In 1873 at the start of a campaign in the Gold Coast the fact that they sold 'a large portion of their rations' was even given official recognition. For the duration of the campaign the 2nd WIR, instead of drawing standard rations along with the other regiments in the British force, were issued with 'the native levy ration' together with a cash sum of ninepence a day. As the rations supplied to the Gold Coast levies was made up of the very foodstuffs the 2nd WIR troops would have bought for themselves anyway they were 'well pleased' with the arrangement. Regrettably, the campaign was over within a few months and they then had to revert to their normal way of supplementing army stodge.

Another bonus enjoyed by the 2nd WIR at the same time was that the men were issued with a special uniform, considered to be more appropriate for the conditions under which they were required to fight. Although this was a short-lived experiment, lasting no longer than the campaign itself, it represented a decided advance on much of the thought previously given to a combat dress for the West India regiments. For many years after 1795, besides having to exist on a largely unsuitable diet, the troops were expected to fight in equally inappropriate uniforms. Right at the beginning it was envisaged the regiments would be used as light infantry. Units such as Malcolm's Rangers had shown how adept black irregulars were as skirmishers, and it was expected that the men of the new regiments would be used as fast-moving raiders, living off the land when necessary, and engaging in less conventional forms of warfare such as ambushes and hit-and-run raids. This concept was fostered by various senior officers in the Westindies, in particular by Brigadier-Generals John Moore and Thomas Hislop, both of whom arrived there in 1796 as part of an expeditionary force under General Abercromby. Moore, whose fame as a military commander was to be immortalized by his untimely death at Corunna during the Peninsular War, is recognised as the founder of the light infantry and rifle regiments of the British Army. While it would be too much to say that he obtained his inspiration for the development of this arm of the service from seeing black troops in action, he was well aware of their value in unconventional warfare. While in command in St Lucia in the middle of 1796 he wrote to Abercromby:

> In this country much may be made of Black Corps. I have had occasion to observe them of late. They possess, I think, many excellent qualities as Soldiers, and may with proper attention become equal to any thing. Even at present as they are, for the W. Indies they are invaluable.

Five years later, in his all-embracing memorandum about the West India regiments, Hislop argued that their soldiers were natural light infantrymen and should be dressed accordingly:

> It having always been evident to me that not only from the local circumstances of the Country to which their services are confined, they will be required to act as such, but that they are also from their constitution & natural habits, better calculated for that species of Warfare in this Climate

> than Europeans. If they were put entirely on the footing of Light Troops, by being appointed and Cloathed accordingly, the establishment would in my idea be found to be more congenial to the service required of them.
> Dark Green, instead of Red, would be the colour best adapted to render them unobservable by an Enemy, which for the duty of a Light Infantry Soldier, is a matter of the greatest consequence.

His very sensible proposals written in 1801 were made too late.

By the time his paper reached London there were twelve regiments in existence, with a total strength of perhaps 10,000 men. The prospect of such numbers of blacks, mostly slaves, not only armed but also trained to exercise their skills independently, and encouraged to think for themselves, was too much for anyone in authority to even contemplate. Apprehension about what it all could lead to killed all thought about a special role for the regiments. Instead of being developed into part of an elite corps of light infantry, each West India regiment was to be organised and trained as any other line regiment of the army, and instead of adopting a dark green uniform the rank and file would continue wearing the familiar red.

The infantryman's uniform consisted of a red jacket with lapels to the waist, worn with a white waistcoat, jodhpur-type white breeches, white stockings, short black gaiters, black shoes, and a black stovepipe hat with a large furry crest. Each West India regiment had a different colour for the collar, lapels and cuffs for the jacket, and distinctive cap and belt badges. Some modifications were made as time went by, in attempts to provide the Westindian soldier with a more suitable uniform, but for over fifty years to the untrained eye he was dressed in very much the same way as any other British infantryman. After 1858, when a radical change to his uniform took place, he was dressed like no other soldier in the British Army.

The general standard of accommodation provided for black soldiers was no better for their health and well-being than their food and uniforms. Comfort was unknown, and a barrack-room was usually no more than a dark, badly-ventilated chamber intended to house twenty to thirty men, who slept on wooden platforms or the floor. Hammocks were introduced in the early 1800s and it was another twenty years before iron bedsteads became available. As part of his initial outfit each recruit was issued with a straw-filled mattress, a pillow, a pair of sheets and a blanket. Fresh straw was provided once a quarter, the sheets got washed once a month, and the blanket perhaps once a year.

Forts and other military establishments in the Westindies were needed to protect harbours, sheltered anchorages and landing places. Inevitably this meant that most were sited in low-lying, swampy areas where the risk of contracting a disease was greatest. One such post, and one with which the West India regiments became very familiar from their earliest days, was situated on the west side of Kingston harbour in Jamaica. The rivers and streams draining into this side of the harbour entered the sea through a huge, mosquito-breeding mangrove swamp, on the southern side of which a long, low peninsula had been formed. Fort Augusta had been built at the end of this peninsula during the latter half of the eighteenth century at a place called, appropriately enough, Mosquito Point. It was armed with eighty or more guns, sited to cover the narrow channel leading to Kingston from Port Royal, and

> constructed on a scale becoming its importance, with accommodation for two or three regiments, and the regiments were sent thither, and they perished, regiment after regiment, officers and men, from the malarious exhalations of the morass. Whole battalions were swept away ...

The eminent English historian James Anthony Froude recorded this observation in this now infamous book, *The English in the West Indies*, after visiting the fort in 1887. Even at this late date, long after it had ceased to have any military use other than 'a powder magazine', it was still manned by men of the 2nd WIR:

> A guard is kept there of twenty blacks from the West Indian force, but even these are changed every ten days - so deadly the vapour of the malarious jungle is now understood to be.
>
> I never saw so spectral a scene as met my eyes when we steamed up to the landing place - ramparts broken down, and dismantled cannon lying at the foot of the wall overgrown by jungle. The sentinel who presented arms was like a corpse in uniform. He was not pale, for he was a negro - he was green, and looked like some ghoul or afrite in a ghastly cemetery.

The quarters provided for the regiments in West Africa, once they began serving there on a regular basis, were no better than those in the Caribbean. If anything they were less well-constructed and, because of more severe climatic conditions, tended to deteriorate more rapidly. Even before 1850 the barracks at Bathurst in the Gambia were described as 'literally tumbling to pieces':

> The [officers'] apartments, in respect to their size, are tolerable, and this is

> all that can be said of them; for what with the filth of bats falling from the decayed ceiling and the destructive visits of the Bug-aBug, nothing like comfort .... could possibly be found there.
> The skill and judgement of the architect in design are equally praiseworthy in the construction of the Soldiers' quarters, which have the appearance of a row of wine vaults more than the habitations for human beings. There is no external protection against bad weather, so that ... the men [are] either to be exposed to wind and rain without mercy, or immerse themselves in nearly total darkness.

At the time this was written most of the barrack accommodation in the Westindies would probably have given the men of the West India regiments equal cause to grumble. Fifty years earlier, closer to the time such buildings were erected and when the majority of the soldiers were still slaves, this would not have been the case. Then, no matter how comfortless and lacking in amenities, the accommodation provided was of a higher standard than that available to slaves working in any of the islands. Just as importantly as far as the black soldiers were concerned, the white troops expected and enjoyed nothing better. This assisted the army authorities in their policy of indoctrinating the men to consider themselves in all respects superior to the general black population. It also quickly produced among the soldiers the beginnings of the necessary *esprit de corps.*

On account of their acceptance of one day's pay, the 'King's Shilling', which was the recognized token of enlistment throughout the army, the few free blacks who joined right at the beginning were known as 'King's Men'. This served to differentiate them from the mass of involuntary slave recruits who, when they were enfranchised in 1807, all adopted the term in order to distance themselves even further from slavery. It survived both the general abolition of slavery in 1834 and the accession of Queen Victoria three years later, as was noted, quite independently, by observers on opposite sides of the Atlantic in the early 1840s. In British Honduras, at the start of his travels in Central America, an American noted that the men of the 2nd WIR

> carry themselves proudly, call themselves the "Queen's Gentlemen", and look down with contempt upon the "niggers".

At much the same time in Sierra Leone an English traveller reported that the soldiers of the 1st WIR

> are proud of being called "Queen's Men", and scornfully address the civilians with - "Me no Niggur, me Queen Man".

While it is open to question whether anything can be read into the preference of the 2nd WIR to be known as 'gentlemen', rather than the mere 'men' of the 1st WIR, such observations make it clear that all the soldiers had pride in their calling and a marked sense of superiority over their civilian compatriots.

It was all very well for the army to foster this attitude: no-one in authority wanted to see disciplined, trained and well-armed troops making common cause with the Westindian slave population as it existed until 1834, nor with a disgruntled and sometimes disaffected labour force after Emancipation: but for the individual soldier it was not without its drawbacks. Once he had got through the rigours of basic training, mastering the rudiments of English when necessary, and acquired his not unimpressive uniform, the new member of a West India regiment sooner or later came into contact with civilian society. And this society of course was composed of both men and women.

From the time the regiments were raised, and for many, many years afterwards, the Westindian soldier suffered from the army's reluctance to acknowledge that he might desire a wife and family, or want any female companionship other than that of prostitutes. This denial of a basic human need applied throughout the army and in any regiment, black or white, only six out of every hundred men were permitted to marry 'on the strength'. This entitled their wives to live in barracks and draw army rations, but in return they were expected to carry out tasks such as washing and cooking for the regiment as a whole. Other men could marry if they so wished, but they then had to make all their own arrangements for housing and feeding their families. As Britain's world-wide military responsibilities led to the frequent movement of regiments, with prolonged periods of service in foreign parts, the plight of 'unofficial' wives was often extremely desperate, many being abandoned completely when their husbands were posted abroad. This policy remained in force throughout the whole of the nineteenth century, and after the West India regiments started to serve in West Africa caused great distress to many of the men and their families.

But, if the problems which faced a Westindian soldier who wanted to marry were difficult in the late 1890s, how much more difficult they were a hundred years earlier. His barracks in any part of the Westindies, if not in or close to a town, were surrounded by plantations, and female slaves were constantly importuned. This led to endless friction between the civil and military authorities, with soldiers being accused of attempting to lure women away from their work or from existing domestic relationships. The question of soldiers' wives, like so much else to do with the West India regiments, was given some thought by Hislop in 1801:

> Among other ideas which have occurr'd to me, with a view of improving the establishment ... is that of purchasing and attaching a certain number of women, to each Company, who should have liberty to choose a Husband, from amongst the most regular and well behav'd Men belonging to it, with the approbation of the Commanding officer of the Regiment ...The Children [who would result] ... should remain constantly with the Regiment ... Boys would be trained to arms, and become in time excellent Soldiers ... The Girls, when at a proper age, would be allowed to marry in the Regiment, and during their younger years be taught such employment as would make them useful to it. It would also be but just to allow the same rations of provisions to them, as to the Wives and Children of Soldiers in European Regiments.

If today this particular 'idea' of Hislop's seems altogether outrageous it should be remembered that when he wrote it there was no practical alternative to his suggestion, and at least it shows he recognized that in the matter of wives and families black soldiers deserved no less than white troops. There is some evidence that attempts were made to put his proposal into effect but not to any great extent. Matters improved slightly after 1807 when partners could sometimes be found among the free black community, and again of course after 1834. However an increase in the number of married men after Emancipation was not accompanied by much improvement in the way they were treated. This is illustrated very well in the memoirs of Lieutenant-Colonel Balcarres Ramsay, who served briefly in the 3rd WIR in 1847. He records an incident which took place shortly after he joined as a captain in British Guiana, and which began with a conversation with the Regimental Sergeant-Major:

> "I hear, sir, you are only going to stop a few weeks with us. I fear you will have a good deal of trouble with some of the men unless you compromise with them". I said, "What on earth do you mean?" He replied, "Sir, if the men behave well we allow them their mammys (*Anglice,* wives) in barracks; if not, they are kept out". Whereupon I took his advice, and sent for the men he pointed out, whose names were of the strangest character, mostly taken from illustrious and public characters. Several I found were named after men who had been governors. Amongst them was that of my grandfather, the Earl of Balcarres. I addressed them as follows, according to the sergeant-major's

recommendation: "Julius Caesar, Duke of Wellington, Pompey, Sir Robert Peel, Earl of Balcarres, Scipio, Duke of Manchester, etc., you all d..d bad men. I stay here two week; you behave well that time, you have mammy every night; you not behave well, you not have mammy".

This anecdote, recorded by Ramsay over thirty years after the event, says more for the stoicism and fortitude of the men it was intended to deride, than it does for the wit and humanity of the author. The soldiers he spoke to in his patronizing pidgin English, if their preposterous names are anything to go by, may well have joined the army before he was born. To answer to such names, day in and day out, was probably bad enough. To marry, and then have to endure further humiliation as a result, must have been extremely hard to bear.

Some slight mitigation for his insulting behaviour may be found in the knowledge that Ramsay had no wish to serve in the 3rd WIR, joined it unwillingly, and stayed only a few weeks before transferring into a Scottish regiment. In this he was doing no more than many another young officer did throughout the history of the West India regiments. For them, like Ramsay, service with black troops was something to be endured for as short a time as possible before gaining entrance into a more prestigious regiment.

CHAPTER 4
'THE FINE UNISON OF FEELING'

> The fine unison of feeling, the splendid record and tradition of unity and goodwill between the black men in the ranks, and the white men as officers in the W.I.R. form evidence and an emblem, a sign and a pledge of that which, through all differences of race and colour, makes the Empire a fact and a continuing strength, and without which vainly would her cannon thunder or her wealth accumulate.
>
> **Thomas MacDermot (1923)**

Captain Balcarres Ramsay obtained his commission in the 3rd WIR in England in 1847. He had no intention of remaining one of its officers for very long, and even before he sailed to join a detachment of the regiment in British Guiana he had arranged a transfer to the 75th Regiment. The ship in which he crossed the Atlantic called first at Barbados, and Ramsay took the opportunity of going ashore to pay his respects to Major-General Sackville Berkeley, the officer commanding British Forces in the Westindies. It was a particularly opportune call as Berkeley 'was colonel of the regiment I was about to exchange into', and Ramsay lost no time in asking for his transfer to be brought forward. He had no desire to serve with black troops or to spend time in the backwoods of the colony on the South American mainland. Berkeley was sympathetic but, 'as these regiments were only made stepping-stones for promotion to officers from other corps, who exchanged immediately afterwards, [and] he never could lay his hands on a captain', Ramsay would have to join the 3rd WIR as planned. He reached Georgetown at the end of the year and immediately assumed acting command of the detachment, as the proper officer in command, a major, 'was under arrest'. He stay was very brief and after a few weeks he departed for Barbados and the more congenial company of the 75th Foot. Whether his disgracefully condescending treatment of the married men in his detachment was typical of how officers of the West India regiments behaved during this era it is difficult to say, but it seems not unlikely. What was typical, and had been since the regiments were raised, was his use of a commission in one of them purely as a means to an end.

From the beginning it had been intended that although the troops were black all the officers would be white, all with permanent commissions and entitlement to half-pay if and when their regiments were disbanded. It was inconceivable that any black soldier could hold a commission; regardless of any other factors, none could ever have afforded the life of an officer. Until 1871 many commissions and promotions up to and including the rank of lieutenant-colonel were only obtained by paying for them. An official price existed for each rank, with different rates for the Regiments of Horse, the Dragoons, the Foot Guards and the Infantry. In 1795 a commission as an infantry ensign (the lowest rank) cost £450; that of a lieutenant-colonel was ten times as much. In an age when skilled tradesmen were doing well if they earned £100 a year, and many professional men considered £500 to be a substantial annual income, the career of an army officer was restricted to a very small part of the community. The cost of the commission was only part of the expense. An officer had to buy his own uniform and equipment, and was required to live up to a certain standard within his regiment. This standard invariably was one which could not be supported by his pay alone, and a private income was a prerequisite for any officer. Even as late as 1900 a subaltern in the least fashionable infantry regiment still could not get by without at least £60 a year on top of his pay.

The decision to raise the first eight West India regiments created the need for several hundred officers. One lieutenant-colonel and one major, together with something in the order of eight captains, twelve lieutenants and up to twenty ensigns, were needed for each regiment. Even though each commission had to be purchased once the requirement was made known in Great Britain there was a rush to fill the vacancies. By the beginning of July 1795 the 1st WIR already had its full complement, with more than half coming from Scotland or Ireland. However, keen as the purchasers were to acquire their commissions in the 1st WIR or any other, the majority showed no great inclination to take up their regimental duties. Only a few dozen had arrived in the Caribbean by the end of the year. This was brought about to some extent by the evil reputation acquired by the Westindian climate, and the risks involved in soldiering in that part of the world, but in the main it was due to the value of the new commissions as investments which could be traded or sold in the same way as any other.

The exchange of commissions between officers of the same rank in different regiments was a regular occurrence. An officer in a more prestigious regiment who, as was often the case, was in urgent need of funds, could be persuaded to exchange with a suitable cash inducement;

some more determined fellow relishing blood and the prospect of glory, might be willing to risk the climate in order to see some action; there were all sorts of possibilities, but most could only be realised by staying safely in Great Britain. By going out to the Westindies the holder of a commission in, say, the 1st WIR not only reduced his chances of making an advantageous trade but, because of the dangers involved in soldiering there, risked losing his investment altogether. Absenteeism among the officers remained a feature of all the West India regiments throughout the early decades of their existence and, as General Berkeley's comments to Captain Ramsay illustrated, was still a problem in the late 1840s. There was of course another reason for the widespread reluctance of officers to take up their appointments. The appreciation of the worth of black soldiers voiced by a number of senior officers serving in the Westindies was not a view widely shared. The great majority of army officers could hardly have failed to subscribe to the anti-Abolitionist views of the propertied classes from which they were drawn, and for most of them actual service with black troops would have been anathema.

A shortage of officers serving with the men, as opposed to just being borne on the books, became a feature of all the regiments and was highly detrimental, especially in the early years. As it was raised each regiment, consisting as it did of untrained slaves or partly trained irregulars, or a mixture of both, speaking in English, French and a whole variety of African tongues, needed a proper hierarchy of officers. They were required, not only to oversee every aspect of the organization and training necessary to turn such raw material into useful soldiers, but also to present the result to the rest of the army. Without enough dedicated officers to look after their interests the regiments had no chance of acquiring any status other than that of 'a temporary convenience [which] may be found a future evil', condemned to remain at the bottom of the pile even in such basic matters as the issue of clothing and equipment. The shortfall in officers was reflected among the troops by a shortage of everything from caps to muskets which lasted throughout most of the war period.

The high rate of absenteeism among the officers, together with the poor quality of some who did eventually fetch up with their regiments, caused concern among the senior officers in the Westindies who had argued for the raising of the regiments in the first place. In September 1796 Brigadier-General John Moore wrote to the Duke of York, the Commander-in-Chief of the Army, complaining that the West India regiments

> should not be given to General Officers to make jobs of, but clothed by Government and given to Lt Colonels and Majors, who are to command and serve with them. These officers must be chosen and possess certain qualities which render them peculiarly fit for such an Office.

There is nothing in Moore's later career to show that he was prepared to practice what he preached. He left the Caribbean in May 1797 and a year later accepted the colonelcy of the 9th WIR, retaining it and the double pay that went with it until the end of 1799. There is also no evidence that his advice was followed with respect to the other regiments. They continued to be given to 'General Officers to make jobs of', regardless of whether or not such officers were in the Westindies and their suitability for such appointments. The one most unsuitable of all became Colonel of the 8th WIR in June 1798.

The career of Andrew James Cochrane Johnstone typified all that was wrong with the army's method of finding its officers, and many of the worst aspects of late eighteenth century patronage and jobbery. He was born in 1767 as Andrew Cochrane, the eighth son of the Earl of Dundonald. At age sixteen a commission as a cornet in a regiment of Light Dragoons was bought for him and he was packed off to India. Three years later he transferred to another regiment as a lieutenant, and four years after that more of his father's money changed hands and he became a captain in an infantry regiment. In 1791, aged twenty-four, family money and influence got him elected to Parliament as the member of Stirling, and two years after that he married one of the daughters of James Hope Johnstone, the third Earl of Hopetoun. It is not clear just why, when he married, Cochrane should have assumed the name Johnstone, but from what is known of the rest of his life it is highly likely that it was only done with the accompaniment of a sizeable cash inducement. For whatever reason he was known from then on by the surname of Johnstone. By 1794 he was a lieutenant-colonel, and in 1797, by which time he was serving in the Westindies, he was promoted to colonel - the first rank for which he did not have to pay. He was then a few months short of his thirtieth birthday.

Soon after his promotion he was offered the governorship of Dominica. He accepted at once; the opportunities the appointment offered for him to make his fortune were too good to miss. Once he had taken over he not only bought an estate but entered with enthusiasm into the business of buying and selling slaves. When in April 1799 he was again promoted and given command of all the troops in the Leeward Islands it must have seemed that his accumulation of rank, privileges and wealth was set to continue indefinitely. If so, it merely reinforced a similar view formed the year before when he was made Colonel of the 8th WIR, with all the pecuniary opportunities that then still went with such an appointment.

Towards the end of 1801 the 8th WIR, which had been in Dominica for most of the time since 1798, was stationed in the north of the island in a fort guarding the important anchorage in Prince Rupert's Bay. Fort Shirley was superbly sited on Prince Rupert's Bluff, the hilly extremity of a peninsula which formed the northern side of the bay, separated from the mainland by a large area of marshland on the neck of the peninsula. Early in 1802 Johnstone received orders to have clearing and drainage work carried out in the marshes, in order to make the area more healthy and to improve the landward approaches to the fort. His orders contained specific instructions that, if black troops were to be used on this work, they were to be paid the extra ninepence a day which white soldiers received when doing work which would otherwise have to be carried out by civilian labour. Johnstone was not a man to obey an order without first considering what advantage, if any, its execution might bring to himself. After entering into a syndicate which bought up uncultivated land in the vicinity of the marshes, he set the 8th WIR to work in clearing access to this rather than in improving the outer reaches of the fort.

Long before the work started Johnstone, as Colonel of the regiment and with the connivance of several of its officers, had worked out methods of defrauding the men by diverting regimental funds and keeping their pay in arrears. To even consider now paying each man an extra ninepence a day was out of the question, and the funds with which he had been provided to meet this expense were put to his own use.

While it is possible that the troops doing the work might not have known they were entitled to extra pay, they would have objected to such employment in any case. To be set to work with hoes, spades and billhooks went against all the effort made during their training to make them feel superior to plantation slaves, and they were immediately suspicious of the motives of their officers in ordering such menial employment. Their suspicions turned to fear and anger in March after some of them had been in contact with slaves from the nearby plantations. The latter, who were understandably jealous of black soldiers, spread the rumour that the 8th WIR was about to be disbanded, and that the soldiers were being used as labourers in preparation for being sold to plantation owners. Those most affected by such tales were the men most recently entered into the regiment, and who were still far from fluent in English. With memories of enslavement, slave ships and slave masters not yet faded, any departure from the orderly routine to which they had become accustomed was bound to create doubt and unease. When half-understood rumours began to circulate among them, this unease quickly turned into panicky distress. The arrival of two warships in Prince Rupert's Bay on 9th April brought matters to a head. During their day's work the story circulated that the ships had come to carry them away into plantation slavery, and on return to their barracks in the evening a full-scale mutiny broke out.

The regiment's officers, none of whom had been sufficiently close to the men to have detected any change in their demeanour during the previous days, were taken completely by surprise. The remainder of the garrison, officers and men of the artillery, and of the commissariat and ordnance departments, were just as unprepared. Within a couple of hours the mutineers were in full control of the fort, and in the general confusion which had taken place seven officers had been killed. All the other white personnel, including a few women, had either been captured or had managed to escape in the darkness. It was not only the distant attitude of the regiment's officers which helped the mutineers; as was so often the case in any of the West India regiments, the number of officers actually serving was well below the authorized establishment. On this particular day there were only eleven officers in charge of almost five hundred men. Even the commanding officer was absent, 'having gone to Europe, for the recovery of his health'. Major John Gordon, who had assumed temporary command, was one of three who managed to escape and raise the alarm. Five of the others were amongst those killed, and the remaining three were held as hostages.

When news of the mutiny reached Roseau, the island's main town, the next morning, Johnstone declared martial law, mobilized the Militia, and called out the 68th Regiment from Morne Bruce just outside the town. As road communication on the island was so poor he requisitioned various small vessels in the roadstead, and these transported the troops and himself to Prince Rupert's Bay the same evening. The two warships, the *Excellent* and the *Magnificent*, which had only anchored in the bay the previous day to embark firewood and fresh water, were still there, and Johnstone found that their marines had already been landed in order to prevent anyone from leaving the fort. The *Magnificent* was despatched for reinforcements from among the troops occupying the Iles des Saintes off Guadeloupe, and when she returned on 12th April Johnstone was able to muster a total of 1300 men. Preparations were then put in hand to storm the fort. Before this could take place the mutineers, using one of their hostages as a go-between, agreed to an unconditional surrender. Arrangements were made for Johnstone and his force to take over the fort at five o'clock in the afternoon, by which time the mutineers would be drawn up on parade where they would 'lay down their arms, on receiving word the from the governor'.

The British troops, including a detachment of artillery, with Johnstone riding at their head, and followed by 'all the civilians attached to the army ... anxious to be spectators of the approaching scene', entered the fort at the time agreed. They found the 8th WIR in place on the parade ground, with 'the three officers (their prisoners) standing in front of their respective companies, to the command of which, it appeared, they had been restored'. At this point, instead of merely giving the order for their arms to be grounded, Johnstone felt called upon to make a speech and to chastise the regiment for disloyalty. His harangue, delivered from the saddle while backed by ranks of fully-armed white troops and several pieces of artillery, turned what should have been a quick and painless operation into a bloodbath. Many of the mutineers could have had no understanding of what Johnstone was saying, and all of them must have been extremely tense and nervous. As their mumbles of discontent increased in volume Johnstone realised he had made a mistake, and 'without losing further time, gave the word for them to order, and ground their arms'. It was too late. Only a few men obeyed and when one of the others called out that 'Governor Johnstone would cheat them', the British troops 'scarcely waiting for orders, fired a volley'. The three company commanders managed to escape unhurt but a least seventy of the men were killed or wounded. The remainder panicked; a few returned fire, killing or wounding a number of white soldiers, but the great majority attempted to flee from the parade ground. They were pursued through the fort and out to the end of the bluff, 'from the top of which, two or three hundred of them precipitated themselves into the sea'. Incredibly, very few were killed by their fall, and eventually all the others struggled ashore to be taken into custody. Some who managed to escape from the fort in the opposite direction avoided capture by hiding in the very swamps which Johnstone had been told to have cleared, but eventually all were hunted down by the Militia. By the time order was restored and all the regiment accounted for at least fifty had been killed and a similar number wounded.

Three days later, after Major Gordon had identified the ringleaders, seven soldiers were court-martialled, found guilty of 'exciting and joining in mutiny' and sentenced to death. Soon afterwards they and the rest of the regiment were transported to Martinique, where the executions took place on 27th April. As it was still not clear to the army authorities why the mutiny had taken place a Court of Inquiry was convened at Fort Royal at the end of the month. The evidence obtained from the interrogation of Major Gordon and the other officers, and from some of the men, and which then formed part of the report sent to the Secretary of War, contained references to various irregularities in the way the men had been employed and paid. At the time of the mutiny none of the men had received the extra allowance they were entitled to, and most of them had not received their regular pay for several months. Although these facts were considered to be no more than incidental to the major cause of the mutiny - which was recognised as being the fear of the men of being sold as field slaves - they marked the beginning of the end for Johnstone.

On 24th May, by which time the 8th WIR had been shipped to Barbados, another Court of Inquiry was convened, in order to investigate the state of the regimental accounts. The evidence that this unearthed of unusual and irregular transactions, involving both pay and rations for the troops, was enough to show that the actions of some of the officers, Johnstone in particular, had contributed much to the outbreak of the mutiny. This was confirmed in June, when another twenty-four men were court-martialled, and it was asserted 'that short pay and want of money, were the general cry among the soldiers on the eve of the mutiny'. All those tried, most bearing the foolish names they had had hung around their necks just a few years earlier - Mars, Congo Jack, Martyr, Manly, Lively - were found guilty and executed. Punishment of the rest of the regiment, now reduced to under four hundred, took place three months later. The one hundred and eighty-four men adjudged to have taken an active part in the mutiny were sent as pioneers to various white regiments where, no doubt, they were soon worked to death. The remainder, considered not to have been directly involved, were drafted into some of the other West India regiments. Although the 8th WIR remained in being for another fourteen years, from September 1802 it consisted of officers and men of the 11th WIR, which had been renumbered.

Out of the officers of the 'old' 8th WIR who could be held culpable, only Johnstone and Gordon remained alive. Gordon was not given the opportunity of transferring into another regiment, but sent back to England on half-pay. Johnstone, who was dismissed from his post as governor of Dominica, lost his appointment as a brigadier and was put on half-pay as a colonel. He followed Gordon to England determined to revive his fortunes, and began by having Gordon arrested and court-martialled, charged with embezzlement, misuse of public funds and general dereliction of duty. The trial took place in London in February 1804, with Johnstone prosecuting. It lasted two weeks and involved the prosecutor and the accused in a series of charges and countercharges, each trying to blame the other for what had taken place two years earlier. In the end, even though Gordon was acquitted on all charges, the officers who formed the court obviously reached their verdict with some reluctance. In finding him not guilty they recorded that he 'procrastinated', showed 'culpable neglect', was 'very irregular, in not keeping an account of the monies which he received', and also 'negligent, and to have subjected himself to censure, in not having taken further measures in order to have accounted for the whole of the monies which he had received'. He remained on half-pay and was never employed again.

A year later, largely as a result of the accusations made by Gordon at his own trial, Johnstone himself was court-martialled for various 'irregularities'. Although he was eventually acquitted it brought his army career to an end. He was passed over for promotion to major-general and so resigned in order to try his luck elsewhere. In 1807, again through family influence and string-pulling, he secured a 'lucrative appointment' in Tortola. There he entered wholeheartedly into a new career of fraud, larceny and embezzlement, which he pursued both in the Caribbean and Great Britain for the next seven years. In 1814 he was the prime instigator of a plot to defraud the London Stock Exchange, in which he involved and ruined the reputation of his nephew, Admiral Thomas Cochrane, the tenth Earl of Dundonald. While awaiting trial for his part in the conspiracy Johnstone fled the country and disappeared from history.

Although out-and-out rogues, such as Johnstone certainly was, were not unknown among army officers of the late eighteenth and early nineteenth centuries, the West India regiments suffered more from men like Gordon. There were many like him who, if not genuinely venal, were lacking in leadership and responsibility, and also in common decency and humanity - perhaps what in more recent times came to be called 'officer-like qualities'. It was unfortunate that such men, out of all those officers holding commissions in the regiments, were usually the ones who actually wanted or needed to take up their appointments. They were rarely of the type who took a true interest in the troops they commanded, or had any pride in their achievements. The men of the 8th WIR, only a year before the mutiny, had taken part in the seizure of the island of St Martin. Afterwards the expedition's commander, Lieutenant-General Thomas Trigge, had extolled their fighting ability and praised their behaviour as that which 'would do honour to any troops'. There seems little doubt that, had they not under Johnstone's malign influence later been reduced to the status of unpaid field-hands, forced to labour under the indifferent eyes of an insufficient number of officers, the mutiny would not have taken place.

The prospect of making one's career in a West India regiment throughout the time they remained part of the British Army, but particularly during the first few decades of their existence, was attractive to only certain kinds of officers, and a fairly small number at that. For one or two of the more ambitious, keen for action and adventure, such a career did hold out the promise of independent commands, brevet promotions and, after such things were introduced, the award of medals or the membership of Orders for bravery: it meant serving in places where diseases were rampant, but it was always someone else who was going to fall sick and that would increase one's own chances of achieving something worthwhile. For others, perhaps less ambitious, the pleasures of peacetime soldiering in a warm climate and the more louche aspects of colonial society provided the attractions. In his old age Major William Ross of the 1st WIR recalled the balls which used to be given in Jamaica in the late 1840s:

> As a result of these Entertainments, it sometimes occurred that a young officer became engaged to a Jamaica damsel, when our good Colonel would undertake all the marital expenses, if needed.
> At this period of the purchase system, there was a large and wealthy Jewish population in the Island and officers eager for rapid promotion, could, by aid of the marital tie, become Field Officers in about six years; otherwise advancement in West India Regiments was very slow. Many officers from the Line - it is interesting to note - came solely for that purpose!

There were other, rather more unusual attractions available to those who served with the regiments in West Africa, as Ross remembered from his time at Cape Coast Castle, on the Gold Coast in 1850:

> ...there existed a curious custom. In the town itself, there resided a Fantee-lady - a Mrs Swanzy ... Being very well-to-do, she had numerous domestics and soon after the arrival of a new European official, whether civil, military or mercantile, by way of a welcome insisted on him accepting one of her damsels, generally covered with gold ornaments, to look after his household! .... one was generally warned not to refuse ... and the lady at once assumed all responsibility and remained with the individual until he went home and died.

That was not all the benevolent Mrs Swanzy provided for young British officers so far from home:

> She had a troupe of dancing girls and it was customary, after dinner, to proceed to the dwelling of this lady to witness their performance which took

place nightly and their dancing was certainly very graceful. She was always most hospitable, and during the entertainment, champagne and other refreshments were freely supplied, whilst to her special favourites, Mrs. S. exhibited her valuable collection of native jewellery.

Major Ross was one officer apparently who found the 'damsels' of West Africa more to his liking than those of Jamaica; having resigned his commission in 1871 he settled in Freetown and was still there forty years later, recording his reminiscences for a regimental magazine at the age of eighty.

Among the fire-eaters, the remittance men, the Rosses, and other long-serving officers there were some who found life in a West India regiment so congenial that they remained until forced to leave by death or age. In some cases they even managed to pass on their attachment to other generations: William Nicholls of the 2nd WIR joined in 1824 and died in command in Jamaica twenty years later, leaving two sons in the regiment; Henry Whitfeild, who joined the 2nd WIR in 1828 remained for forty years, the last twelve in command; he was succeeded as commanding officer by William Hill, whose father and grandfather had also served in the same regiment. Regrettably men like these were always a minority. For most a period of service as an officer in a West India regiment was seen as nothing more than something to be endured before moving on to better things. As a result the regiments always suffered from having many officers who had no feeling for regimental pride or tradition, no liking for the countries in which they served, and little but disdain for the troops they led. Their general attitude in turn is reflected in the way the regiments were viewed by the rest of the British Army, in which they always ranked at the bottom of the infantry order of precedence.

Problems associated with a shortage of officers, career men or otherwise, remained with the regiments until the end. Even towards the end of the nineteenth century, when there remained only a single regiment of two battalions, it was very rare for either battalion to be able to muster all its officers, fit and healthy, in one place at any one time. In 1888 the author or a book about Sierra Leone, to which he gave the not inappropriate subtitle *The White Man's Grave*, observed that the officers of the battalion then in Freetown 'are generally a nice set of fellows, but there are not nearly enough of them'. He then went on to state what effect this had on the men, but without being aware that what he was saying was far from being original:

Owing to the unhealthiness of the climate in which they serve, many [of the officers] are constantly on sick leave and furlough, and junior lieutenants are frequently compelled to take charge of companies ....

The results of having junior officers in positions of responsibility for which, by virtue of their youth and limited experience, most of them were unsuited, were bad both for them and they men they commanded. The assumption of a position to which he was not yet temperamentally suited, nor fully competent to hold, could not fail to leave a young officer very susceptible to received wisdom, and the ready acceptance of other people's opinions and biases. A junior lieutenant placed in command of a company of eighty to a hundred men, and dependent on senior, white, NCOs for advice and assistance, would have had to be exceptionally mature not to have imbibed at the same time the prejudices and racial views many of such NCOs must have held.

The sort of patronizing attitude towards their men which was induced among such officers, unable to see much beyond the colour of a man's skin, was demonstrated in the lecture delivered by Captain Ramsay to some of the married men of the 3rd WIR. The general opinion of Westindian soldiers which he and many other officers held was given to a visitor to St Kitts in the late 1840s:

"The black troops are as courageous as the white", said an officer of the ..... West India regiment to me; "but once fairly excited, they are beyond control. They are willing to obey an order, as far as they can be made to comprehend it, but their intellect is so limited, and their powers of reflection are so slight, that we can trust little or nothing to the [black] non-commissioned officers; so that in addition to our normal duties, we have to do that which, amongst the whites, would be done by colour-sergeants, corporals, etc. Their ideas on discipline, dress and neatness, are extremely lax, so that we have great trouble in keeping them in anything like military order. They have furious animal passions, and were we to restrain them too far, they would mutiny".

These comments, complete with the sexual innuendo without which no discussion of blacks by whites can ever be contemplated, probably say more about the quality of the anonymous officer then they do about the quality of the men he so halfheartedly commanded: read in the late twentieth century, they much resemble an 'expatriate' wife's views of her Westindian maid, and have similar validity.

Fortunately for the black troops who manned places like Brimstone Hill in St Kitts and Fort Augusta in Kingston Harbour in the last century, there were some officers at least who did not subscribe to such bigoted views and racial prejudice (or if they did, not to any serious extent), and the interest which they took in the men went some way towards making up for the indifference of the rest. Colonel Alfred Ellis, whose *History of the First West India Regiment* has already been mentioned, was one such officer. He joined the 1st WIR in 1873 and as well as becoming a most able soldier also made a reputation as an ethnographer. The studies he made during his time in the regiment of various West African tribes were considered at the time to be 'models of what books should be that are written by people studying native customs in their native land'. He was certainly one officer with a reasonable understanding and clear perception of the various elements, influences and traits which helped form the African, and hence black Westindian, character. In his history of the regiment he recorded his opinion that

> The English-speaking negro of the West Indies is most excellent material for a soldier. He is docile, patient, brave and faithful, and for an officer who knows how to gain his affection - an easy matter, requiring only justness, good temper, and an ear ready to listen patiently to any tale of real or imaginary grievance - he will do anything.

Evidence that Ellis was correct in his assessment of the attributes of the Westindian soldier, as he was in his summary of those needed by his British officer, is to be found throughout the history of the West India regiments. The quality of the leadership provided for the 'excellent material' was an essential factor in every one of the campaigns in which the regiments took part, beginning with those of the French Revolutionary War in the Windward Islands in 1796.

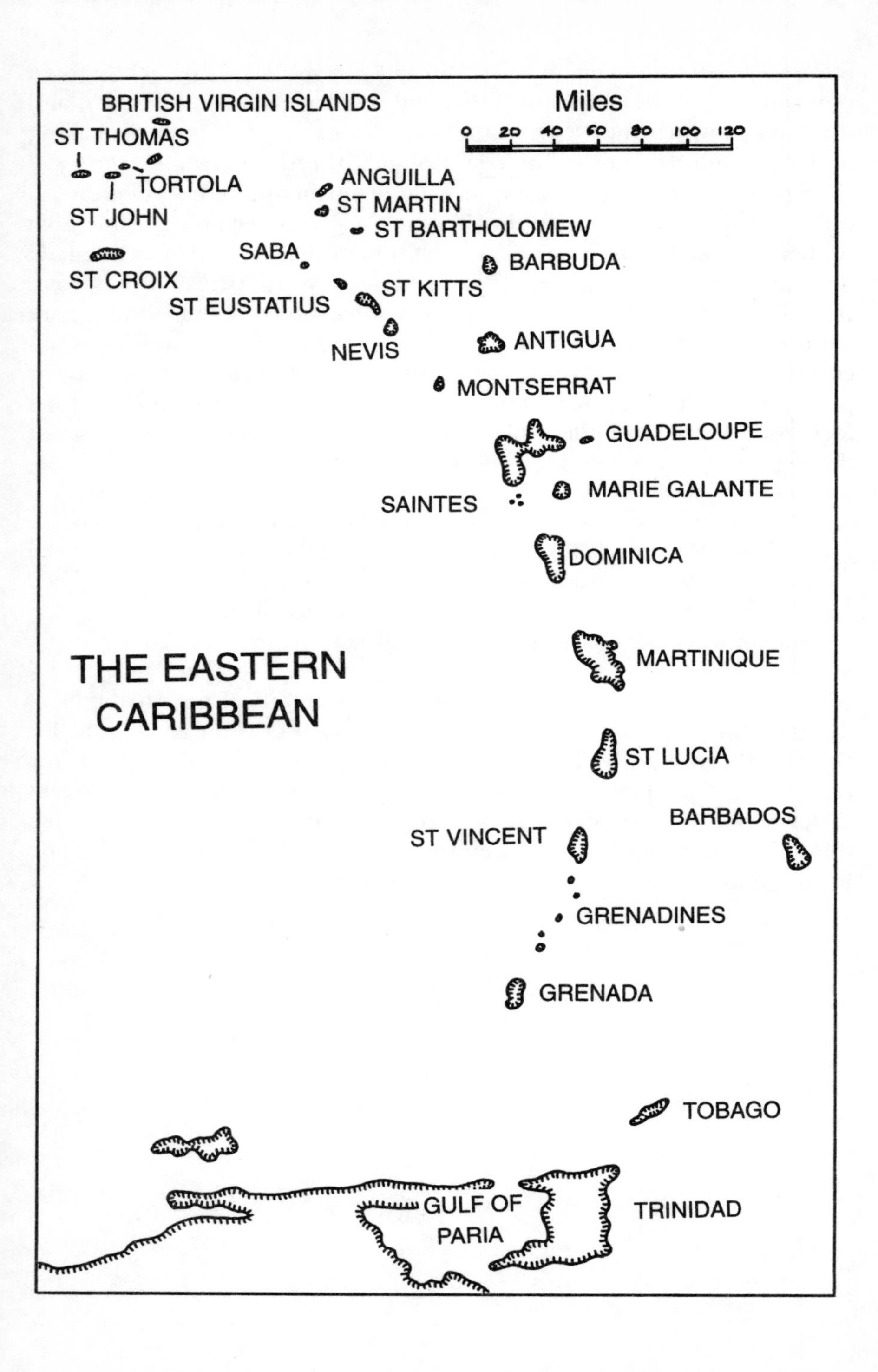

BRITISH VIRGIN ISLANDS
Miles
0 20 40 60 80 100 120
ST THOMAS
TORTOLA
ST JOHN
ANGUILLA
ST MARTIN
ST BARTHOLOMEW
SABA
BARBUDA
ST CROIX
ST KITTS
ST EUSTATIUS
NEVIS
ANTIGUA
MONTSERRAT
GUADELOUPE
MARIE GALANTE
SAINTES
DOMINICA
THE EASTERN
CARIBBEAN
MARTINIQUE
ST LUCIA
BARBADOS
ST VINCENT
GRENADINES
GRENADA
TOBAGO
GULF OF
PARIA
TRINIDAD

PART TWO

PERFECTING THEIR DISCIPLINE

Besides the white troops employed in the West Indies in wartime, there were eight West India regiments, composed of negro soldiers, commanded by regular white officers. The embodying and employing of such a corps in the West Indies is considered by the inhabitants, and doubtless with much reason, as an impolitic step. The more perfect these troops may become in their discipline, the more dangerous and formidable they would be in case of defection ...

J Stewart
A View of the Past and Present State of the Island of Jamaica (1823)

CHAPTER 5
PROVING THEIR UTILITY

Whatever prejudices may have existed, or may still be entertained, among the Planter or other Residents in the West India Colonies, against the establishment of Black regiments, the utility of them, has in every instance been fully proved, whether by their services in the field or by their capability of performing every other description of Military duties.

Brigadier-General Thomas Hislop (1801)

The letter authorizing the formation of two regular regiments of black troops was signed by the Secretary of State for War and the Colonies, Henry Dundas, on 17th April 1795. It reached Lieutenant-General Vaughan, C-in-C of the British forces in the eastern Caribbean, in the middle of June.

By that time the British and French had been fighting in the area for over two years, having begun with the British capture of Tobago in April 1793. In the following year an expeditionary force under Lieutenant-General Charles Grey had invaded and captured the far more important islands of Martinique, St Lucia and Guadeloupe. Unfortunately the total number of troops at Grey's disposal, constantly being reduced by sickness and death from disease, was insufficient for the task of garrisoning these islands and for providing adequate protection for all the British possessions at the same time. In October 1794 Guadeloupe was effectively retaken by the French, leaving one fort only in British hands for another two months before it, too, was surrendered. Once this island was safely back in French hands a campaign was begun to stir up trouble in Grenada, St Vincent, Dominica and St Lucia, each of which had a strong French element in its population. The French inhabitants of Grenada were inspired to revolt in March 1795; the 'Black' Carib population, assisted by some of the French, rose at much the same time in St Vincent; a small force invaded Dominica but was repulsed on 16th June; a larger force sent to St Lucia forced the British to evacuate three days later.

The arrival of the letter from Dundas at the British headquarters in Martinique at just about this time must have given General Vaughan some encouragement, but he was not to live long enough to see any result, or even to learn that more than two regiments of black troops were to be raised. He died suddenly in July, another victim - like so many of his troops - of the Westindian climate. The formation of the regiments was now left to his replacement, Lieutenant-General Sir Ralph Abercromby, who was to lead another, much larger expeditionary force then being assembled in Britain.

Abercromby arrived in Barbados in March 1796, a couple of weeks ahead of the main body of his force, expecting to find a considerable number of trained black soldiers waiting to join his expedition. Instead he discovered he could draw upon about 1500 men, most of them armed but by no means all yet properly trained for active service in conjunction with white troops. Most of them belonged to units such as Malcolm's Rangers or Drualt's Rangers (the French corps raised in Guadeloupe which had been taken into British pay before the evacuation of the island eighteen months earlier). Out of the eight black regiments which had by then been authorized, only the first, Whyte's, and the second, Myers', had any strength to speak of, and they could only muster about 400 rank and file between them. Of these the greater proportion belonged to Myers' Regiment, which since September of the previous year had been in St Vincent.

The formation of both regiments (which from now on it is more convenient to refer to by their designated West India Regiment numbers) had taken place in Martinique and the 1st WIR was to remain there, not seeing any action, until the end of 1798. During this time, even after the incorporation of Malcolm's Rangers at the end of 1796, the total rank and file was never to exceed 350. Because of this it fell to the 2nd WIR to have the honour of being the first of the new regiments to experience active service.

The Carib revolt, or 'Brigands' War', broke out in March 1795, at a time when the number of British troops in St Vincent was too small to contain it. When a French force of about 800 men landed to support the rising in September the British were forced to withdraw into the capital, Kingstown, leaving the remainder of the island outside their control with

> the works and buildings of almost every estate ... either burnt or destroyed by the Caribs, assisted by some of the old French inhabitants and the Republicans from Guadeloupe.

A relief force which included the nucleus of the 2nd WIR was rushed from Martinique on 29th September, but proved to small to do much more than clear the enemy from the ridges and hills overlooking

Kingstown. Having done that, nominal control was re-established over that part of the island lying to the south of a line between Kingstown and the mouth of the Colonarie River on the east coast, perhaps one quarter of the island in all. A stalemate then existed from early October for three months.

Among those who had landed with the relief force was Lieutenant-Colonel Samuel Graham, who had been appointed as the first commanding officer of the 2nd WIR, together 'with the officers and noncommissioned officers requisite for the formation of the regiment', in the middle of 1795. Having had little success in finding suitable recruits in Martinique they had now been sent to St Vincent in order to enrol a body of 'trustworthy negroes' raised by the Governor some months earlier to assist in fighting the Caribs, and known as the St Vincent Rangers. Once ashore Graham had lost no time and: 'According to his own memorandum to form the regiment, he received a number of slaves the property of planters, some French blacks from Guadeloupe, some Carolina [Corps] blacks, in all amounting to 400 rank and file'. And so, at the beginning of October 1795, the first of the new regiments to consist of more than a name, a selection of officers and NCOs, and the odd drummer, came into existence. Graham then had just three months in which to try to turn his somewhat motley collection of irregulars into a useful unit of the British Army.

The 2nd WIR went into action for the first time on 8th January, 1796, when two companies led by Graham formed part of a small force stationed on the eastern side of the island. An outpost on a ridge overlooking the Colonarie River was attacked in the early hours of the morning and completely overrun: 'The rout was indeed complete - nothing was saved - guns and stores were all abandoned to the enemy'. Graham and his men, who were encamped about a mile away, were hurriedly called in to cover the ensuing retreat which, because everything had been abandoned, took place all the way to Kingstown, a distance of over twelve miles. They performed this task very creditably but at great cost, suffering no less than 152 casualties, a figure which represented nearly forty per cent of the total British casualties. Once the survivors reached the capital there was nothing more any of them could do but tend the wounded, and await the arrival of General Abercromby's expeditionary force.

The fleet with the British force arrived in the Caribbean in early April. The troops, many of whom had been cooped up in the transports for several months, were given little time to recover. Abercromby began his campaign to restore British supremacy in the region before the end of the month by attacking St Lucia. None of the West India regiments was involved as such, but nearly 1200 black troops were an integral part of the 9000-strong force. The bulk of them belonged either to Malcolm's Rangers, later to be transferred into the 1st WIR, or to Drualt's Rangers, which became the 9th WIR in 1798.

Malcolm, aged twenty-eight and recently promoted to lieutenant-colonel, was shot and killed on 3rd May while leading his men in the storming of one of the outlying batteries on Morne Fortune, the main French stronghold overlooking the capital, Castries. He was undoubtedly an extremely competent and courageous officer, with an outlook and lack of prejudice remarkable for his time. His outstanding leadership ability and strong attachment to the men he raised and commanded can be sensed - allowing for eulogistic hyperbole - in the obituary which appeared in *The London Chronicle* in June:

> Deeply indeed will his loss be lamented by the common soldier; for he was their friend and protector! While he habituated them to the strictest discipline, he rivetted their affections; and of the black corps which he raised and formed entirely ... he never lost a single man by desertion out of 700, in the whole campaign!

Although he does not quite merit the description of him in Sir John Fortescue's incomparable *History of the British Army* as 'the father of our African regiments' (a distinction which either of the Frenchmen de Soter or Drualt, both of whom raised their black ranger units a year before Malcolm, can lay better claim to) he certainly played a key role in establishing the credibility of black soldiers. His connection with the early history of the West India regiments was important, and most of Fortescue's panegyric holds true:

> His name is justly remembered as the founder of the First West India Regiment, but it deserves record rather as one of those officers, fortunately not uncommon though too easily forgotten amongst us, whose skill, courage and magic of leadership can turn the rawest of material into the most devoted and efficient of soldiers.

The campaign to recapture St Lucia lasted exactly one month and the French surrendered on 26th May. Brigadier-General John Moore was left to secure the island (and to ponder on the 'many excellent qualities' of the black soldiers he had 'had occasion to observe') while Abercromy turned his attention to the relief of Grenada and St Vincent, dividing his forces accordingly.

Some three thousand troops, including Malcolm's Rangers, were sent to Grenada and after a brief campaign lasting nine days forced the French to surrender on 19th June. The relief of St Vincent took place simultaneously and was equally brief. Abercromby himself, with another three thousand men, landed at Kingstown on 7th June and began driving the enemy out of their positions overlooking the town three days later. This was achieved at the expense of 38 dead and 145 wounded in two days. Nearly 700 French prisoners were taken but their Carib allies all fled, some to give themselves up a week later while the more intransigent retreated into the mountains.

Who better after this to reconnoitre and assess the situation than Lieutenant-Colonel Graham and the 2nd WIR? On 18th June, 'having pursued the line formed by the bed of the Colonarie River to a considerable elevation', they discovered a large gathering of Caribs in a well-fortified stronghold. Graham attempted to parley with them under a white flag, but as he approached 'he received a desperate wound through the lungs from a musket-ball, and soon afterwards, a second in the hand from another ball'. Several of the soldiers with him were also killed but the rest behaved with great coolness and courage. The unconscious Graham was carried back down the riverbed until out of range of the stronghold, put into a makeshift stretcher and then carried four miles to a camp occupied by the 42nd Regiment. After receiving some rough and ready attention in the field for the wounds caused by the ball which 'had entered his side three inches from the backbone, and passing through, had come out under his breast' he was taken back to Kingstown. Three weeks later he was evacuated to England with 'the wound in his side discharging matter from both orifices'. After his departure, with Captain Andrew Thompson in acting command (the regiment's only major having not yet joined) the 2nd WIR became engaged in a lengthy period of guerilla warfare which lasted until the middle of October.

By then the Caribs had had enough and resigned themselves to the awful fate which they must have known awaited them. Back in July Abercromby had ordered those who had surrendered initially to be shipped to Balliceaux, one of the smaller Grenadine Islands about eleven miles south of St Vincent, from where they would eventually be transported to some more distant place. This move had been authorized by the British Government in response to petitions from the planters and merchants of St Vincent, who had their eyes on the Carib lands and saw banishment of their owners as the best means of acquiring them. After the final surrender another 5000 or more Caribs were sent to Balliceaux where they remained, living under primitive and disease-ridden conditions, until March 1797. By then only 2200 remained alive to be shipped into permanent exile in the Bay Islands, over fifteen hundred miles to the west. The troops sent to escort them were under the command of Major John Wilson of the 7th WIR (who later became the absent commanding officer of the 8th WIR during the mutiny in Dominica).

The 2nd WIR remained in St Vincent until June 1797. A new commanding officer, Lieutenant-Colonel Hugh Carmichael, was appointed in January when Graham, still not fully recovered from his wounds, transferred to command of the 27th Regiment. Although Graham's subsequent history is unconnected with the West India regiments it is pleasant to record that he made a full recovery:

> on the evening of the illumination for the battle of Camperdown [October 1797], the smoke of so many candles and flambeaux affecting his breathing, he coughed with great violence, and in the exertion threw up a piece of cloth, left, no doubt, by the ball in its passage through his body. From that day he recovered as by a charm.

Carmichael assumed command of a regiment which all but existed in name only, having been reduced to no more than about 120 all ranks. He was ordered to concentrate on recruiting.

This proved to be just as difficult in St Vincent as it was in other parts of the Caribbean for the other seven regiments. The 1st WIR by this time had incorporated Malcolm's Rangers, but was not to return a strength of more than 350 for another two years. The 3rd WIR even by the end of 1797 'had no non-commissioned officers, no privates, and only two drummers'. The 4th, 5th and 6th WIR were only slightly better off. The 7th WIR, raised in Barbados from among slaves brought there from other islands, had nearly 400 rank and file before the end of 1795, but had then been sent to join the British force attempting to gain control of St Domingue, the French portion of Hispaniola. It remained there, finding very few more recruits and steadily losing in action those it arrived with for the next three years. The poor 8th WIR had such little success in recruiting that it was disbanded in 1796, but re-raised two years later to absorb the Loyal Dominica Rangers. Carmichael did his best but the 2nd WIR was still less than 200-strong when it was sent to Grenada in June 1797. It remained there for the next three years, during which time the policy of buying slaves direct from agents, rather than from ill-disposed and reluctant planters, greatly reduced the recruiting problem for all the regiments.

The kind of attitude they faced before this policy came into effect is exemplified by the treatment received by the 4th WIR in St Kitts in 1797. There, while still less than 250 in number, and safely confined in the imposing fortress on Brimstone Hill, some minor disturbance occurred which was quickly blown up among the civilian population of the island as a conspiracy to mutiny. Although the commanding officer of the fort thought the whole affair 'trifling', and the island's Chief Justice, who investigated the matter reported that

> this rash Design has been confined to a very few: that it originated from no preconcerted plan, but was the rash impromptu idea of a foolish Drunkard communicated, in his cups, to three or four of his Comrades, upon the Hill, by whom it appears to have been received with its merited contempt ...

the local legislature was determined to make the most of it. In the Chief Justice's report, sent to the Home Secretary in London, he recorded that the members of the House of Assembly were 'anxious only for the Consumation of their own Plan, which was to get rid of the 4th West India Regiment at all events'. And it was their view which prevailed: the regiment was transferred to St Vincent early in 1798 and a handful of the supposed ringleaders were court-martialled; leading to one man being executed and three others being flogged.

Permission to purchase slaves 'for Government' was received by General Abercromby near the end of 1796. By the time suitably discreet arrangements had been entered into with the necessary agents, and the recruits - 'commonly called "New Negroes" never having been employed in any of these Islands or plantations' - began to be supplied in reasonable numbers, the requirement for black troops had become even more pressing. Spain had declared war on Britain in October 1796 and Trinidad, the only Spanish possession in the eastern Caribbean, was captured by Abercromby without any fighting in the following February. An attempt by the Spanish in September 1798 to eject the small British community from the settlement at Belize in Central America was defeated by a scratch force, which included a detachment of the 6th WIR. The puppet 'Batavian Republic' set up in Holland by the French had declared war in 1795, and this led to the British acquisition, usually without any fighting, of the major Dutch colonies: Demerara, Essequibo and Berbice in 1796, Surinam in 1799 and Curacao in 1800. By the end of the century there were so many British garrisons required throughout the Caribbean that this would have justified the creation of the West India regiments if nothing else.

The original eight were augmented in September 1798 when four existing units, The Trinidad Rangers (known as Drualt's Rangers until 1797), de Soter's Royal Island Rangers, the South American Rangers, and O'Meara's Rangers, all already in British pay, became respectively the 9th, 10th, 11th and 12th WIR. At the end of 1800 the total strength of all twelve was in excess of 5000 men, which was just as well as, at the beginning of the following year, even more islands were to fall into British hands.

In August 1800 the 2nd WIR was ordered from Grenada to Trinidad, which was thought to be threatened with an imminent French invasion from Guadeloupe. The threat turned out to be illusory, but the regiment's sudden transfer involved it in the first of a series of accidents, all connected with ships, which were to dog it throughout the nineteenth century. The entire regiment including 'ladies, women, and children', embarked in HMS *Dromedary* for the short passage but as the ship approached Trinidad

> Light winds and strong currents baffled the first and second attempts to enter the Gulf of Paria; but on account of the urgency of the service, a third attempt was made at night. However, the wind falling at a critical moment, the ship was swept away by the strong currents .... and carried with great force on to the [P]arasol rock ...

Fortunately good order, naval and military discipline, and sound seamanship all prevailed. The women and children were put into boats, and 'the whole of the troops and crew, amounting in all to over 500', were able to scramble ashore onto the uninhabited island of Huevos. The boats reached Port-of-Spain the next day and the castaways were all rescued a day later. Considerable courage and superb discipline were displayed by the troops with 'many officers' lives ... saved owing to the attachment of their men, who swam with, and supported them through the heavy surf'. As if this was not enough

> although all their kits and baggage were lost, the men succeeded in saving nearly all their muskets, only sixty-four out of four hundred stand of arms being missing on their arrival at Trinidad.

The preservation of most of their arms under such circumstances was quite outstanding; the standard infantryman's weapon, the flintlock musket, being both heavy and cumbersome. It was also unreliable and inaccurate. It fired a round lead ball, weighing over an ounce, wrapped in a paper cartridge with a small charge of gunpowder, which first had to be rammed down the forty-two inch barrel. This reduced the rate of fire, even for the most experienced marksman to no more than three rounds a minute. In battle, because of the amount of smoke produced by the ignition of the powder and the absence of proper sighting arrangements, the hit rate was probably no better than fifteen per cent of rounds fired. It had a killing range of around 300 yards but, as a British ordnance officer commented in 1814:

> a soldier's musket, if not exceedingly ill-bored as many are, will strike the figure of a man at 80 yards ... but a soldier must be very fortunate indeed who shall be wounded by a common musket at 150 yards, provided his antagonist aims at him, and as for firing at 200 yards you might as well fire at the moon.

Be that as it may, the 'Brown Bess' as the musket was called remained the infantryman's weapon until the early 1840s, when the first rifles began to be introduced. It was certainly the only firearm the West India regiments were issued with and, as black troops came last in the line for the issue of any equipment, the men of the 2nd WIR probably had more reason than most soldiers for hanging on to their weapons. In the event the regiment was not required to repel a French invasion of Trinidad, but allowed to recover from the shipwreck in peace, being re-kitted and re-equipped with a grant approved by the C-in-C with his 'marked approbation'.

The Commander-in-Chief by this time was Lieutenant-General Thomas Trigge, who had taken over from Abercromby soon after the capture of Trinidad. At the beginning of 1801 he was ordered by the British Government to seize the Westindian possessions of Denmark and Sweden, in view of the participation of those countries in an 'armed Neutrality' with Russia which had been instigated by the French as a possible means of counteracting the British blockade of Europe. In March, after embarking troops in Martinique and Antigua - among them the 8th WIR - he sailed for the tiny Swedish island of St Bartholomew. The equally tiny garrison surrendered without fighting shortly after Trigge arrived on 20th March. Three hundred men drawn from the 3rd Regiment and the 8th WIR were left as the British garrison, and Lieutenant-Colonel Wilson, the commanding officer of the latter, installed as the Governor. The rest of the force, now supplemented by the arrival of the 2nd WIR (diverted from being transferred from Trinidad to Jamaica), sailed a few days later for the neighbouring island of St Martin. Shared between Holland and France it lay on the direct route from St

Bartholomew to the Danish Virgin Islands and, although its dual garrison had been left unmolested so far during the war, it now seemed prudent to make sure it was neutralized.

Early on 24th March a force of 1500 men, made up of the 64th Regiment, six companies of the 3rd Regiment, and the four remaining companies of the 8th WIR, all commanded by Brigadier-General Frederick Maitland, landed in Cole Bay on the southern, Dutch, side of the island.

The subsequent attack on Fort Amsterdam, guarding the main town of Philipsburg, was carried out by the 64th Foot under Lieutenant-Colonel Edward Pakenham, supported by the men of the 8th WIR acting as skirmishers. The Dutch defenders sortied out with 300 men and two field guns as the British approached, and a very brisk action took place during which the black troops 'evinced ... the greatest courage and steadiness'. The Dutch suffered some fifty casualties and lost both guns before being forced to retreat into the fort. Pakenham, who on this occasion showed considerable military aptitude combined with a reasonable amount of consideration for the welfare of the troops under his command, was to find himself in command of men of the West India regiments again in the future. On that occasion, as will be seen, even though he had by then earned plaudits from the Duke of Wellington in the Peninsular War and risen to the rank of major-general, he was to be found wanting in both attributes.

In the late afternoon, after Philipsburg had been occupied, Maitland called upon the Dutch Governor to surrender the fort and end the fighting. In reply he was told that this would depend upon how the French viewed the situation from their side of the island. As by this time another large British force, made up of the 1st and 11th Regiments and the 2nd WIR had surrounded the main French town of Marigot the French Commissioner had little hesitation in agreeing to a general surrender. Arrangements were made to garrison the whole island with the 1st Foot and the remainder of the 8th WIR, and Trigge sailed on 26th March for the Danish possessions to the west. All three, St Thomas, St John and St Croix, later surrendered without a fight.

On completion of the campaign the 2nd WIR was released to continue its passage to Jamaica. The 8th WIR remained as part of the garrisons of St Bartholomew and St Martin for several months before being returned to Dominica where, in the following April, the mutiny already described took place. That this sad event was brought about primarily by the machinations of the regiment's Colonel, Johnstone, abetted by poor leadership among too few officers, is surely borne out by the opinion of the men expressed by General Trigge in the report of his expedition:

> I have particular satisfaction in being enabled to add that the 8th West India Regiment, formed within the last three years, and composed almost entirely of new negroes, who never had before seen an enemy, engaged with a degree of gallantry, and behaved in a manner, that would do honour to any troops.

Following the capture of the Danish Virgin Islands a stalemate developed in the conflict in the Caribbean, although a state of war continued to exist between Britain and France and her allies for another few months. In the end the French agreed to a ceasefire and preliminary articles of peace were signed with Britain on 1st October. These were ratified in March 1802 by the Treaty of Amiens. Under its terms most of the fighting which had taken place in the Westindies during the previous nine years turned out to have been for nothing. Every island taken from the French, Dutch, Danes or the Swedes was returned to its previous overlord. Surinam, Demerara, Essequibo and Berbice were handed back to the Dutch. The Spanish came off worst: Trinidad was ceded to Britain and the settlement of Belize had to be recognized begrudgingly as an embryo British colony.

With the end of hostilities some rationalization among the West India regiments was seen to be necessary and before the end of 1802 their number was once more reduced to eight. In July the 7th, 9th, 10th and 12th WIR, all of which were well below strength, were disbanded and their rank and file re-mustered in a new 7th WIR. In September, following the mutiny in Dominica, the 11th was renumbered as the 8th WIR.

The seven-year apprenticeship of the regiments can be said to have come to an end with the signing of the Treaty of Amiens. Eight out of the twelve had had combat experience, even if this was gained by some while still serving as Ranger units prior to being numbered. The recruitment problem had been overcome, albeit at the cost of involving the British Government and the army directly in the slave trade. Detachments of disciplined and properly trained black troops were to be found throughout the Westindian islands, as well as in South and Central America and the Bahamas. Even the antagonism of the various colonial authorities to the regiments had been overcome - or, as in the last bastion of such opposition, was about to be brushed aside.

CHAPTER 6
HARD AND SEVERE WORK

> From the day of the regiment landing, to that of the enemy's surrender, it [the 1st WIR] served with the greatest credit under all the disadvantages to which a West India regiment is exposed. The hard and severe work is generally performed by them, which the European soldiers could not undergo from the climate.
>
> **Lieutenant-General George Beckwith (1809)**

In September 1800 in Trinidad, while still recovering from being shipwrecked, the 2nd WIR received two documents from Grenada. These recorded the 'unanimous resolutions' passed separately by the Council and the House of Assembly to mark 'their sense of the benefits derived from the service of the 2nd West India Regiment' during the period it had been stationed in the island, and which had ended a month earlier.

The sentiments found in these addresses could not have contrasted more strongly with those expressed by the Jamaican legislature the following year, after the regiment's transfer to Jamaica in April 'awoke a storm of indignation'. The House of Assembly had opposed the idea of such regiments from the start and its members now persisted for over a year in the view that

> having black troops raised or sent here, or, in other language, armed slaves to defend and protect the rights, the liberties, and properties, not only of free men, but of British subjects, [is] a measure not only considered to proceed from ignorance of our local circumstances, of our laws, and of our constitution, but [is] viewed with that abhorrence and indignation which it could not fail to excite.

Eventually the British Government realized the only way to solve the problem was by threatening the pockets of the plantocracy. It was agreed to remove the regiment provided the Jamaican authorities undertook to cover the entire expense of defending the island with white troops, and on 14th June Carmichael and his men were embarked in a transport

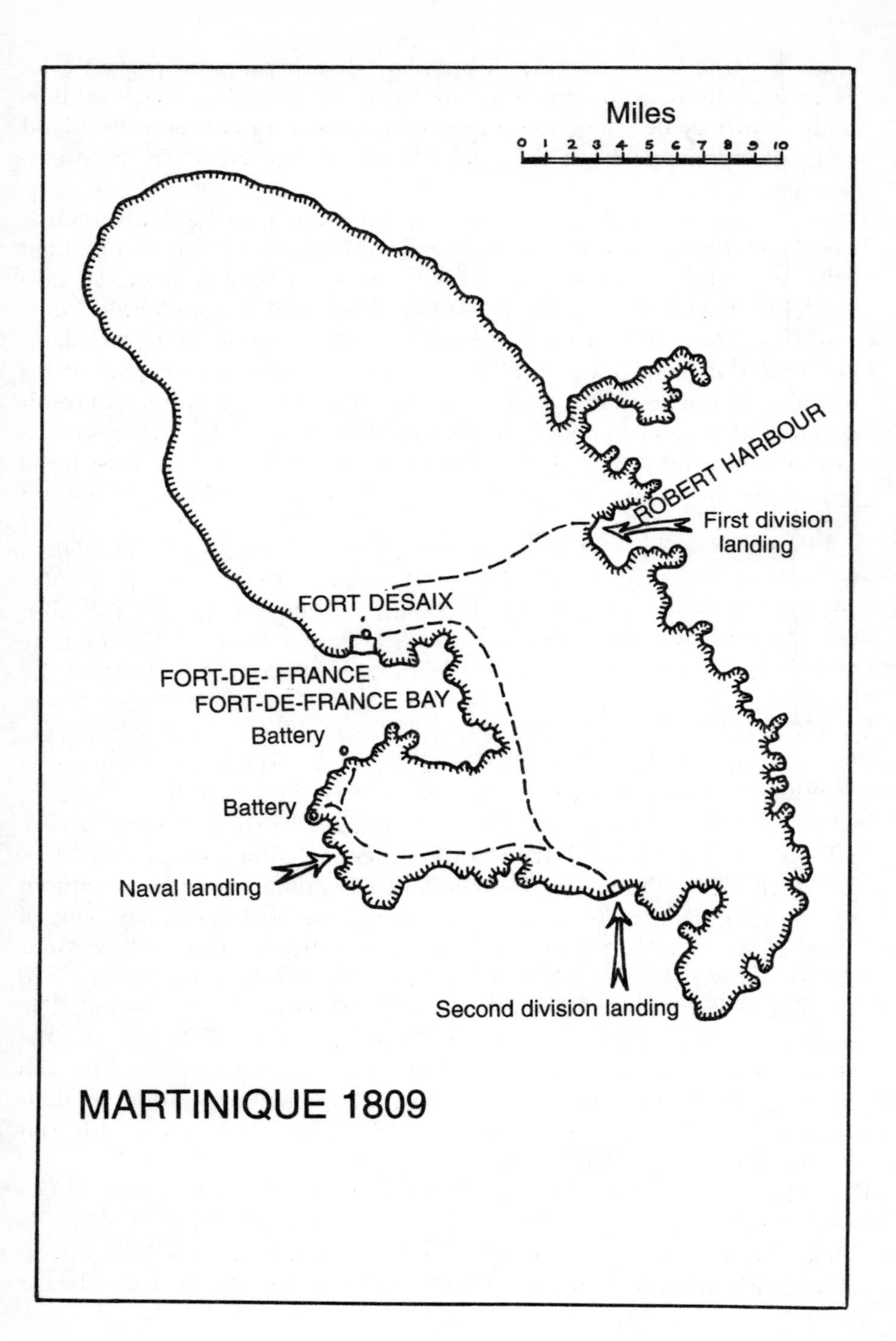
Miles
0 1 2 3 4 5 6 7 8 9 10
ROBERT HARBOUR
First division landing
FORT DESAIX
FORT-DE- FRANCE
FORT-DE-FRANCE BAY
Battery
Battery
Naval landing
Second division landing
MARTINIQUE 1809

ready for transfer to another island. The British proposal proved even more obnoxious to the Assembly and so the six hundred black soldiers came ashore again; this time to begin a connection between the island and such troops which was to last until the second quarter of the twentieth century.

It was just as well that the animosity of the Jamaican Assembly towards the regiments was not allowed to prevail: the Treaty of Amiens provided little more than a fourteen month-long ceasefire and the conflict, now thought of and more properly referred to as the Napoleonic Wars, resumed in May 1803. This time there was to be no peace until Napoleon was removed from power twelve years later. In the interim part of his overall plan was an extension of the French Westindian empire. As a result much of what had taken place in the Caribbean during the earlier war was now about to be repeated; and this time the services of the West India regiments - now beginning their journeymen years - would be in constant demand.

The British C-in-C, Lieutenant-General William Grinfield, lost no time in taking the offensive. On 21st June he attacked St Lucia with a 3000-strong force made up of the 1st, 64th and 68th Regiments, together with the 3rd WIR. Once again Morne Fortune had to be stormed, but this time it was carried out with such enthusiasm that the French capitulated the next day. The 68th Foot and three companies of the 3rd WIR were left to garrison the island, while the remainder of the force sailed for Tobago. French resistance there was even weaker and the island was surrendered after a little nominal resistance had been offered on 1st July.

The Netherlands, which were still under French domination, were also at war with Britain, so their South American colonies were turned on next. All three, Demerara, Berbice and Essequibo, capitulated without any fighting on 17th September. The close business links which many of the planters had developed with merchants in Britain during the previous British occupation had fallen into disarray during the interregnum, and the opportunity to repair these made the takeover very welcome. The inhabitants of the adjacent colony of Surinam were not so keen to see the British return and, when a force of 2000 men, including part of the 6th WIR, appeared off the coast in April 1804 some opposition to their landing was offered. This fizzled out after a few days and by 4th May Surinam was also in British hands.

After this Grinfield was in no position to attempt other conquests. The total number of troops at his disposal was not large enough for him to tackle Martinique or Guadeloupe, and in any case the white regiments were still constantly being reduced by sickness and death from disease.

But perhaps more importantly, in spite of the renewal of the naval blockade of France, the British did not yet possess control of the sea - in the Caribbean or anywhere else.

Part of Napoleon's grand scheme was that his Navy should break the blockade and then enter the Caribbean in such strength as to destroy any opposition found there, and enable his land forces to overwhelm the British possessions. In January 1805 one of his admirals, the Comte de Missiessy, managed to escape from Rochefort and with ten ships, packed with troops, headed across the Atlantic. He arrived at Martinique a month later, embarked another thousand troops and - presumably based on whatever intelligence the local forces had of the relative strength of each British island - decided to attack Dominica. His fleet, flying false colours to delay any defensive preparations for as long as possible, arrived off the island early on 22nd February. Troops under General Joseph La Grange were then landed two miles or so to the south of Roseau.

The garrison consisted of four companies of the 1st WIR, three companies of the 46th Regiment, and a few companies of Militia, perhaps one thousand men in all. The 46th Foot and one company of the 1st WIR were at Morne Bruce, the fort overlooking Roseau, while the remainder of the 1st WIR were at Fort Shirley (more usually referred to at the time as Prince Rupert's) some twenty-five miles to the north. All the troops were under the command of Brigadier-General George Prevost, who had succeeded the disgraced Johnstone as Governor. He had been in the Westindies since 1793 and had had plenty of experience in fighting the French; most recently in the retaking of St Lucia. As soon as it became clear that an invasion was about to take place he sent Captain O'Connell and one company of the 1st WIR, together with a company of the 46th Regiment and another from the Militia, to try to prevent French troops from landing.

They arrived just in time. 'The first boats were beat off, but the schooner and one of the brigs coming close on shore to cover the landing, compelled our troops to occupy a better position'. This was among some ruined buildings in the village of Pointe Michel, a little north of the landing area, from where they could cover the narrow pathway around the point 'bounded by inaccessible heights on the right, and a broken and rugged shore on the left'. O'Connell could not have chosen a better position to make a stand, just as La Grange could not have picked a less suitable beach on which to make a landing. While the French were coming ashore the defenders were joined by the rest of the 46th companies with two field guns and more militiamen, and Major Nunn of the 1st WIR arrived to take over the command. For the next five or six hours the entire invasion force was prevented from advancing past Pointe Michel. By early afternoon, by which time Nunn had been shot and killed and O'Connell, although himself wounded, had resumed command, La Grange had had enough and his troops were 'obliged ... to retire from their position with great slaughter' having suffered over three hundred casualties.

Having failed to take Roseau from the south the French general now took the balance of his troops still embarked to Woodbridge Bay 'and a considerable force was landed near Morne Daniel', a small redoubt on the northern side of the town. Prevost had no troops other than about one company of the Militia to oppose this landing and no sooner were the French ashore than Morne Daniel was overrun. As Roseau was already in flames by this time, having been bombarded by the largest French man-of-war for some hours, Prevost had little option but to abandon the town. In order to 'attempt to keep the sovereignty of the island, which the excellent troops I had, warranted' he set off with two staff officers for Prince Rupert's, reaching it 'in twenty-four hours, with the aid of the inhabitants and the exertions of the Caribs'. Captain O'Connell, 'bringing in his wounded, with a few of the Royal Artillery, and the precious remainder of the 46th and the 1st West India Light Company', joined him after 'four days continued march through the most difficult country', having had to travel well inland through the mountains to bypass Roseau.

A demand for the surrender of Prince Rupert's Garrison, received from La Grange on 25th February, was immediately rejected by Prevost. Two days later, presumably having decided that the reduction of Fort Shirley and its defences would take too long or prove too difficult, the general destroyed the fortifications of Roseau, extracted 'a contribution of £5500' from its inhabitants, and re-embarked his men. Missiessy's fleet hovered off the island for a day or two and then departed. The total British casualties among the regular troops comprised 21 dead, 21 wounded and eight taken prisoner; the 1st WIR losses amounting to one officer and nine men killed with two officers and eight men wounded.

Dominica was never threatened again. Roseau was soon rebuilt and its fortifications repaired. Prevost was created a baronet later in the year and would have the 1st WIR serving under him again before the war ended. Captain O'Connell was promoted to major in the 5th WIR and voted £100 for the purchase of a sword by the grateful members of the Dominica House of Assembly. The rest of the regiment had to make do with the Assembly's vote of thanks 'for their gallant conduct', and the subsequent award of 'Dominica' as a Battle Honour - the first to be won by any of the West India regiments.

Although Dominica was saved Missiessy's fleet was still at large, and it next appeared off St Kitts on 5th March. The admiral and La Grange, perhaps weighing the 'contribution' of £5500 against the lives of three hundred or more soldiers, made no attempt to invade but demanded £18,000 from the burghers of Basseterre in return for the town being spared from destruction. As this sum was immediately forthcoming the same demand was made on the townspeople of Charlestown in Nevis, which netted another £4000, and then on the citizens of Plymouth in Montserrat, who had to part with £7500: a grand total of £29,500 [the equivalent of perhaps two million pounds today] and all without a drop of blood being spilt. After these acts of extortion Missiessy could chance his arm no longer and, realizing that no other part of the French Navy was about to join him to clear the British from the Caribbean, he paid a swift visit to Santo Domingo to replenish the French garrison and then returned to France. The Battle of Trafalgar on 21st October put paid to any possibility of the French depriving the British of control of the Caribbean Sea. Although small squadrons of French warships did still visit and raid from time to time thereafter, none of the British possessions was ever again in any serious danger.

Throughout the islands, in the captured South American territories, in Belize and in the Bahamas, the West India regiments - often in detachments of only one or two companies - gradually settled into routine garrison duties and the never-ending business of training new recruits. The establishment of rank and file had been increased from 600 to 1000 in 1804, enough to give each regiment from then on eight 'battalion' companies in addition to its two 'flank' companies. One flank company, the Light, was made up in general of short, nimble men who were useful as skirmishers, and fell in on the left of the line when the regiment was on parade. The right flank, the senior position, was taken by the Grenadier company, consisting of the tallest and strongest men and considered as the regiment's storm troops. Not that any of the regiments was able to parade all its companies in any one place at any one time, except on the rarest of occasions: the army had forts and outposts throughout the Westindies which needed to be manned, and it was long going to remain politic for black troops not to outnumber whites in any island or mainland territory. This splitting up of a regiment was something which was to continue throughout most of the nineteenth century. Even as late as 1885 the commanding officer of the 1st WIR could complain

> No lieutenant-colonel of a West India regiment can ever see the whole of his regiment together. The largest number that, under present circumstances, he

can ever have under him at any one station is four companies; and the most he can have under his actual command at any one time is six companies on board a troopship.

For the company commanders the employment of the regiments in this way was probably a mixed blessing. Many a captain or lieutenant, vested with an independent command in some remote corner of a colony well away from regimental headquarters and all that went on there, must have enjoyed the experience. Others probably resented having to forego the pleasures of garrison life in towns such as Kingston or Bridgetown, and resented being sent to some dull backwater. A few, such as the officer observed by a lieutenant from an English regiment at Fort Andries on the Berbice River in 1806, obviously found such duty all too much:

> One of the officers whom I found here, Lieutenant Dudgeon, 4th West India Regiment, used to turn out for morning parade as drunk as when he tumbled into a soldier's hammock in which he slept at night. At the end of six months he killed himself by drinking rum; and I have often heard him, when he could say nothing else, stammer out: "Drunkenness is a bewitching devil, a pleasant poison, and a sweet sin ..."

While poor Dudgeon was drinking himself to death from boredom up the Berbice the Royal Navy was establishing control of the Caribbean Sea. The prolonged lull in land warfare which had existed since the failure of the French to take Dominica lasted until December 1807. Three months before, for reasons having far more to do with the Baltic than the Caribbean, war had broken out again between Britain and Denmark. On 21st December the events of March 1801 were repeated, when British ships carrying a sizeable body of troops once again arrived off St Thomas in the Danish Virgin Islands. The islands still had no defensive capability to speak of and, after terms had been agreed, St Thomas and St John were surrendered on 22nd December, and St Croix three days later. No fighting took place and the episode is only of interest here because among the troops embarked were men of both the 1st and 3rd WIR, and because the ships were under the overall command of Rear-Admiral Sir Alexander Cochrane, an older brother of the infamous Cochrane-Johnstone, the ex-Governor of Dominica. Although there is little to indicate that the admiral was in any way corrupt like his brother, he has been accused of being 'as too often happened in the Navy, keener after prize-money than real injury to the enemy'. That Johnstone was then the Naval Agent in nearby Tortola, and that the prize goods the admiral

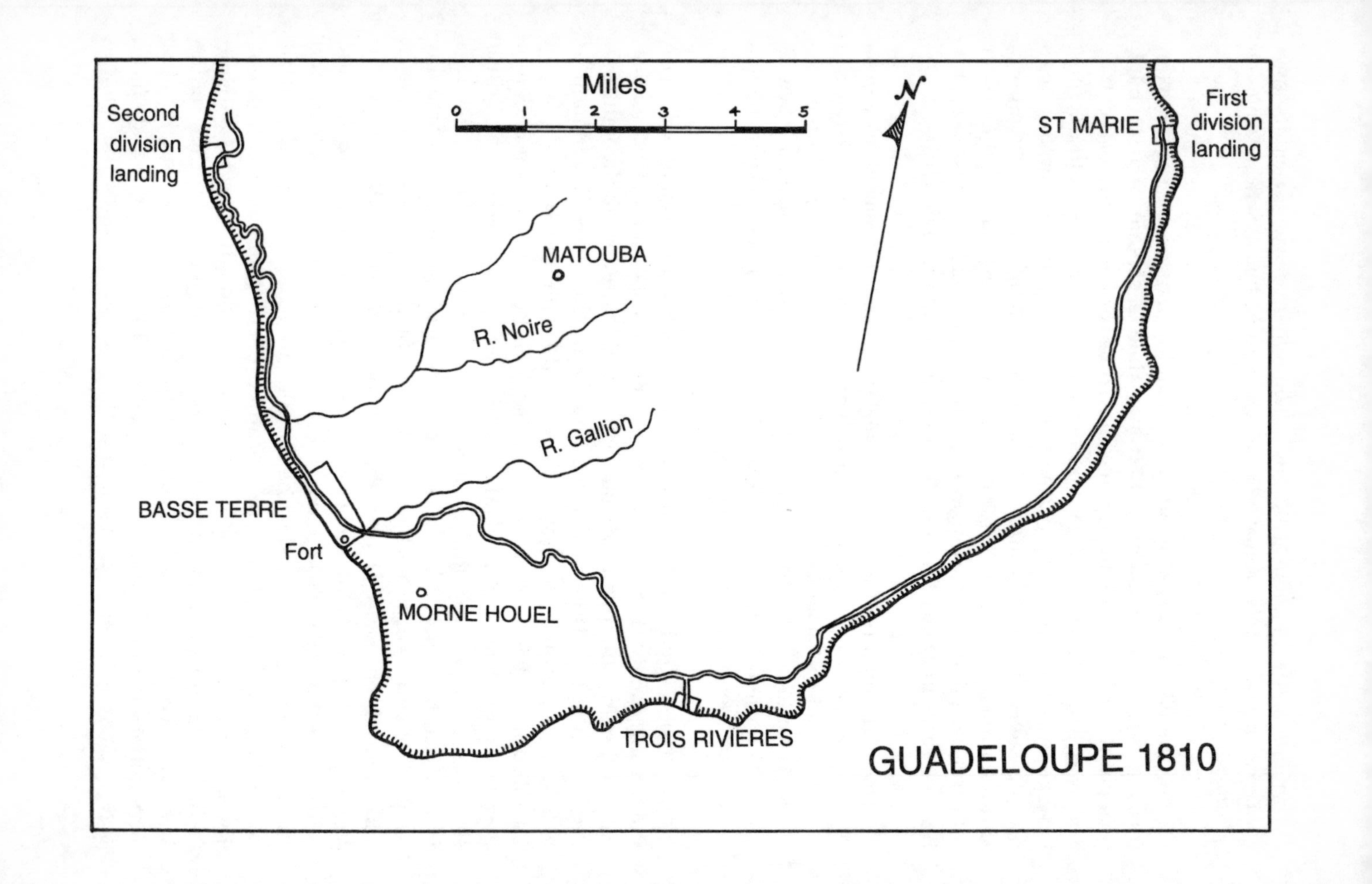
Miles
0
1
2
3
4
5
N
Second division landing
First division landing
ST MARIE
MATOUBA
R. Noire
R. Gallion
BASSE TERRE
Fort
MORNE HOUEL
TROIS RIVIERES
GUADELOUPE 1810

extorted from the Danes were sent there for disposal, and that Johnstone then embezzled the proceeds, is all neither here nor there. What is relevant to the history of the West India regiments is that Admiral Cochrane seems to have had a dislike of soldiers, or a least a total lack of interest in the welfare of any he had dealings with. Seven years later his craving for prize-money and disregard for land forces were to play a large part in bringing about a military fiasco outside the Caribbean, with accompanying calamity for two of the regiments. Meanwhile, inside the Caribbean, the capture of the Danish islands marked the beginning of a long and determined effort by the British to increase their supremacy throughout the Westindies.

In March 1808 the Navy seized the island of Marie Galante, about halfway between Dominica and Guadeloupe, in order to deprive the French of a base for their privateers. Another island, Desirade, taken at the same time and much closer to Guadeloupe, was small, barren and of such little value that its seizure could be ignored. Marie Galante on the other hand was too valuable to allow the British occupation to remain unchallenged, and on 23rd August a force of about two hundred French troops crossed over from Guadeloupe and landed near Grand Bourg, the main town. Before they could retake the fort or do any damage their presence was detected by the naval guardship, their boats were seized, and they were chased inland by seamen and marines. The Navy then had no alternative but to appeal to the Army for assistance in hunting them down. Six days later three companies of the 1st WIR, under Lieutenant-Colonel Nathaniel Blackwell, arrived from Barbados and landed at Grand Bourg. Blackwell added the marines and a few sailors with a six-pounder gun to his force and set off in

> a pursuit of the enemy for five days and nights, and having during that period ... four engagements with him, in each of which he was repulsed, and obliged to make most precipitate retreat, leaving behind his arms, ammunition, etc.

On 3rd September the French finally gave up, having by then lost nearly forty men and most of their equipment. The 1st WIR casualties were one private killed and another wounded. Back in Barbados, where the headquarters of the regiment had been since April of the previous year, Blackwell was presented with a sword for his services by the C-in-C, Lieutenant-General George Beckwith. The other ranks as always had to make do with a few words of praise in the general's despatch to London:

> The perseverance and temper of the three companies was respectable, and the fatigue they underwent at this season of the year unusually great.

As he received his sword it is possible that Blackwell may well have thought that the men he had led during the operation had been under some obligation to perform well. At just the time earlier in the year when he had been promoted from major in the 1st WIR to lieutenant-colonel in the 4th WIR (he had still been awaiting transfer to his new regiment in Surinam when called upon to go to Marie Galante), an event at the opposite end of the Caribbean had threatened to disturb the confidence that senior officers such as Beckwith were now placing in the West India regiments.

In May 1808 the 2nd WIR, which by now had been in Jamaica for seven years, was concentrated in the grim, isolated surroundings of Fort Augusta near the entrance to Kingston Harbour. Early in the morning of 27th the regiment was being paraded on the beach about three hundred yards from the fort (presumably because there was not enough space within), while inside the latest batch of recruits were being drilled by a sergeant and a corporal. Shortly after the parade had been drawn up 'a terrible war whoop was heard', and hundreds of pairs of eyes watched in amazement as the recruits, brandishing their muskets with fixed bayonets, ran out of the fort amid the sound of gunfire, leaving behind seven of their number who had been shot down by the barrack guard.

The adjutant, Lieutenant Ellis, who like Major Darley the officer in temporary command, was mounted, turned and rode towards the disturbance. As he met up with the running, whooping men, and before the horrified gaze of the entire parade, he was knocked off his horse with the butt end of a musket and bayonetted to death. A moment or two later Darley, who had ordered the parade to stand firm when some of the men had broken ranks to give him protection, was also dragged down and bayonetted. He died shortly afterwards but not before one of the sergeants had been sent into the fort for ammunition. The mutinous recruits meanwhile tried to escape along the beach but were prevented from doing so by the grenadier company which, being positioned on the right of the parade and so furthest from the fort, was in the best position to stop them from making their way along the peninsula on which the fort was situated. The end came as soon as ammunition was available and had been issued to another company:

> a fire was opened on the mutineers; fourteen of them were killed, five wounded, and twenty-four taken prisoners. The remainder fled to the bushes.

The dozen or so fugitives were soon rounded-up, placed with the rest of the survivors in captivity, and order restored. Seven were later executed after being court-martialled. The remainder were pardoned and

> by their subsequent good conduct, redeemed their character. Some of them were, in 1833, highly esteemed respectable non-commissioned officers.

To use the words 'mutiny' and 'mutineers' in connection with this violent and distressing incident, while of course perfectly correct in any military context, is to ignore reality. The men who took part, still in only the first stages of their training, must have been among the very last to have been purchased by the Army, the slave trade having been made illegal five months earlier. Most of them were Asante or, as they were miscalled at the time throughout the Westindies, 'Coromantees' or 'Coromantines - names derived from Cormantine (now Kormantine), the fort on the Gold Coast from where they were shipped. It is very probable that they would have been confined in chains in such a fort for weeks, if not months, before having to endure the terrifying ordeal of an interminable sea voyage under bestial conditions into the unknown. To then find, when the voyage ended, that they were once again confined in a fort, admittedly no longer in chains, but being kicked around from morning to night by brutal NCOs, must surely have been enough to produce uncontrollable violence amongst even the most docile of men. And the Asante were far from docile (as the West India regiments, as will be seen, were to keep on finding out throughout the next ninety years or more). Throughout the miserable history of Westindian slavery, 'Coromantees' had instigated or led many revolts and insurrections, and a book published in 1803 warned that as they brought with them from Africa 'lofty ideas of independence, they are dangerous inmates on a West Indian plantation'. They had now demonstrated they were equally dangerous inmates of a military installation, but the action of those at Fort Augusta is surely more clearly seen, not as a breakdown in discipline leading to participation in the gravest of military crimes, but as a bid for freedom by proud men tormented beyond endurance. Credence for this view was provided at their court martial, when the main reason given for the murders of Darley and Ellis was that the perpetrators were 'influenced by some wild idea that, if they killed the officers, they would then be able to return to their own country'.

Such a delusion, that it would be possible for slaves to escape and somehow find their way back to their homelands on foot, was not uncommon among those newly brought to the Westindies. Such unfortunates had no way of knowing where they were in relation to West Africa, and their knowledge of the world, like that of the majority of mankind at the beginning of the nineteenth century, was limited in the extreme. However, in case it is thought that considering it possible to walk from the Westindies to the African continent showed a degree of ignorance confined solely to black men, it is well to recall that white convicts, transported to Australia at just this same time, 'believed that China was only a hundred miles to the north of Parramatta, and separated from Australia by a river', and that many died trying to walk there to freedom.

Needless to say, the mutiny (to return to the appropriate military terminology) had immediate repercussions. Although it had been confined solely to the new recruits, the rest of the regiment being 'enraged by the deaths of their officers' and remaining 'steady in every respect', the white population in Jamaica was outraged and rushed to sign petitions begging for the removal of black troops from the island. The Governor forwarded these to London, adding his comment that the petitioners' 'utter dislike and distrust of them will never be diminished'. No notice was taken and the 2nd WIR remained at Fort Augusta. Hugh Carmichael, who had left the regiment in January when placed in command of all the forces in Jamaica as a major-general, made his own opinion of the brouhaha known by ordering the 2nd WIR to provide the daily guard on his official residence in Kingston. He also refused to supply the House of Assembly with details of the mutiny and subsequent court martial until ordered to do so by the Secretary of War, although he was later humiliated for this by being made to apologize to the Assembly at the bar of the House.

While the storm in the Jamaican teacup was still being stirred in the early months of 1809 by Carmichael's refusal to provide the Assembly with the court martial papers, more serious events were taking place in the eastern Caribbean. The C-in-C, Lieutenant-General Beckwith, was at last ready to tackle the French in their few remaining possessions. Cayenne, the colony close to Surinam in South America, was taken by British and Portuguese troops in the middle of January, at the same time as a large expeditionary force was being assembled in Barbados. This comprised nine regiments of Foot (four having been brought from Canada for the operation), the 1st WIR, 3rd WIR, 4th WIR and three companies of the 8th WIR - some ten thousand men in all, split between two Divisions. The larger, under Lieutenant-General Prevost, consisted of three Brigades. The first brigade contained the 7th and 23rd Regiments together with half of the 1st WIR. The other half of the 1st WIR, less the light company, was in the second brigade with the 8th and 13th Regiments. The light company, together with those of the other West India regiments taking part, formed the major part of a Light Infantry Battalion in the reserve brigade - a brigade which also contained the 4th WIR. The 3rd WIR and 8th WIR were in two of the three brigades which made up the smaller, Second Division under the command of Major-General Maitland.

The entire force left Barbados on 28th January and reached its objective, Martinique, two days later. Control of the island called for securing the use of Fort-de-France Bay by putting the batteries which guarded its approaches out of use, and for the capture of Fort Desaix, the stronghold which dominated the town of Fort-de-France on the north side of the bay. Beckwith disposed his two Divisions accordingly. He himself landed with Prevost in Robert Harbour on the east coast to accompany the First Division, which was expected to fight its way overland, a distance of about twelve miles, in order to attack Fort Desaix from the rear. At the same time Maitland landed with his Division at the little port of Saint Luce on the south coast, with orders to seize the coastal batteries at the entrance to Fort-de-France Bay, and to then march on the capital.

Out of the West India regiments taking part, only the 1st WIR and the troops in the Light Infantry Battalion saw any real fighting. The first brigade of the First Division led the advance from Robert Harbour, 'the French skirmishers falling back slowly before them, while keeping up a smart fire'. In the hills behind Fort-de-France the opposition increased and the advance was halted on 1st February as the leading troops came across a large enemy force 'well placed on the crest of [a] ridge, with a mountain torrent in their front, and a strong force of artillery drawn up on their left flank'. Prevost was determined not to lose momentum:

> The flank companies of the 7th were ordered to turn the French right, while the light battalion ... moved against his left, and the grenadiers of the 1st West India Regiment, with the remainder of the 7th, advanced against the centre. The troops rushed forward, fording the stream under a heavy fire, and attacking the enemy, who was greatly superior in numbers, with the bayonet, drove him from his position.

After his second brigade had caught up Prevost continued the advance and, after pushing aside another attempt by the French to make a stand, 'forced them to take shelter under the guns of [the] redoubts' of Fort Desaix. Much heavy fighting then took place on 2nd and 3rd

February before the French were at last driven from their outposts and retired inside the fort.

The investment of Fort-de-France was completed on 5th February when Maitland's Division arrived. Only one of the constituent regiments had been needed, with the help of the Navy, to capture the batteries which had threatened British use of Fort-de-France Bay, and the rest of the Second Division had moved through the southern part of the island entirely unopposed. A large group of Militia encountered on the way had surrendered immediately and been told to go home.

It was two weeks after the island's governor and all the French forces had retired into Fort Desaix before Beckwith had enough artillery in place to begin an attempt to bombard them into submission. Firing by over forty cannon and mortars from six well-constructed batteries began in the afternoon of 19th February. It was returned by the French, briskly at first but then intermittently, until 22nd when a magazine blew up. This caused terms for a surrender to be proposed by the commandant of the fort the next day, but as these were unacceptable the bombardment recommenced. The Governor, Admiral Villaret de Joyeuse, capitulated twenty-four hours later, and Martinique passed into British hands for the rest of war. The admiral must have been particularly mortified: in 1794 he had been in command of the French fleet trounced by Lord Howe at the Battle of the 'Glorious First of June' - the first victory of the Royal Navy over the navy of Revolutionary France.

The operation had cost the British over 550 casualties among all ranks. The 7th Regiment suffered worst of all, losing 31 killed and 122 wounded. The Light Infantry Battalion, 'composed chiefly, if not entirely, of black troops' came off little better, with 28 dead and close to 100 wounded. There are no figures available for the number of the wounded who recovered but, while this is no place to go into the failings of the army's medical service of the time, a contemporary soldier's comment bears repetition:

> The medical men we had were not always ornaments to their profession. They were chiefly I believe composed of apothecary's boys, who having studied a session or two were thrust into the Army as into a huge dissecting room where they might mangle with impunity until they were drilled into an ordinary knowledge of their profession.

Among those with serious wounds it is most unlikely that more than a small minority survived. The trauma involved in evacuation from any early nineteenth century battleground, with the type of doctoring and surgery available afterwards, was acute; in the Westindian climate it was deadly.

All four of the West India regiments which had taken part in its capture were kept in Martinique as part of the 3000-strong considered necessary by Beckwith, although for about a week in April the garrison consisted of little more than the men of the 1st WIR. All the rest were required for a short operation carried out by Major-General Maitland to assist the Navy. At the beginning of the month ships of Admiral Cochrane's fleet had come across five French warships, sent to boost the defence of Guadeloupe, now the last French Westindian possession of any importance. Being too weak to offer any challenge to the British fleet the French ships had taken refuge among the group of small islands called The Saints, not far from the south coast of Guadeloupe. As the only way then left of driving them back to the open sea was by gunfire from the islands, Cochrane had sent an urgent request to Beckwith for The Saints to be captured so that this bombardment could take place.

Maitland left Martinique on 12th April with about 2800 men, of whom about 1000 belonged to the 3rd and 8th WIR. They landed two days later in a bay at the western end of Terre-de-Haut, the most easterly of the islands, entirely unopposed except for some cannon fire from another of the islands, Cabrit, over a mile away. The landing left the troops at the base of a very steep hill, a thousand feet high, with a French outpost on the summit. Once this outpost had been taken - something which required an enormous amount of perspiration and hardly any fighting - two heavy howitzers were brought ashore. Hauling these into a position from where the French squadron could be menaced involved more sweat and foul language, and was not completed until the early evening. Once firing began however it was extremely effective and all five ships were driven out of the anchorage within an hour.

On the following day, while Cochrane dealt with the French Navy, Maitland set about the reduction of the island which, for such a small place, was very well fortified. He was hampered by first having to set up a battery in such a position that its guns could both bombard Fort Napoleon, which protected the main town, and also return the fire of the battery on Cabrit. Once this was established and in action a move could be made against Fort Morel at the north end of the island. The approaches to the latter were cleared and during the night of 16th April two companies of the 3rd WIR with one from the 8th WIR were established in an outpost on a ridge overlooking the two forts. The next morning the post was attacked in strength by troops from both forts but 'though under fire of grape [and] round shot [the West India regiments] held their own most gallantly, and repulsed the enemy with loss'. Later the same morning the French commandant asked for terms and surrendered his forces. Nearly eight hundred prisoners were taken, at a cost among the British forces of six men killed and seven wounded. As soon as the surrender was complete the islands were turned over to the Navy, and Maitland and his force were back in Martinique a few days later. From then on Cochrane, the Naval Commander-in-Chief, administered The Saints together with Marie Galante, 'both of which the Admiral treated as an appanage of the Navy, appointing Governors, raising taxes, and establishing custom-dues with the freedom of an independent sovereign'.

In May action switched to the other end of the Caribbean, when Major-General Carmichael in Jamaica was ordered to mount an expedition to assist the Spanish (who had been allied with the British against France since the middle of the previous year) in evicting the last French garrison from Hispaniola. The French occupation of the Spanish part of the island had begun in 1802, but disease and a revolt by the inhabitants had by this time succeeded in reducing their forces to less than 1500, all now besieged in the capital, Santo Domingo. As no reinforcements could be spared from outside Jamaica, Carmichael was told to use 'all the available troops in that Island'. Among the 1400 he assembled were the flank companies of the 2nd WIR and another hundred men of the regiment who during the previous two years had been trained as artillerymen.

The expedition sailed for Santo Domingo on 3rd June in a number of small, crowded transports. The ships ran into such bad weather, beating into the prevailing easterly wind, that the troops spent over three weeks at sea, and in the end were put ashore at Puerto Palenque, nearly thirty miles short of the capital. The ship carrying the 2nd WIR fared even worse and had to put into the Haitian port of Jacmel to carry out repairs. There

> the light company under Captain Ross, volunteered a march of more than 300 miles over the mountains, to join the British Forces, then before the enemy; on being informed that it was impracticable by land, they proposed subscribing four dollars each to be stopped out of their pay, to hire a vessel to carry them more rapidly to join the Army.

Whether this offer represented a genuine desire on their part to get to grips with the enemy, or merely a desperate attempt to escape the foul conditions in the leaking tub of a transport (another example of the regiment's luck with ships), will never be known. In any case it was not taken up and they eventually joined the rest of Carmichael's force at Palenque on 28th June in the same vessel in which they had left Kingston.

The next day Carmichael joined the Spanish forces besieging the city and having reconnoitred the fortifications himself decided they could be carried by assault. His troops joined him on 1st July having

> been delayed by heavy and incessant rain, and swollen rivers, and had suffered the greatest fatigue in dragging the artillery along bad roads.

The 2nd WIR companies were very much involved in this task, the other troops in the force apparently suffering 'to the extremity from a sudden and fatal sickness' so that 'the most severe and fatiguing duties devolved upon this [the 2nd WIR] regiment'. Their exertions paid off, and before preparations for the assault had been completed the French opened negotiations. After much toing and froing the garrison surrendered on 8th July. Although this pre-empted any fighting it did not bring the 'fatiguing duties' of the 2nd WIR to an end. Many of the sick white troops had to be hospitalized and the men of the regiment were obliged to act as 'orderlies and attendants on the hospital' throughout the rest of the time the expedition remained in Santo Domingo. Eventually, and presumably after a much shorter and somewhat smoother passage, they all returned to Jamaica by 31st August.

With the ousting of the French from Santo Domingo only the island of Guadeloupe was left still to be tackled. Since its recapture by the French in 1794 it had become the focal point of their intervention elsewhere in the eastern Caribbean, and the centre of privateering activity. General Beckwith was in no two minds about the need for its capture, but it took him until the end of September to obtain the necessary approval from London. After that it was a question of finding enough troops to take on the job. The regiments borrowed from Canada had long since gone back, and his remaining regiments were, as always, being wasted by disease, desertion and the repatriation of invalids. It was not until January 1810 that he could muster the size of force he felt was required, and only then by calling on the services of no less than five of the West India regiments.

The expeditionary force which sailed from Barbados on 22nd January numbered 6700 troops, of whom some 2500 belonged to the 1st, 3rd, 4th, 6th and 8th WIR. As with that which had invaded Martinique, it was again split in two with the First Division commanded by Major-General Hislop, and the Second Division under Major-General Harcourt. Each division consisted of two brigades, and a fifth brigade was created as the Reserve.

Because of the numbering system adopted, and the way the West India regiments were divided up between the brigades, the compilation of the force is best shown in a table:

FIRST DIVISION

3rd Brigade	8th WIR
	90th Regiment
	2nd Battalion Light Infantry *(composed of the light companies of the 1st, 3rd, 4th, 6th and 8th WIR)*
4th Brigade	4th WIR
	York Light Infantry Volunteers
	Composite Battalion from 13th and 63rd Regiments

SECOND DIVISION

1st Brigade	3rd WIR
	15th Regiment
	1st Battalion Light Infantry
2nd Brigade	6th WIR
	25th Regiment
	Grenadier Corps *(composed of the grenadier companies of 1st, 4th and 8th WIR)*

RESERVE BRIGADE

	Grenadier Corps
	Royal York Rangers
	Royal Artillery
	Royal Military Artificers

It can have been no accident that the 3rd Brigade under Hislop's command contained the troops it did. He was Colonel of the 8th WIR and, having been responsible for raising their forerunners the South American Rangers in 1796, had been closely associated with the regiment for fourteen years. Then, remembering his opinions of 1801 on how the men of the West India regiments should be trained and used, it must have done his heart good to see who now made up his Light Infantry Battalion. He was not to be disappointed by their performance in the field.

The key to the capture of Guadeloupe was the capital Basse Terre, on the southwest coast of that part of the island confusingly with the same name; once the town and its garrison were taken the island would fall, just as Martinique had after the surrender of Fort Desaix. Beckwith's plan was a repetition of that used the year before: to land the First Division on one coast, the Second on another, and to attack the capital from opposite directions. He himself landed with Hislop and the First Division at the port of St Marie on the east coast of Basse Terre on 28th January, with no opposition by the French being offered. Because of the extremely rugged nature of the interior the only practical approach to the town of Basse Terre was along a road around the south coast - a distance of about twenty miles. As soon as the division was ashore 'the light infantry battalion was ordered forward as the advance guard' and the march began. The Reserve Brigade landed later, but 'remained at St Marie to cover the landing of munitions and supplies'.

Two days later Hislop halted his advance at Trois Rivieres, a port about twelve miles from Basse Terre, in order to obtain further supplies from the Navy. The French had done little to impede the movement of the division along the coast and the skirmishers of the Light Infantry Battalion had had no trouble in clearing the route. Nor was there much of an attempt to prevent the use of Trois Rivieres: the day before the Second Division had made a feint of disembarking there which had caused most of the defenders to take refuge in prepared positions in the hills overlooking the port. Those that remained were 'dispersed ... after a short conflict' by the advance guard before the main body arrived. On the following day the French redoubts in the vicinity were cleared by the Light Infantry Battalion who,

> advancing along the high road towards the enemy's position, alarmed him to such a degree as to induce him to open fire from all his batteries and entrenched lines ... from which he kept up for some time an incessant fire, without doing any other injury than killing one man, and wounding another.

Just before nightfall troops were seen leaving their positions, and at daybreak on 1st February

> not a soul was to be seen near the enemy's works; and, it having been ascertained that they were evacuated, the light company of the 1st West India Regiment was ordered to march at noon and take possession.

Meanwhile, three days later, the Second Division had sailed up the west coast and made an unopposed landing about fives miles to the north of Basse Terre. The day afterwards Harcourt moved south for a while, before having to turn inland to attack an enemy position in the hills which threatened his flank. His troops found the going extremely hard and on 31st January he was obliged to call a halt about half a mile from the French redoubt and send for artillery. For the next two days many of his troops, with the help of the Navy, were employed in hauling two howitzers, two six-pounders and two mortars, and all their ammunition, a distance of about five miles and up to a height of around 1500 feet.

By now it was apparent that the French commander, General Ernouf, had all but abandoned the town of Basse Terre and its fortifications, and established two strongholds in the mountains near Matouba, about three miles from the sea and at a height of about 2000 feet, which threatened the flank of each British division as it approached. Having reviewed the situation, Beckwith ordered Harcourt to stay where he was, blocking off any escape to the north, and to begin a bombardment of Ernouf's positions, while Hislop continued his advance from the southeast.

The road to Basse Terre left the coast at Trois Rivieres, ran alongside a river for some way, climbed steeply to the flat 1600 feet-high Plateau du Palmiste, and then dropped down another river valley into the town. A French position which had been established on the plateau to block the road was also sited to cover the only practicable crossing of the River Gallion, an obstacle which had to be overcome before the Matouba strongholds could be attacked. On 2nd February, by moving the First Division up to the plateau in two columns and attacking the outpost from two directions, Hislop ended the day at the Gallion and with detachments of his troops manning road blocks on all the roads leading inland from Basse Terre.

The Gallion was crossed the next morning and the division moved on towards Matouba until halted by another obstacle, the River Noire. During this movement, Harcourt's artillery opened fire on the French strongholds and stirred the enemy into action:

> The 2nd Division had, during the night ... pushed forward the grenadiers of the 2nd Brigade and a detachment of the 6th. West India Regiment to occupy [a] ridge .... on the upper part of which the strong post of Bellair was situated. On the morning of the 3rd the enemy perceived what had been done, and moved out in force to dislodge the British. The 1st Brigade was immediately ordered up in support; but, before it could gain the heights, a smart action had taken place and it only arrived in time to complete the defeat of the enemy.

While this action was taking place, costing both sides many casualties, the advance of the First Division on the other side of Matouba had come to a complete stop. The right bank of the Noire had been so well fortified that a general assault across the river was out of the question without the help of a strong flanking movement.

The was provided the next day by the Royal York Rangers, from the Reserve Brigade, who had been sent overnight to cross the river nearer its source and to turn the French defences from the north. As this was taking place part of the 4th Brigade made a feint to the south towards the only bridge over the river. The action of the Royal York Rangers, which cost them nearly 120 casualties, carried the day and General Ernouf surrendered a few hours after the Noire was crossed and an all-out assault launched. Some two thousand prisoners were taken, and it was discovered that nearly six hundred French troops had been killed or wounded since the British landing a week earlier. The total number of British casualties amounted to 52 dead and about 250 wounded; losses among the West India regiments being seven dead and 91 wounded.

Nothing then remained to be done by Beckwith except to send a small force to seize the islands of St Martin, St Eustatius and Saba. Only the first two were garrisoned and they surrendered as soon as the British ships appeared. By 21st February French colonial rule in the Westindies had been brought to an end.

The capture of Guadeloupe was effectively the end of the war in the Caribbean. The West India regiments which had played an important part in bringing it to an end received no words of praise, or any special mention from Beckwith, either in his general orders issued within a day or two of the island's fall, or in his despatch of 9th February to London. To their rank and file by this time, if they had any thoughts on the matter at all, it was probably no more than they expected. The C-in-C had had to refer to the 'perseverance and temper' of the 1st WIR being 'respectable' after the episode in Marie Galante in 1808, because they were the only troops which took part. After the capture of Martinique his praise had been limited to that of the 'hard and severe work' carried out by the regiments, 'which the European soldier could not undergo'. Long before Guadeloupe it must have been obvious to them that they had been trained as soldiers only in order to do what the white soldier could not.

At the beginning of the Martinique campaign, as Prevost set off from the east coast to cross the island:

> the roads were in a wretched condition from the rains, and the horses being done up from the length of time which they had been on board ship, the troops were obliged to drag the guns themselves.

It requires no great stretch of imagination to work out which troops, out of a division made up from four European regiments and the 1st WIR, then hauled the guns up hill and down dale to Fort-de-France. Again, a year later when Harcourt required artillery in the mountains of Guadeloupe to fire on the French strongholds, it is not difficult to work out whether it was the men of the 15th and 25th Regiments, or of the 3rd and 6th WIR, who ended up with the job of getting them into position. The experiences of the 2nd WIR in Hispaniola, as hospital 'orderlies and attendants' as well as haulers of guns, only reinforces the view that, although black soldiers had long proved their skill and versatility in the field this was always considered secondary to their usefulness to the rest of the army as general dogsbodies, humpers and carriers. Some consolation may have come to those who took part in the capture of Guadeloupe from knowing that it was Hislop's 3rd Brigade, which contained twice as many black as white troops, which had led the advance and done all the dirty work in clearing the way for the rest of the First Division. Their efforts were acknowledged eventually when the Battle Honours 'Martinique' and 'Guadeloupe' were awarded to most of the regiments which had taken part, including the 1st WIR. Sadly, by the time this happened, the other West India regiments involved had all been disbanded.

Once the new administration had been established in Guadeloupe the 1st WIR and all the rest returned to their garrison duties, in places as far apart as Surinam and Belize, Curacao and the Bahamas. The dislike of them, which most of the white population in any of these places had displayed to begin with, gradually faded into a begrudging acceptance. Provided the troops kept out of trouble, better still if they kept themselves to themselves in the barracks, their presence - even in Jamaica - could be tolerated. That some of the slave-owners were not above cashing-in on the situation, and that life in these garrisons was perhaps not quite as dull and monastic as might have been expected, could be construed from a notice which appeared in the Kingston newspapers in November 1813:

> The Commanding Officer of Fort-Augusta, being desirous to prevent as much as possible Runaway Negro women from being permitted to remain in or about the Fort, thinks it necessary to acquaint those persons, who are in the habit of granting passes to their women slaves, to resort to the Garrison, that after the present month, every woman found there, who cannot produce a regular pass, countersigned by a Magistrate, will be taken up, and forwarded to one of the Workhouses.

The war between Britain and France continued in other parts of the world until 1814, when Napoleon was forced to abdicate and sent into exile. Under the terms of the Treaty of Paris signed in May of that year, everything in the Westindies returned to the way it had been after the Treaty of Amiens twelve years earlier - or very nearly. The victors had to come out of it better off than the losers, so France gave up St Lucia and Tobago, and the Dutch ceded Demerara, Berbice and Essequibo.

The signing of the treaty meant little to the West India regiments. Ever since the capture of Guadeloupe life for them had gone along much the same, whether stationed at Fort Augusta in Jamaica, in St Anne's Garrison in Barbados, on Morne Fortune in St Lucia, even at Fort Andries on the Berbice, or anywhere else. Only three of them went into action again during this period; two of them to experience warfare at its worst. This was brought about by the entry, incredible as it seemed to many at the time, and certainly to more or less everybody ever since, of Britain into another war in 1812.

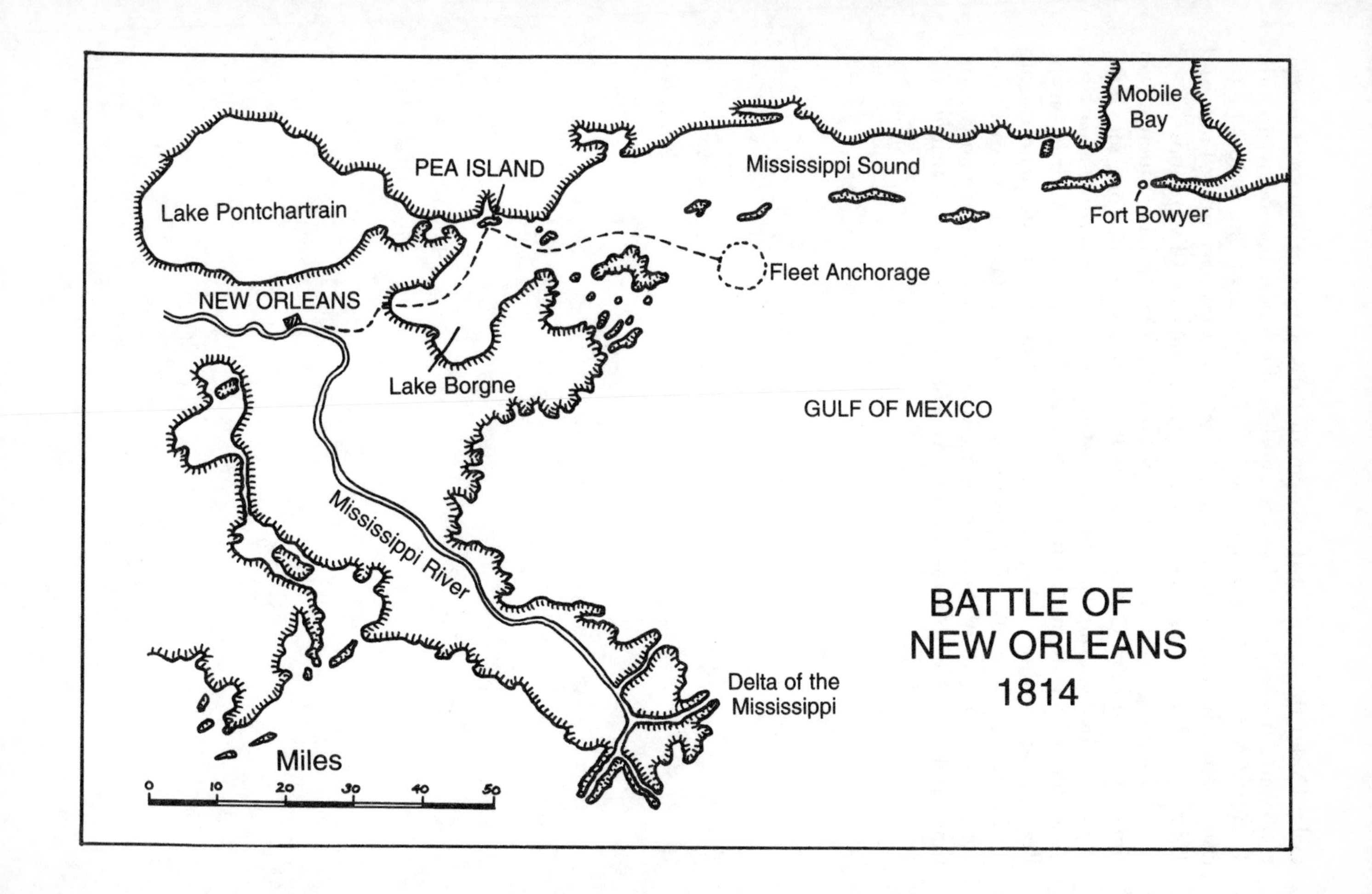
Mobile Bay
PEA ISLAND
Mississippi Sound
Lake Pontchartrain
Fort Bowyer
Fleet Anchorage
NEW ORLEANS
Lake Borgne
GULF OF MEXICO
Mississippi River
BATTLE OF
NEW ORLEANS
1814
Delta of the Mississippi
Miles
0
10
20
30
40
50

CHAPTER 7
SO MAD A VENTURE

> There are times and circumstances in which ... risks must and should be taken by commanders; but to put the country to the expense of sending six thousand men across the Atlantic for so mad a venture was little short of criminal.
>
> **Sir John W Fortescue (1911)**

The Anglo-American War, or the War of 1812 as it is usually called, began after a lengthy period of increasingly strained relations between the United States and Britain which developed during the Napoleonic Wars. It was brought about primarily through British efforts to prevent neutral countries from trading with France. After the Battle of Trafalgar the Royal Navy had complete control of the Atlantic and ruthless exercise of this, leading effectively to a blockade of American ports, created great resentment. A particular source of annoyance was the British insistence on claiming the right to stop and search any American ship, in order to impress British subjects and to arrest naval deserters found in its crew. In the end, after a demand in 1811 for trade restrictions to be lifted had been ignored until it was too late, the USA declared war in June 1812. It lasted for two and a half years, was one of the most unnecessary wars ever fought, and brought very little credit to British arms.

Although the war lasted for this length of time, it is only the events of the final few weeks that have any relevance here. In August 1814 a British fleet under Vice-Admiral Cochrane (the 'sovereign' of Marie Galante) had entered Chesapeake Bay on the east coast of the United States, and landed an expeditionary force under Major-General Robert Ross with instructions to do as much damage as possible. This led to the infamous burning of all the public buildings in Washington, followed by the death of Ross during an unsuccessful attempt to capture Baltimore. The force then withdrew and was taken to the Caribbean in order to refit and await reinforcements and a new commander from England, before attempting a similar expedition in the Gulf of Mexico. Admiral Cochrane was now worried that the war might end before Britain had made any territorial gain or he himself had made sufficient financial gain. Taking advantage of the lack of any Army commander-in-chief, and the lack of seniority of the officer left in acting command of the troops, he 'persuaded the authorities to sanction an attack upon New Orleans, estimated to contain sugar, cotton and tobacco to the value of three or four millions sterling, of which he hoped to obtain a good share for himself'.

New Orleans is almost one hundred miles up the Mississippi from the delta, and over fifty miles from the open sea in any other direction. In choosing it as a suitable target Cochrane ignored military considerations, apparently giving little thought to the difficulties which would be involved in supplying an expeditionary force at such a long distance from a base at sea, and even less to how the campaign would be conducted once the troops had been dumped ashore. That his concern for their safety and well-being ended as soon as they stepped off his ships was something that all, officers and men, black and white, who took part were to find out.

The decision to include any of the West India regiments in the force followed the admiral's receipt of an intelligence report from one of his naval subordinates:

> The Population of the slaves in the Southern Provinces of America is so great, that the People of Landed Property would be panic-struck at the sight of a Black Regiment on their coast, and nothing would effectually tend to make the war with this country unpopular, than of such a measure being in contemplation.

It is not clear whether this sort of information influenced the decision or not, but both Cochrane and Major-General John Keane, who was in temporary command of the troops, were probably only too glad to get their hands on another thousand or so seasoned soldiers. These belonged to the 5th WIR, which was part of the Jamaica garrison, and the 1st WIR, which had been in Guadeloupe since July. Both regiments joined up with the expedition off Negril on the west coast of Jamaica, shortly before the fleet left for the Gulf coast towards the end of November. The replacement Army C-in-C had not arrived by then but Cochrane, who was aware that peace talks were already taking place in Europe, could wait no longer. Ignoring his hankering for prize money, the seizure of as much American territory as possible was essential to Britain's negotiating position, and capture of New Orleans could even lead to revocation of the Louisiana Purchase - the legality of which the British Government had never recognized.

The fleet of over 40 ships, including 8 men-of-war, 15 frigates, and transports of all sizes, carrying over 5000 men and all their supplies, arrived off Ship Island in Mississippi Sound to the east of New Orleans by 10th December. As the river route to the city from the delta was well protected by forts, it was the admiral's intention that the attack should take place from the east. This would involve an approach through the swamps and creeks which separated New Orleans from a large lagoon called Lake Borgne. Unfortunately, although open to the sea not too far from the fleet's anchorage, the lake was so shallow that none of his ships could enter it. This meant that before they could begin to advance through the five miles of swamp which lay between the lagoon and their objective, some five thousand troops had to get from the ships to the lagoon entrance, and then all the way from one end of Lake Borgne to the other - a total distance of no less than seventy miles.

Preliminaries to an assault of this magnitude were enough to daunt the most seasoned campaigner, and the force contained a number of regiments filled with veterans of the Peninsular War. For the men of the West India regiments the prospect was much worse. Even before the vessels which transported them from Jamaica arrived in Mississippi Sound they must have realized that their welfare was of small concern to the rest of the force, and that they had not been prepared or equipped for the task ahead of them. The weather along the Gulf coast was at its worst when they arrived, already shrivelled with cold. Their uniform, though similar to that worn by the rest of the infantry, had been modified slightly for the tropics, and each man wore little more than an unlined waist-length jacket, lightweight gaitered duck trousers and light leather shoes. Before they left Jamaica

> no attempt was made to furnish the men with warm clothing, and their sufferings from this cause, they being all natives of the tropics, can be better imagined than described. During the voyage they had been much scattered in small craft, where the soldiers were obliged to sleep on deck, exposed to the torrents of rain which fell by day and to the frosts that came on at night...

As a result, even before any of them set foot ashore, 'large numbers of them died from cold and exposure, the 5th West India Regiment suffering equally with the 1st'.

Worse was to follow. After Lake Borgne had been cleared of some small American gunboats on 14th December the way was clear to begin the immense task of ferrying the troops ashore. This was done in two stages, using the ships' boats manned by the seamen. Each was filled with troops, crowding in as many as possible, and then rowed a distance of thirty miles to a staging post off the northern side of the lake. It took ten hours or more to make the passage to the 'small desert spot of earth' known as Pea Island:

> Than this spot it is scarcely possible to imagine any place more wretched. It was a swamp, containing a small space of firm ground at one end, and almost wholly unadorned with trees of any sort of description. The interior was the resort of waterfowl; and the pools and creeks with which it was intercepted abounded in dormant alligators.

It took five days to assemble all the force on the island, and one can only marvel at the fortitude of men left 'without tents or huts, or any covering to shelter them from the inclemency of weather' in a place 'incapable of furnishing even fuel enough to supply our fires'. The unfortunates belonging to the West India regiments suffered most of all:

> as night closed in, the rain generally ceased, and severe frosts set in, which, congealing our wet clothes upon our bodies, left little animal warmth to keep the limbs in a state of activity; and the consequence was, that many of the wretched negroes, to whom frost and cold were altogether new, fell fast asleep and perished before morning.

Their piteous condition was such that it even managed to evoke a trace of sympathy among the other troops. An officer of the 95th Rifles noted loftily

> some of the poor blacks also, I understand, suffered in consequence of the severe cold, a thing with which they were totally unacquainted, and against which they were ill provided, having nothing but their light and thin West Indian dress to keep it out.

It also, incredibly, caused some amusement and the same young officer thought

> It was laughable the next morning to see them examining so intently the ice which had been formed on the pools near our bivouack. They could not conjecture what it was; some of them asserting it was salt; while the greater part were totally at a loss respecting it.

Whether there was anything humorous in this scene or not, by the time the force was ready to move on neither West India regiment had much to laugh about. The 1st WIR 'which had left Negril Bay 500 strong, was now so reduced by mortality and sickness that barely 400 men were in a condition to take the field', and the 5th WIR was in no better shape.

Before beginning the next part of the odyssey the troops were formed into three brigades, the 1st WIR joining the 21st and 44th Regiments in the Second Brigade, while the 5th WIR and the 93rd Regiment formed the Third. It took three days, starting at daybreak on 22nd December, for the entire force to be ferried across Lake Borgne and landed at the mouth of the Bayou Mazant. This was a creek which when followed to its source through the swamps gave access to a road alongside the Mississippi, only seven miles or so down-river from New Orleans.

For each man as he waded ashore the entire undertaking must by then have assumed a grotesque nightmarish quality: the passage from Pea Island for some of the boats had taken nearly twenty-four hours, and none had made it in under twelve. Each boat had been so crowded that the soldiers could do nothing but sit in benumbed, half-starved misery, unable even to relieve their bladders or bowels except with supreme difficulty, and when not sitting in torrential rain they had been lashed by an icy wind. For the men of the West India regiments the horrors of the 'middle passage' could have been no worse. It is impossible to say that they, out of all the sodden, shivering soldiers who eventually staggered ashore, had suffered most since leaving the fleet nine days earlier, but it is difficult to believe any could have suffered more.

The First Brigade, formed from the 4th and 85th Regiments with the 95th Rifles, and acting as the Advance under Major-General Keane, had landed first to clear the route along the bayou. When it ran into American pickets the alarm had been raised in New Orleans where General Andrew Jackson had arrived earlier in the month to conduct its defence. Jackson, 'a rancorous hater of the British', whose achievements in the days that followed were to help him eventually to become the seventh president of the United States, immediately organized a force of about two thousand men to check Keane's advance. The encounter which ensued took place at the position established by Keane near the river bank, beginning late in the afternoon of 23rd December. Both sides were fairly evenly matched, with the local knowledge of the Americans combatted by the superior discipline and experience of the British. After five or six hours of very confused fighting in the dark, an American flanking movement, which might have succeeded, was interrupted by the arrival of the first units of the Second Brigade. These 'took the enemy in flank, and a hand-to-hand conflict took place', which continued until the early hours of the next morning when 'the enemy retired, beaten off at all points'. Each side suffered over two hundred casualties. The losses incurred by the 1st WIR during this action, when added to all 'the deaths from cold and exposure that had occurred during the passage from [Pea] Island ... so thinned the already attenuated ranks .... that on the morning of the 24th, only 16 sergeants and 240 rank and file were available for duty'.

On Christmas Eve the American forces withdrew a couple of miles closer to the city and established a defensive line, the 'Jackson Line' , flanked by a two-gun battery, between the Mississippi and the edge of the swamps. At the British position, about two miles down-river, once all the troops had arrived all Keane could do was organize his defence and wait for all the guns, ammunition, stores and equipment needed for an assault to be brought up. Every item required had to be transported some seventy miles in boats manned by weary sailors, before being hauled several miles through the cypress swamps to the river bank by equally tired and miserable soldiers. Keane was also expecting at any moment the arrival of the new commander-in-chief.

Major-General Sir Edward Pakenham, fresh from glory in the Peninsular War, finally caught up with his army on Christmas Day, 'bringing some guns with him'. He was understandably horrified at what he found. In effect his force was trapped on a bank about a mile wide between the Mississippi and the dense swamps which separated the solid ground of the river bank from Lake Borgne. Between his troops and their objective the Jackson Line was being made into a formidable obstacle across the bank by the erection of a high barricade and the digging of a ditch which could be enfiladed by a battery. Two armed vessels on the river were able to cruise up and down and fire on the British at will. And, to cap it all, his only supply base was over seventy miles away, and at sea.

His first action was to do something about the ships in the river. On 26th December the guns which had arrived the previous day were brought into action with heated shot. One vessel was destroyed, but the other managed to move out of range upstream and anchor abreast the Jackson Line, from where it could still interfere with any British attack. Two days later Pakenham attempted just that. His forces moved forward in two columns, only to be brought to a halt as they came within range of the by now substantial breastwork and the fusillade which poured from it. As there appeared to be no way around the left of the American line where it ended in the swamps, the troops withdrew before the carnage became too great. Pakenham was then left with no alternative it seemed but to try to blast his way through the barricade, using some of the heavy guns carried by Admiral Cochrane's men-of-war.

It took until the end of the year to bring ten 18-pounder guns and four 24-pounder carronades ashore and into position. The amount of labour this must have involved is almost impossible to envisage by anyone living in a world filled with mechanical aids. It must have been difficult enough to get the guns into the mouth of the bayou, but at least they were carried that far slung under or between boats. After that they had to be manhandled all the way, 'on which duty' it comes as no surprise to learn 'the two West India Regiments and the seamen were employed'. Just how they accomplished this Herculean task is not recorded, but the sheer quantity of brute physical effort needed to move such heavy, awkward pieces of metal through even a mile of creeks and bogs must have been enormous. The officers as well as the men were fully exercised and 'Major Weston and Lieutenant Magee, 1st West India Regiment, died from exposure and fatigue while engaged in this work'.

The bombardment began at dawn on 1st January from makeshift batteries only 500 yards or so from their target. The Americans retaliated quickly and an artillery duel developed which, even after only an hour, had given the defenders the edge. The British batteries, made mostly from sugar casks (some of the prize goods Cochrane had set his heart on), had been blown away and their guns were being knocked from their carriages. At the same time it was apparent that the British cannonade was having little effect on the American breastwork, where the shot was being absorbed by the cotton bales (more of Cochrane's prospective loot) from which it was built. When the supply of ammunition began to run out Pakenham was forced to accept another failure and withdraw the gunners. With thought processes a hundred years ahead of his time, he now adopted a view which was to be found among many British generals on the Western Front during the First World War, that the only follow-up to a futile bombardment was a full frontal infantry attack.

This could not take place immediately, nor until a mile-long canal had been excavated between the bayou and the Mississippi to permit some of the ships' boats to be used to take part of his force across the river. A battery on the west bank, unless seized by this force, would otherwise menace the main assault with flanking fire. It took until 7th January to finish the canal and complete the rest of the preparations, time which Jackson and the Americans used to repair and strengthen the barricade, deepen and extend the ditches, and ensure they had plenty of ammunition. Pakenham, now in a great hurry to get things moving, gave orders for the attack to begin the next day.

Nothing went right from the word go. A crucial dam in the new canal gave way, allowing only half the number of boats needed to be floated into the Mississippi, and so only half the planned number of men needed to take out the west bank battery could be ferried across. Negligence on the part of the C-in-C's staff brought about the failure to provide the 44th Regiment with the ladders and fascines it was supposed to carry into the field, and the commanding officer of the regiment chose to proceed without them, deluded into believing he and his men were foredoomed to sacrifice. In fact the whole of the attacking force from Pakenham downwards was doomed. As the troops approached the American defences, looking around for the missing fascines and ladders, they were mowed down from the high barricade. The men of the two West India regiments, who had been put on the far right of the line, fared slightly better and managed to cross the ditches where they ran into the swamp, but they were then still unable to surmount the breastwork.

While this carnage was taking place Pakenham, who was prancing up and down in the rear on a horse he had obtained trying to rally the remnants of broken regiments, 'received a slight wound in the knee from a musket-ball'. The same shot killed his horse and he was deposited on the ground. A few moments later 'a second ball took effect more fatally, and he dropped lifeless into the arms of his aide-de-camp'. When two of the three brigade commanders were severely wounded some minutes afterwards

> All was now confusion and dismay. Without leaders, ignorant of what was to be done, the troops first halted and then began to retire; till finally the retreat was changed into a flight, and they quitted the ground in the utmost disorder.

The West India regiments ran with the rest, and they were all, black and white alike, saved from annihilation only by the cool and responsible action of the Reserve Brigade. This was comprised of the 7th and 43rd Regiments, which had only joined the force two days earlier. They made an impressive feint 'by which the enemy were so much awed that they did not venture beyond their lines in pursuit of the fugitives'.

With more than 300 dead, nearly 1200 wounded - many mortally - and another 400 or so taken prisoner, the British were now in no position to do anything but hope they could get back to the fleet without suffering any further. Command had devolved upon Major-General John Lambert, who quickly arranged a short truce with General Jackson in order to bury the dead and collect the wounded. When this had been done he brought back the troops who had been sent across the river, destroyed all the heavy guns, and put a full-scale retreat in motion.

This was no easy matter. It was unsafe to use the route along the bayou, there were the numerous sick and wounded to look after, and when the remains of the force reached Lake Borgne there would not be enough boats to take them off in one go. Lambert decided on a new route to the lake and

> to make a road from the firm ground to the water's edge, a distance of many miles, through the very centre of a morass, where human foot had never before trodden. The difficulties experienced in making this road were immense. Sometimes for miles together no firm soil could be found, nor trees to furnish brushwood, and all that could be done was to lay down bundles of reeds ......

Nine days of filthy, backbreaking labour were needed to create the road. While it was being laid Jackson, sure of his victory and with nice perception, limited his attentions to harassing the British outposts by day, and keeping up a noisy artillery bombardment all night to add sleeplessness to his enemy's woes. On 17th January the sick and wounded were able to be moved along the road to the edge of the lake, and the remainder of the troops began to retreat along it the following evening:

> Leaving the campfires burning as if no movement were taking place, battalion after battalion stole away in the darkness in the most profound silence. Marching all night over the fragile road of reeds, through which the men sank knee-deep into the mud, the army reached the borders of the lake at dawn.

It took until the end of the month to ferry the entire force and whatever equipment it still possessed back to the ships. Jackson paid no attention to the encampment on Lake Borgne as it gradually emptied, and with the exception of one boat which was captured, the procession of boats moving back and forth across the lake was also left unmolested. It was all a long, slow, undignified and humiliating process: an inglorious ending to an inglorious campaign, not quite the final act in an inglorious war.

Even after he had been given all the details of the disaster, and seen for himself the bedraggled state of the returning troops, Cochrane was still not prepared to give up. He bludgeoned Lambert and Keane (who had made a rapid recovery from his wounding) into agreeing to an attack on Fort Bowyer at the entrance to Mobile Bay. This began on 7th February and ended with the surrender of the fort four days later. On

14th February a despatch vessel arrived from England with the news that on 24th December a peace treaty had been signed between Britain and the United States: the sweat, filth and blood of the New Orleans debacle, even the thirty casualties incurred during the vindictive seizure of Fort Bowyer, had all been for nothing.

The shattered remains of the two West India regiments, each with less than half its rank and file fit for duty, were returned, the 1st WIR to Barbados and the 5th WIR to Jamaica, in March. They probably arrived at just the same time as men of the 2nd WIR were returning to the Bahamas from another part of the United States, where they had been involved in an operation only slightly less futile than the one at New Orleans.

Even after the British expedition to Chesapeake Bay in the summer of 1814 had ended in failure it was still felt necessary to maintain some sort of offensive against ports on the east coast. The task was given to a squadron of ships under Rear-Admiral George Cockburn. As he needed troops in addition to the marines carried by his ships if he was to achieve anything worthwhile, the 2nd WIR which had been stationed in the Bahamas since the end of 1809 was ordered to help. On 13th December 1814 the flank companies embarked in HMS *Rota* at Nassau, and the ship sailed to a rendezvous point off Cumberland Island at the extreme southern end of the coast of Georgia. There they found other ships but 'neither the Admiral, nor General, with the remainder of the troops' had yet arrived.

The senior naval officer present, the captain of HMS *Dragon* 'deemed it expedient to strike a blow' without waiting for the main force, and a landing was made on Cumberland Island. This was carried out by the ships' marines, supported by the 2nd WIR. They met little opposition and what defenders there were soon retired by boat to the mainland, under cover of fire from Fort Peitrie at the mouth of the St Marys River. The next morning the British force crossed to the mainland and, supported by the ships' boats, marched on the fort with the 2nd WIR skirmishing ahead. The column was attacked before reaching its objective but 'after a sharp struggle' that attackers 'fled, so closely pursued, that both British and Americans rushed pellmell into the fort along a narrow causeway, raised above the level of the swamp'. The Americans rapidly abandoned the fort and took refuge in the town of St Marys, some way up the river, but evacuated it as soon as the 2nd WIR and the marines approached. By the time they entered the town they had been 'employed without rest or intermission for twenty-two hours'.

The town remained in British hands until the end of February, its location among the swamps of south-east Georgia having the usual impact of such places on the health of white troops. At the beginning of the month Admiral Cockburn had written to the commanding officer of the 2nd WIR:

> In consequence of the distinguished and gallant conduct of the two flank companies of your Regiment ... I am induced to ... request [the Governor of the Bahamas] will permit such further numbers of the Regiment under your command to come to me, as may be deemed prudent to spare from Nassau.

Three more companies were embarked on 15th February, but by the time they reached the coast of Georgia it was too late. The imminence of an attack by a large American force from Savannah had caused the garrison to withdraw from St Marys, and an evacuation took place instead of a landing. As news of the peace agreement between the United States and Britain arrived at the same time no further operations took place, and all five companies of the 2nd WIR were returned to Nassau by the middle of March.

The three West India regiments that had been involved in the war with America returned to their regular garrison duties in the knowledge that, for the first time in twelve years, there were no hostilities, or even preparations for hostilities, taking place anywhere in the Caribbean. Unfortunately, any feeling of complacency which this may have induced was dispelled within only a week or two of their return, by arrival of the news that Napoleon had escaped from exile in Elba.

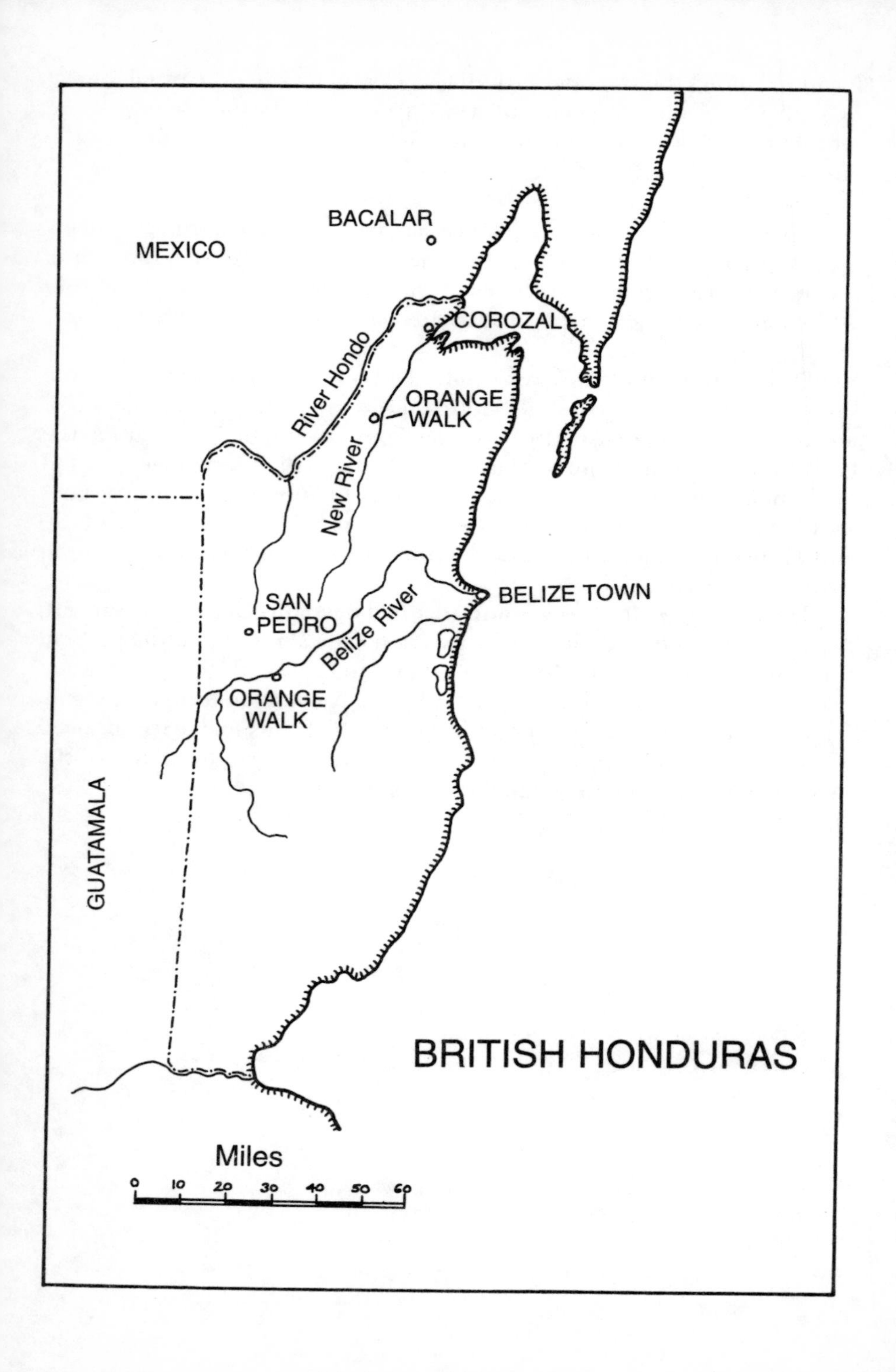
BACALAR
MEXICO
COROZAL
River Hondo
ORANGE
WALK
New River
SAN
PEDRO
BELIZE TOWN
Belize River
ORANGE
WALK
GUATAMALA
BRITISH HONDURAS
Miles
0
10
20
30
40
50
60

CHAPTER 8
HABITS OF OBEDIENCE

> These Negro yeomen-veterans, let it be said in passing, are among the ablest and steadiest of the coloured population. Military service has given them just enough of those habits of obedience of which slavery gives too much - if the obedience of a mere slave, depending not on the independent will, but on brute fear, is to be called obedience at all.
>
> **Charles Kingsley (1870)**

News of Napoleon's return to France reached the Caribbean in April 1815, and had an immediate effect in Martinique and Guadeloupe, both of which the year before had been turned over to representatives of King Louis XVIII under the terms of the Treaty of Paris. The Republican faction in each island - sizeable in Martinique, but bigger and more forceful in Guadeloupe - gave every indication of rebelling in the Emperor's favour. An appeal for assistance from the authorities in Martinique brought British ships with the Army C-in-C, Lieutenant-General Sir James Leith, and several hundred troops to the island on 5th June. This show of strength defused the situation, and after landing a contingent of troops Leith returned to his headquarters in Barbados. Martinique afterwards remained loyal to the French crown but the Governor of Guadeloupe, supported by a large percentage of the population, declared for Napoleon on 18th June, unaware that he had been defeated at Waterloo and was already on his way to St Helena. But, even with Bonaparte in exile a Bonapartiste regime could not be allowed to exist and so, for the third time in twenty-one years, the British prepared to invade the island.

The force assembled by General Leith was divided as usual into three, only brigades this time, using troops drawn from Barbados, St Lucia, Martinique and Dominica. In the Second Brigade were '400 picked men of the 1st West India Regiment' from the Barbados garrison. For some of these men, as with some of the hardier members of the 15th, 25th and 63rd Regiments, which were also part of the force, it would be their second assault on Guadeloupe in six years.

This time the whole operation took only two days. The First and Second Brigades were put ashore on the southeast coast of that part of the island called Basse Terre on 8th August. Their landing place was much closer to the port of Trois Rivieres than in 1810, and after 'a short but sharp skirmish with a body of the enemy' they advanced inland towards the Plateau du Palmiste. On the following afternoon their advance on the French positions on the plateau caused the defenders, 'after the exchange of a few shots, to evacuate [the] works and retire to Morne Houel', a fortified position on a 1400-foot hill which overlooked the town of Basse Terre from the east. The town itself was already in British hands, having been occupied that morning after a short struggle by the Third Brigade, who had landed earlier a little to the north. While the other two brigades were taking over the abandoned redoubts on the plateau, reports were received of troops from Grande Terre, the eastern part of the island, moving through the mountains behind the plateau, in an attempt to join up with the defenders of Morne Houel.

> The detachment of the 1st West India Regiment was at once despatched to reinforce the rearguard, and to occupy in force all the passes of the Gallion, a river running through a formidable ravine at the foot of [the] plateau. The troops from Grandeterre being thus cut off, endeavoured to form a junction by unfrequented paths through the woods; but, being met at every point by the skirmishers of the 1st West India Regiment, who searched the woods in every direction, they were compelled to abandon the attempt and retire at dusk.

Early on 10th August, after a night spent in pouring rain, 'bivouacked on the ground, without shelter, and drenched to the skin', the First and Second Brigades started the ascent of Morne Houel. As they neared the summit a British flag was waved from the French position, and the defenders made an immediate and unconditional surrender. The administration of the island was then returned into Royalist hands, although a British garrison was required for several months afterwards as 'Guadeloupe was not at once reduced to a state of tranquillity'.

The main source of disturbance came from French army deserters who had taken to the mountains before the surrender, and who persisted in 'a desultory and ferocious war against the British posts'. The 1st WIR was left as part of the British garrison and,

> being composed of men better able to support the hardships of a guerilla war, carried on in a country naturally difficult, during the height of the tropical rains, was continually employed against these insurgent bands, and several men were killed and wounded in unknown and forgotten skirmishes.

The regiment did not return to Barbados until October.

And so, right up until the very end, months after the Congress of Vienna had brought the Napoleonic Wars to an end, the 1st WIR continued to fight exactly the kind of war which had brought it, and all the other West India regiments, into existence some twenty years earlier. Time after time the men had demonstrated what tough and resilient soldiers they were and, provided they were not expected to function in subzero conditions wearing only tropical clothing, how well suited they were to irregular war as light infantrymen. The most unfortunate aspect of their future was that, although it was only this type of warfare they would have to cope with during the remainder of their existence, they were never going to be considered or organized as anything but standard British infantry regiments. That is, those that had any future: within five years of the return of the 1st WIR from Guadeloupe, five of the eight would be disbanded. But before that took place there were other aspects of soldiering to be learned or experienced.

In the process of being turned into useful soldiers the recruits of any West India regiment suffered one major disability not shared by the recruits of the any white regiment. Considering that the former were drawn from a variety of tribes and regions in West Africa all the regiments they were drafted into suffered acute language problems. That the recruits were also illiterate was of less importance than the fact that they spoke a variety of tongues; it was doubtful after all if more than a handful of the rank and file in any British regiment could read or write. An attempt was made in 1812 to improve the situation when each West India regiment was ordered to open a regimental school, but these were slow to be established - usually because no suitable instructors could be found, or because the regiment was too dispersed, or because other matters were too pressing. The ending of the war provided an excellent opportunity for this situation to be remedied but, although there was some improvement, no genuine sustained effort to teach recruits English, let alone to read and write, was ever made. This says little for the officers and senior NCOs who remained content with having to issue orders through interpreters or to demean the men and themselves by resorting to pidgin English. At the same time it says much for the aptitude and natural abilities of the men, that they were able to perform their duties and master the art of war as well as they did while under such a disability.

The collective illiteracy of the troops of the West India regiments throughout the war period was not quite so universal among the slave population of the Westindies as a whole. Even though to teach slaves to read and write was illegal in some islands, and hardly considered as less than a crime in all the others, there were slaves who managed to find teachers. By 1815 it is likely that one or two out of every hundred had acquired some ability to read if not to write. One such was a female slave on an estate in Barbados who, at the beginning of 1816 set in motion a series of events which eventually brought men of the 1st WIR into direct conflict with many of her fellow slaves.

A bill calling for the compulsory registration of all slaves in the British colonies, as another step towards the abolition of slavery, was introduced in the British parliament in 1815. It met such violent opposition from the Westindian plantocracy's representatives in London that it was withdrawn, and this soon became common knowledge among the slaves, but only in a distorted form. In Barbados, where slave conditions in general were worse than in other islands, snippets of printed material concerning the bill and its fate were read by a woman called Nanny Grigg and relayed to her fellow plantation workers, who in turn spoke to other slaves. This soon produced a widespread impression that emancipation was imminent, but was being held up by the intransigence of the estate owners and the legislature. Spurred on by this a number of the more authoritative slaves, drivers and rangers, began plotting a revolt. The chief ringleader, Bussa, after whom the revolt is sometimes called, belonged to the owner of an estate near the easternmost point of the island. Because of his position as the overseer's assistant he had more freedom of movement than other workers, and as a result was able to influence slaves holding similar positions on many of the adjoining estates.

The plot developed and the revolt was timed to begin at sunset on Easter Sunday, 14th April 1816.

> A conflagration upon a high ridge of copse-wood ... was the first signal. Shortly after, the canes upon eight or nine of the surrounding estates were set on fire. Some few of the rebels were furnished with firearms, and a scanty supply of ammunition, and the remainder were armed with swords, bludgeons, and such rude weapons as they had been able to procure. Their approach was announced by the beating of the drums, the blowing of shells, and other discordant sounds.

The uprising was widely supported, and some twenty thousand slaves, drawn from over seventy-five estates, the following day took control of virtually the whole of the southeast part of the island. The damage inflicted on the plantation buildings was by no means as serious as might have been expected, and the white families who did not manage to flee to

Bridgetown were not that badly treated: certainly no killing took place. The slaves made no attempt to enter the capital but set up defensive positions on the outskirts, Bussa and the other leaders assuming that the authorities would be prepared to negotiate.

This was the last thing anyone in authority was prepared to do. Martial law was declared, the Militia was called out, and Colonel Edward Codd, commander of St Anne's Garrison, ordered the 1st WIR under Major James Cassidy into the field. Just to the east of Bridgetown Cassidy came across 'a dense mob of half-armed slaves crowning the summits of the low hills' in Christchurch Parish, and

> an advance being ordered, the 1st West India Regiment stormed the heights, and at the point of the bayonet drove the rebels from their position. Not a shot was fired by the regiment on this occasion, Major Cassidy being anxious to save bloodshed as much as possible ...

It was hardly surprising that the rebels, who had been led to believe by some of their leaders that troops of their own colour and ancestry would not be used against them, were incensed by this and many of them rushed back to offer

> a furious resistance, closing with and aiming blows at the soldiers with their rude weapons, and endeavouring to wrench the muskets from their hands ....

Fortunately for the troops, and most unfortunately for the slaves, the army's training had not been for nothing. With one of his men already dead and seventeen more wounded, Cassidy was obliged to give the order to open fire, and 'a considerable number of the insurgents were thus killed and wounded'. The remainder then fled and the regiment's part in the suppression of the revolt ended. The hunting down of the ringleaders and the cold-blooded reprisals that followed were carried out by the Militia, composed largely of men drawn from the 'poor white' section of society, and encouraged in their excesses by Colonel Codd. Acting on his orders the Militia killed any slaves who offered the slightest resistance, and wantonly destroyed their houses and gardens. About 150 were killed and another 144 were executed later after standing trial. A further 130 were deported, first to Belize where they were prevented from landing by the inhabitants, and eventually to Sierra Leone.

What slaves in Barbados or elsewhere in the Caribbean thought about the use of black troops to suppress this bid for freedom is not recorded. The soldiers' views of this or any other slave revolt are equally unknown, but there is no record of any of them, anywhere, assisting in a plot connected with the general struggle for freedom which broke out in such confrontations from time to time. Bussa's Revolt took place after the men of the West India regiments had been free for nine years and, like their brethren in the 'free black' community, they were not prepared to jeopardize this status, regardless of race, colour, kinship or anything else. White society in Barbados and the other islands must certainly have noted the disciplined way in which the 1st WIR set about restoring order after the revolt had begun, and this may well have helped to reduce the still widespread antagonism towards the regiments. Not that the Westindian legislators, planters and merchants would need to feed their resentment for very much longer: the reductions brought about by the inevitable demands in Britain for cuts in military spending, following the end of the war, began to take effect even before normal life had been resumed in Barbados.

Orders for the disbandment of the 7th and 8th WIR arrived in May, with the officers being granted pay until the end of the year and passages paid back to England, while the majority of the men were drafted into the other six regiments. Soldiers not considered suitable for retention or unfit for active service were sent to Black Garrison Companies, attached to the garrisons in Jamaica, Barbados and elsewhere. Their personnel were fed and clothed, paid threepence a day each, and expected to work as pioneers. Less than a year later the establishment of each of the remaining regiments was reduced to 800 rank and file. Some of the men made redundant could be sent to the Black Garrison Companies, but the majority - who needed to be settled into civilian society - presented a problem.

As there was surprisingly little demand from among the African-born soldiers to be returned to Africa, the plan put forward by the army originally was that each discharged man should be allowed to settle in the island of his choice. This met with such hostility from all the island legislatures, except that of Trinidad where more settlers were needed to add to the labour force, that some other solution had to be found. After the Superintendent of Belize had been persuaded that ex-soldiers would make a valuable addition to the Settlement's work-force, it was decided that all discharged men who had been born in the Westindies or brought from Africa at an early age would go to either Trinidad or Belize, while all the rest would be sent back to Sierra Leone. No sooner had this decision been reached than further cuts and changes came into effect.

In June 1817 the Superintendent of Belize informed the Magistracy, which functioned as the Settlement's legislative body, that

> His Majesty's Government have been pleased to determine on disbanding the 5th West India Regiment, and to provide for five hundred of the men by removing them to this Settlement where they are to receive Grants of Land proportioned to their means of cultivation, or to engage themselves in the service of Wood-Cutters or other inhabitants as they themselves prefer.

The first group arrived in November, and the last in October of the following year, a total of 556 men with 81 women and 54 children. Their arrival in Belize produced a sizeable increase to the population which barely exceeded four thousand. They were settled to the south of the town of Belize, along the Sibun River or in the vicinity of Manatee Lagoon, but colonial inefficiency or perhaps sheer bloody-mindedness prevented any of them from being given a formal grant of land. The lack of title merely created problems for the future, when some of the families were treated as squatters. Even as late as 1868 the Governor was writing to London:

> To the descendents of all these old soldiers, who are now in actual possession of the plots of land ... I would suggest that I should be authorized to give Crown titles, without payment. The whole extent of the land occupied is very small, but I think it would be a great hardship if it were sold (as is alleged in one instance to have been done) over the heads of the present occupiers to large proprietors.

The 4th WIR was also considered for disbandment during 1817 but, as it was 'composed of men principally anxious to remain in the service', the regiment was given a chance to see how it fared in another part of the world. Before any reduction in its establishment had taken place it was transferred to Gibraltar, 'where it was supposed the men would be extremely useful in relieving British soldiers from such duties as subjected men to exposure during the heat of the day': in other words where they could undertake all the hard and unpleasant jobs for the rest of the garrison. The regiment arrived there in August 1817 and in under two years had been decimated by disease, losing 119 men out of an initial total of 1000 all ranks, with a mortality rate four times higher than that of any other regiment stationed on the Rock. The most common afflictions were diseases of the lungs, stomach and bowels, closely followed by 'Rheumatic Affections', surely indicating that it was the standard of accommodation and food, and the sort of fatigues they had to carry out, which brought this about. The Army did not think so, preferring to believe that it showed 'that the constitution of the negro was unfitted for any climate of which he was not a native', and in April 1819 shipped the regiment to Sierra

Leone for disbandment.

The 6th WIR was disbanded at the end of 1817. As it was then in Tobago it was easy and inexpensive to transfer the men who qualified to Trinidad, and one hundred and eighty arrived there the following January. They were given suitable grants of Crown land near Manzanilla Bay on the uninhabited east coast. An order in October 1818 to disband the 3rd WIR, which was then in Trinidad, met with strong objections from Lord Combermere, the Commander of the Forces 'Stationed on the Windward and Leeward Islands', and had to be modified. Instead, the regiment was reduced to five companies with a total strength of around five hundred all ranks. The men of the other companies, having made it clear they did not want to be taken to Africa, were allowed to remain in Trinidad. In the middle of 1819 they were settled in three groups on the Cuare River in the east of the island. Each settlement was organized in quasi-military fashion around one of the former companies, with the senior sergeant appointed as headman. Clothing and rations were provided but the cost of these, together with the other expenses of establishing the settlements, had to be borne by the settlers. Each man received a free grant of eight acres of land, or sixteen if he was married, but was then confined to it and liable to be punished if he went to live and work elsewhere. To administer the settlements a retired lieutenant from the regiment was appointed as Superintendent, receiving a salary of £500 a year as well as his normal half-pay. He was not required to live in the area, but merely to visit the settlements from time to time, and to oversee work on a road the settlers were supposed to clear and maintain from Arima, the nearest town.

The remainder of the 3rd WIR was not disbanded until the beginning of 1825. Some 376 men, with 35 women and 34 children, were then settled under the same conditions, and under the same superintendent, in four groups roughly in a line between the Curare villages (as they had by now become) and the sea at Manzanilla Bay. They too were then expected to create and maintain a road which, when it joined that between Arima and Cuare, would provide access from the more inhabited parts of the island to the east coast for the first time.

In the end, road-building in addition to the clearing and planting of their holdings proved too much for the settlers, and nothing much more than a track could be kept open between Arima and Manzanilla until well after 1850. By that time, although many of the men had long since taken their chances and gone off to live elsewhere, those that remained - like Sergeant Brooke in the village of Turoure - had survived quite well. Brooke, the 'headman of the place', lived in 'a neat and commodious mud-hut, covered with ... one of the rough but efficacious thatches of the country', and offered hospitality to the occasional traveller anxious to see the back-country of Trinidad:

> He furnishes the hungry wayfarer with a fowl, yams, a bottle of porter and a hammock, for which the understood consideration is two dollars. But it must not be overlooked, that the porter has to be carried on the head of a man, or at best on a mule, all the way from Port of Spain - thirty miles; and were it not for this accommodation, the traveller must sleep in the woods, and bring with him a sumpter horse to carry the indispensable supplies.

One or two of the old soldiers were still around in 1870 when the English author, Charles Kingsley, made his visit to the area. A 'middle-sized Negro ... Isaac by name' caught his attention, whom he found out had served in 'one of the East [sic] India regiments' and had 'lived and worked in Trinidad' for fifty-three years. A Sergeant Harrison who died in 1877 must have been among the very last to go; he was certainly the oldest, claiming to have been born in 1759.

But to return to 1819; at the beginning of the year, with the 3rd WIR enjoying a reprieve and now permanently stationed in Trinidad, and the 4th WIR in Gibraltar and fated never to return to the Caribbean, only the 1st and 2nd WIR - as befitted the two most senior regiments - remained in being. The former had its headquarters in Barbados, with detachments in four of the other islands of the eastern Caribbean. The headquarters of the latter were in Jamaica, having been transferred from the Bahamas in 1816. And this, more or less, is how things remained for the next twenty years or so, with one regiment in the east providing detachments as necessary for any island or territory between the Virgin Islands and Demerara, and the other in the west covering Belize and the Bahamas as well as Jamaica; that is, except for one great and far-reaching change.

In March, seventeen years after the 2nd WIR had arrived in Jamaica amid such controversy, and eleven years after all the hullabaloo caused by the mutiny at Fort Augusta, a leader in the Kingston *Royal Gazette* noted

> The departure of the Second West-India Regiment from this island affords a proper occasion for speaking with approbation of the discipline and deportment of that Corps. It is perhaps peculiarly just that this tribute to the good conduct of the Regiment should emanate from the press of this city. No other part of the island has had an equal opportunity with this vicinity of observing the demeanour and regularity of the officers and men. If prejudices have existed toward troops of this description, the conduct of the

Second West-India Regiment has deservedly made a most favourable impression in their favour ...

While this might not have made up much for all those years spent in mosquito-ridden Fort Augusta it was better than nothing. On 23rd March, after sending three companies to Belize and two to Nassau, Lieutenant-Colonel John Ross and the remaining five companies embarked in two small transports and set out for Sierra Leone. This tour of duty was to last for six years, but for the West India regiments in general it was the beginning of an association with West Africa which was to last for a century.

PART THREE

STERN ADMONITIONS

Were they truer, the old songs,
when the law lived far away,
when the veiled queen, her girth
as comfortable as cushions,
upheld the orb with its stern admonitions?

Derek Walcott
Parades, Parades

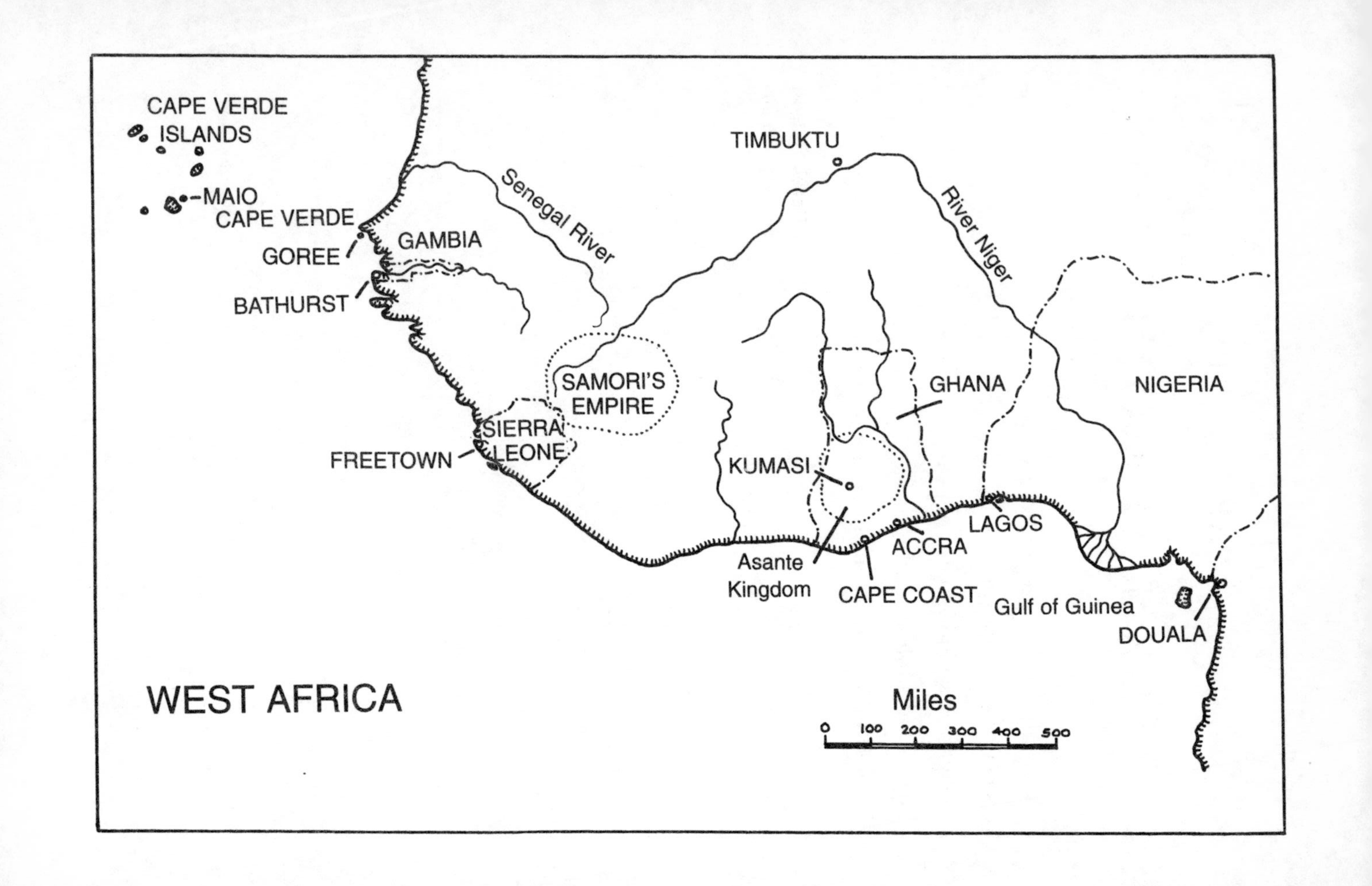
CAPE VERDE
ISLANDS
MAIO
CAPE VERDE
GOREE
BATHURST
GAMBIA
Senegal River
TIMBUKTU
River Niger
SAMORI'S
EMPIRE
SIERRA
LEONE
FREETOWN
KUMASI
GHANA
NIGERIA
Asante
Kingdom
CAPE COAST
ACCRA
LAGOS
Gulf of Guinea
DOUALA
WEST AFRICA
Miles
0
100
200
300
400
500

CHAPTER 9
TO AFRIC'S SHORE

To Afric's shore we're bound again,
In freedom's glory won at large;
In thoughts we claim a just bargain,
To sail in liberty's fair barge.

Marcus Garvey
Centenary's Day

The ships carrying the 2nd WIR across the Atlantic took nine weeks to reach Freetown, arriving within a day of each other towards the end of May 1819. By this time Sierra Leone had been a British possession for thirty-two years, founded as a settlement run by a chartered company to provide a homeland for runaway slaves who had found asylum in England. The original twenty square miles of land had been acquired from a Temne chief for sixty pounds' worth of trade goods. Although the settlement had increased in size since through treaties with other chiefs, it was still little more than a strip of land about 150 square miles in area on a peninsula between the Ribi River in the south and estuary of the Sierra Leone River to the north. Freetown was sited on the north coast of the peninsula, overlooking probably the finest natural harbour on the entire West African coast. A group of five small islands, the Isles de Los, about seventy-five miles to the north of Freetown, had been acquired in 1818, and the four equally small Banana Islands, just off the southwest coast of the peninsula, were to be ceded to Britain in 1820.

Soon after the founding of the settlement it became clear that the surrounding Temne people had no proper understanding of the purpose for which their land had been taken, and certainly no respect for the various 'treaties' by which it had been acquired by the Sierra Leone Company. The complete destruction of Freetown by the French in 1794 was followed in 1801 and 1802 by attacks by the Temne, and these so disrupted the development of the settlement that it became clear it could never succeed as a commercial venture. An appeal was made to the British Government and on 1st January 1808 Sierra Leone had become a Crown Colony.

The troops available for its defence belonged to a unit formed in England some years earlier specifically for service in West Africa, called naturally enough the African Corps to begin with, but the Royal African Corps after 1804. According to their first Colonel its rank and file consisted of

> the sweepings of every parade in England, for when a man was sentenced to be flogged, he was offered the alternative of volunteering for the Royal Africans, and he generally came to me. They were not a bad set of fellows when there was anything to be done, but with nothing to do they were devils incarnate.

They fought well enough, but neither a calloused back nor an immoral character could offer extra protection against the high rate of sickness and death from disease which afflicted all white troops in the tropics. The African Corps suffered so heavily that in 1802 the chairman of the Court of Directors of the Sierra Leone Company appealed to London for a 'Black West India Regiment' to be sent as a replacement.

His request was too premature and instead recruiting for the African Corps was instituted among the liberated slaves living in the settlement. This was very successful and by 1807 African soldiers, under white officers and NCOs, made up five out of the total of twelve companies, which for the next ten years were responsible for the defence of all the British possessions along the West African coast. Mortality among white soldiers did not decrease however and in 1817 it was decided to transfer all that were left to the Cape of Good Hope, and thereafter depend solely on black troops for all the garrisons in West Africa. The black companies of the Royal African Corps held the fort, literally, for the next two years but within a month of the arrival of the 2nd WIR, and with the exception of the garrison in the Gambia, they were disbanded. Sixty-five men transferred into the 2nd WIR but the remainder were discharged. The companies in the Gambia, after being relieved by men of the 2nd WIR, returned to Sierra Leone and were disbanded in 1821. This was the end of the RAC, but months before the last man was discharged events elsewhere in West Africa, as will be seen, ought to have indicated the need for reconsideration of the decision to disband. In the event it turned out to be a very short-sighted move on the part of the army authorities in London.

The men of the 2nd WIR, as they disembarked after what must have been a tedious and uncomfortable sea voyage, were not the first such troops seen by the inhabitants of Freetown. The recruiting station at

Bance Island had operated for four years until 1816, and a month before the regiment landed the 4th WIR had arrived from Gibraltar to be disbanded. Along with some of the men of the RAC they were given if 'in good health an allowance of fivepence per day for life, and if suffering from wounds or other infirmities, an allowance of eightpence per day'. They were also given land and agricultural implements, and could opt to receive rations instead of the pension. Several areas were set aside for them, all well away from Freetown, and the names given to their settlements - Wellington, Waterloo, Hastings and York - still exist today in the names of the towns which have arisen on the same sites. About three hundred of the men were allowed to remain in Freetown where, remembering the place from which they had been delivered, they founded the suburb called Gibraltar Town. A small number were recruited by the 2nd WIR to replace some of the regiment's 'worn out soldiers', men who on arrival in Freetown 'were found unfit for duty, from age and infirmities, and long service'.

The 2nd WIR arrived in Sierra Leone with 341 other ranks and, as usual, less than the proper number of officers needed to man the regimental headquarters and run five companies. If it had been difficult for any of the regiments to ever muster a full complement of officers in the Westindies, how much more so for one now required to serve where 'the climate is obnoxious to all newcomers on their first arrival' and where

> Few Europeans can reside ... even for a short time without passing through an attack of the endemic bilious remittent fever of the country, what is termed "seasoning", and usually happens within the first two years of their residence...

while knowing that 'no residence, even in other tropical climates, is a security against this fever, nor does a partial assimilation lessen the danger'. Lieutenant-Colonel Ross was probably fortunate to bring another eleven in addition to himself.

The shortage must have made itself felt at once as, besides providing the garrison for Freetown, the regiment was required to send a sizeable detachment to Bathurst, a settlement three hundred miles away at the mouth of the River Gambia which had been 'subject to the Government of Sierra Leone' since 1816. There was also a need to garrison the Isles de Los and, after July 1820, the Banana Islands. (The Isles de Los, interestingly, had been added to the colony with the assistance of a discharged soldier of one of the West India regiments, named Dala Modu.

As a high-ranking native of the islands he had been one of the signatories of the treaty effecting the transfer. He subsequently established his own settlement on the mainland to the North of Freetown and founded a line of rulers who were of assistance to the colony's administration throughout the nineteenth century).

It is not clear why the thirty-four men sent to Crawford Island in the Isles de Los had to be accompanied by no less than three officers, but all of them - officers and men alike - ran into trouble before they had been there more than a few weeks:

> In July ... the middle of the rainy season, the barracks at Isles de Los were burned down and the detachment remained without any proper shelter till the following December. The three officers stationed there were sick the whole time, the European sergeant and his wife died.

As after the accident the three officers lived 'in one room in a native hut which [was] not weather tight' it does not say too much for their initiative, nor is it too hard to envisage the standard of temporary accommodation they considered suitable for the men in their charge. One of the three never recovered from his illness and died the following January. He joined an ensign who had lasted only two months at Bathurst, and was quickly followed by a lieutenant who died in Freetown: in a matter of eight months Ross lost a quarter of his officers.

One reason why it was thought that such scattered handfuls of troops were sufficient to protect the British possessions along the West African coast was because they were backed up by ships of the Royal Navy. The West Africa Squadron was able to make its presence felt anywhere along the coast, or in any part of the hinterland served by navigable waterways. Anti-slavery patrols, punitive expeditions, and retaliatory raids for real or imagined transgressions against British authority, using mixed forces of troops, marines and seamen, were to become regular features of life for the West India regiments, beginning in May 1820.

The Rio Pongo Expedition as it came, rather grandly, to be called was brought about by the seizure of a boat belonging to one of the ships of the Squadron, which was trying to capture a slave ship in the river of that name. The murder of several of the boat's crew by 'natives acting under the orders of a European slave dealer named Curtis, who had large barracoons on the river' could not go unpunished, and the 2nd WIR was asked to assist. Three companies under Captain James Chisholm left Freetown in four ships on 12th May and reached the entrance to what is now called the Rio Pongas, just north of Conakry in modern Guinea, three days later.

On 16th May Chisholm and his men, supported by marines, were taken up river in the two smaller vessels to what in his report Chisholm refers to as 'Curtistown', a village guarded by a 'mud fortification mounting several guns'. An attempt to negotiate for the release of the rest of the captured boat's crew got nowhere. The flag of truce was ignored and 'a heavy fire commenced from the fort, and from parties of men posted in very thick mangrove close to the wharf'. This proved ineffective and return fire by the troops soon cleared the way into the village and its 'fort'. Once inside Chisholm and the senior of the two ships' captains present

> determined upon destroying ... the town, burning the houses, raising the fort, and removing the cannon from it to the vessels of war; and on this being done it was agreed that the troops should proceed to the attack of the adjoining towns in alliance with Curtis.

No sooner had this been done and the troops re-embarked than Chisholm was informed that the 'principal encourager of the attack on the ... boat, and the person at whose command the wounded prisoners were inhumanly treated after their surrender' was still at large, with the captured seamen, in a village well away from the ones which had been flattened. The troops returned ashore and the next day, after floundering about in the thick forest for some time, located the right village. It did not contain the 'chief of considerable power' Chisholm was looking for, nor Curtis, nor any of the missing boat's crew, nor anything more than 'but a few of the inhabitants'. Nevertheless, having 'great reason to believe that they depended upon cooperation of a concealed body of men much more numerous and powerful than themselves' Chisholm ordered his men to open fire on the villagers. Having ensured by this that the inhabitants 'suffered considerably', and after destroying 'a large quantity of merchandise (principally the property of Curtis)', the troops returned to the ships once again. Chisholm and the ship's captains were now obliged to turn for help from another European trader in finding and negotiating the release of the prisoners. This individual succeeded where gunfire, arson and the wholesale destruction of property had failed, and a day or two later six seamen were set free.

As the ships sailed back to Freetown, where they arrived on 24th May, Chisholm had plenty of time to write his report. He could find no fault with the conduct of his men whose behaviour he found 'highly satisfactory', but he was obliged to stretch his imagination in order to claim that their part in securing the release of the boat's crew was in any way justified by the havoc they had wrought at his command:

> The conquest of a large district of wooded country, defended by an armed body of men, which the neighbouring inhabitants say exceeded three thousand five hundred, and the destruction of seven towns, with an inconsiderable loss on our side, is to be ascribed to the resolute conduct of the conjoined forces in the attack on Curtistown.

The conquest of a large district? This was hardly possible in two days, particularly when the troops spent much of one day trying to find Curtis's hideout (which in the end was only four miles from 'Curtistown'). The body of 3500 armed men hiding in the bushes was a chimera, and the 'resolute' attack on the town was little more than the putting to flight of a small group of frightened and leaderless villagers. The 'seven towns' which were razed could have been little more than small villages behind insubstantial palisades. And of course in the end neither the shadowy Curtis, nor his ally the 'chief of considerable power', were ever laid eyes on, let alone brought to justice. This early exercise of 'gunboat diplomacy' cost the 2nd WIR only two men wounded, which was just as well because making war in West Africa was rarely going to be so painless again - for any of the West India regiments.

In May 1821, in order to promote legitimate trade and to further suppress that in slaves, the possessions of the Royal African Company along the Gold Coast were vested in the Crown and placed under the authority of the Governor of Sierra Leone. They consisted of eight towns built around substantial forts and two or three undefended settlements, none closer than about nine hundred miles by sea to Freetown. Nearly all were in the Fante kingdom, a coastal state between the River Pra and Accra, some ninety miles to the east, and otherwise bordered by states owing allegiance to the Asantehene, the King of Asante. Fears that the Fante would be forced to join these other states, which were present throughout much of the previous century, were greatly increased by Asante invasions in 1807, 1811 and 1816. They were still very much in evidence when Brigadier-General Sir Charles MacCarthy, the new Governor, paid his first visit to Cape Coast, the seat of government in the new colony, in March 1822.

As the Asantehene still considered the coastal people as his subjects, and the Royal African Company had long been committed to having to defend the Fante from Asante aggression, one of MacCarthy's first priorities was to reorganize the forces available for their protection. The bands of native levies which had been raised were formed into the first

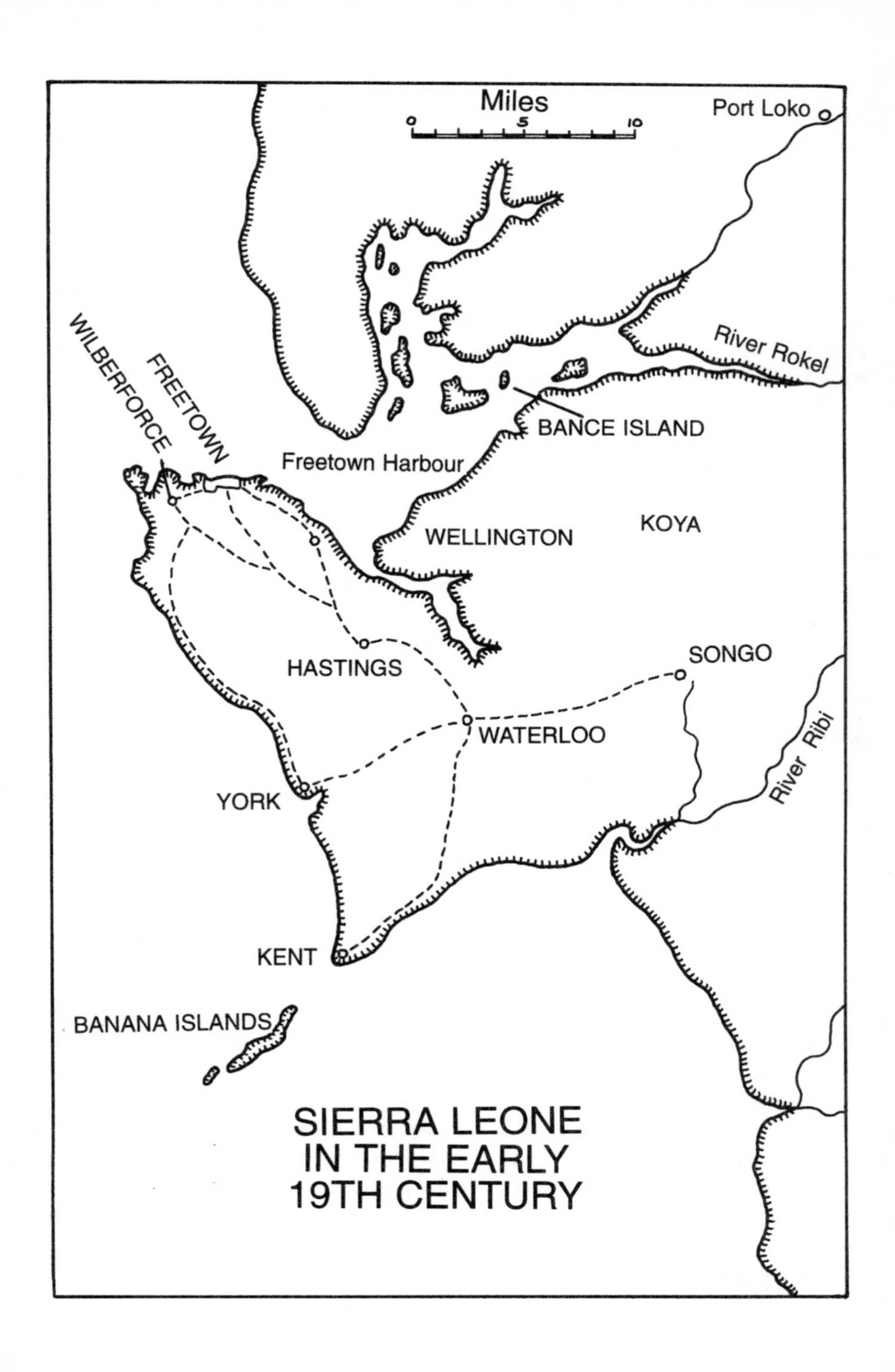

Miles
0
5
10
Port Loko
River Rokel
WILBERFORCE
FREETOWN
BANCE ISLAND
Freetown Harbour
WELLINGTON
KOYA
HASTINGS
SONGO
WATERLOO
River Ribi
YORK
KENT
BANANA ISLANDS
SIERRA LEONE
IN THE EARLY
19TH CENTURY

three companies of a new regiment which, when it was recognized by the army authorities, became the Royal African Colonial Corps and was treated as a re-raising of the old RAC. (For the first few years it even contained a company of white troops - all men sentenced for some military crime or other and, as with the RAC, sent to the regiment as a punishment - but this ended in 1830).

The new regiment required officers and, even though the 2nd WIR was still short - the trickle of replacements from England barely keeping up with the rate at which they succumbed to the dreaded 'endemic bilious remittent fever' - two were transferred to the RACC. One was Captain Chisholm, who was given command in the rank of major, and the other was a Scottish lieutenant, Alexander Laing, who had rejoined the regiment three years earlier. Chisholm's experiences up the Rio Pongas might have had something to do with his selection by MacCarthy, if it was not just a question of seniority, but with Laing it was a different story. His fellow officers were probably glad to see the back of someone so clever, conceited and ambitious. MacCarthy on the other hand, who during the previous year had used Laing on a number of delicate diplomatic missions into the interior of Sierra Leone, was probably only too pleased to get his hands on a young man showing more than average ability. Laing too was promoted and joined the RACC as a captain.

During his initial visit to the Gold Coast MacCarthy had made it obvious that he viewed the Fante kingdom as a British protectorate, and the Asante as barbarians against whom the kingdom was to be safeguarded. The envoys which the Asantehene, Osei Bonsu, had sent to Cape Coast were pointedly ignored and the new governor made no effort to send to Kumasi, the Asante capital, the diplomatic message which the customs of the country required. He was incensed therefore later in the year, after he had returned to Freetown, to learn that a sergeant of the RACC had been kidnapped by the Asante and was being held at Abura Dunkwa, about twenty miles inland from Cape Coast. The sergeant earlier in the year had been heard to curse the Asantehene, a capital crime to the Asante, and was now under sentence of death. The Asantehene, after waiting in vain for three months to see if the British were prepared to negotiate for the soldier's release, ordered him to be executed, and at the same time reaffirmed his claim to the coastal states.

MacCarthy returned to Cape Coast bringing with him one company of the 2nd WIR and, when news of the sergeant's death reached him in February 1823, he decided to mount an attack on Abura Dunkwa which was still occupied by the Asante who had carried out the execution. This the governor considered would provide 'an example [such] as would

Private of the 5th West India Regiment, 1814 *(Anne S K Brown Military Collection, Brown University. Photo: René Chartrand)*

Left: **Captain Francis A Knapp, 2nd West India Regiment, c. 1860** *(Photo: W D Cribbs)*

Below: **NCOs of 2nd West India Regiment, 1861** *(Photo: W D Cribbs)*

Opposite: **The Storming of Tubab Kolon, The Gambia, 1866 Painting by Chevalier Louis W Desanges** *(Penzance & District Museum and Art Gallery)*

The 2nd West India Regiment in Barbados, c. 1880 *(Photo: W D Cribbs)*

Inspection of the 2nd West India Regiment, c. 1885
(Photo: René Chartrand)

Lieutenant R Litchford, The West India Regiment, 1891
(Photo: W D Cribbs)

Lieutenant Edward Lendy DSO, 2nd Battalion West India Regiment, 1890
(Photo: W D Cribbs)

Officer and men of The West India Regiment, c. 1890 *(Photo: W D Cribbs)*

Band of 1st Battalion The West India Regiment, with regimental goat 'Tambi', c. 1893 *(Photo: W D Cribbs)*

The Capture of Toniataba, The Gambia, 1892 *(W D Cribbs)*

Payday for the 2nd West India Regiment, the Gold Coast, 1874 *(Illustrated London News)*

The West India Regiment in action in Sierra Leone, 1894 *(W D Cribbs)*

Sergeant W J Gordon VC, 1st Battalion The West India Regiment, 1897
(Photo: W D Cribbs)

Private of The West India Regiment, c. 1905 *(Anne S K Brown Military Collection, Brown University. Photo: René Chartrand)*

Depot Recruiting Party of the West India Regiment, in Jamaica, 1898. (Note Sergeant Gordon VC on extreme left) *(Photo: W D Cribbs)*

Bandsmen of the West India Regiment, 1905 *(Photo: W D Cribbs)*

Officer of The West India Regiment, c. 1906 *(Photo: W D Cribbs)*

Band of The West India Regiment at British Empire Exhibition, Wembley, England, 1924 *(Photo: W D Cribbs)*

prevent a similar occurrence' and 'render the commission of crime hideous in their eyes'. A force under Captain Laing, made up from the 2nd WIR, the RACC and the Cape Coast Militia, set out in the evening of 21st February, but

> From treachery, however, or imbecility of the Guides, the troops which ought to have reached Dunquah at 4 o'clock in the morning, lost the right road, and after excessive fatigue and want of every sort of provisions were suddenly attacked under a heavy fire ...

The Asante ambush succeeded brilliantly. One officer and six men of the RACC were killed, forty more were wounded or went missing, and the rest of the force had to make a hasty retreat to Anomabu, another of the coastal forts to the east of Cape Coast.

This episode inspired Osei Bonsu to declare that he was going 'to drive the English into the sea', and on 4th June three thousand of his warriors crossed the River Pra about sixty miles inland from Cape Coast (and where the river runs parallel to the coast). The peripatetic governor had already returned to Sierra Leone, leaving Chisholm in his place, so it once again fell to Laing 'with all available troops, and a large contingent of natives' to march north in an effort to head off the invasion. 'On hearing of this the Ashantis at once retired across the Prah', only to return at the end of July. Again Laing set out, and once more the Asante retreated before any fighting could take place. It was not until the very end of the year, a month after MacCarthy had returned yet again, the Osei Bonsu launched a genuine attack. This time a force of about ten thousand was reported to be heading for the coast through Wassa territory to the west of the Pra.

The response to this worked out by Governor MacCarthy involved three lots of troops. A force of militiamen and African levies from Accra was to march across country and attack the enemy from the flank or rear; a large body of Fante under Laing was to head north along the road from Cape Coast to Kumasi to create a diversion; MacCarthy himself would accompany Chisholm and the main body of about 2500 men, including the 2nd WIR company, the RACC and the Cape Coast Militia, which would march directly into Wassa country on the west bank of the Pra.

By 4th January the main force was assembled at Jukwa, about thirteen miles northwest of Cape Coast. Four days later, after Chisholm had moved two thousand of the troops another twenty miles further inland to Ampensasu on the left bank of the Pra, MacCarthy took the remaining five hundred under his personal command, crossed the river and headed west. He was accompanied by two officers of the 2nd WIR, Captain H J Ricketts and Ensign Wetherel, and two privates to act as their orderlies. At Nsamankow, over twenty miles from Ampensasu and directly in the path of the Asante invasion, MaCarthy camped for five days and then, on 18th January, sent off a message ordering Chisholm to join him with the rest of the troops a few hours before he and his gallant five hundred resumed their march to the north. The message took five days to reach Chisholm, arriving when it was much too late for him to do anything; two days earlier MacCarthy had reached the village of Bonsaso and run straight into the bulk of the Asante army.

This was far from the disorganized and ill-disciplined horde of 'savages' and 'barbarians' he was undoubtedly expecting to find. Instead it was a highly developed military organization with scouts, an advance guard, a main body, two wings, and a rear-guard, accompanied by a supply train and even medical orderlies of a sort. The warriors armed with muskets or spears, were highly disciplined, disdainful of personal safety, and under the command of leaders who would normally commit suicide rather than be captured by an enemy. But even if it had been otherwise MacCarthy and his men, of whom no more than half were regular, uniformed soldiers, would have stood no better chance against such overwhelming numbers. A brief stand ended when MacCarthy, already wounded three times, was killed and beheaded.

Eight officers and 178 men also were killed, including Ensign Wetherel and the two privates of the 2nd WIR. Among the few who managed to escape was Captain Ricketts. He was found three days later by the main body as it advanced in accordance with the long-delayed order. 'On seeing and ascertaining from him the disastrous issue of the action of the 21st', wrote Chisholm later

> and also that the small party I commanded was totally unable to cope with the enemy, and being also apprehensive that the Ashantees, flushed with their recent victory, would advance upon Cape Coast Castle by rapid marches, I determined upon retiring upon it.

While this was a sound tactical decision it was just as well that it was based on an incorrect prediction of the Asante intentions as

> all the officers of the party and nearly the whole of the men, were laid up on their arrival at Cape Coast, from the effects of the fatigue and privations undergone by them, and I am sorry to say of the former, all, except two, [in mid-March are] still invalids, and of the latter numbers have died.

Laing and his diversionary force had been recalled as soon as news of the disaster reached Cape Coast, and they were already in the town by the time Chisholm and his men staggered in. Laing was immediately chosen by Chisholm, now once again the acting governor, to carry despatches to London so that the Secretary of State for War and Colonies would be 'in possession of a perfect knowledge of the state of affairs in this quarter'. He left on this mission early in March, never to return. The reason for this has nothing to do with the story of the West India regiments but, because of Laing's earlier connection with the 2nd WIR, merits leaving the Asante war for a moment and following him to London to find out why.

Once in London and with direct access to the Secretary of State, Earl Bathurst, he took the opportunity of putting forward his plan for an expedition to reach the mysterious city of Timbuktu, something he had been trying to interest the Government in by letter for several years. At this time Timbuktu was one of the few places in the interior of Africa known to Europeans by name, but one which no European had yet visited. For no good reason it was thought by many, probably Laing included, to be an imposing metropolis of fabulous wealth and great importance. Earl Bathurst may not have been so convinced but he was sufficiently interested to allow Laing to have his way.

He set off from Tripoli in Libya in August 1825, having made only the most perfunctory preparations, and with great difficulty found guides to take him from one oasis to the next across the Sahara for a distance of well over two thousand miles. He reached the fabled city in September of the following year, having suffered incredible privations, only to find it little more than a squalid town of mud buildings which had lost any importance it had ever had over two centuries earlier. This hardly mattered: the journey alone ensured Laing's fame, and once he had retraced his steps to Tripoli he could forget regimental life and soldiering for ever more. He stayed a few days only before setting off, and was then never seen again. His letters which miraculously got delivered to the British consul in Tripoli brought news of his achievement to the outside world, but his fate remained unknown until the next century. In 1910 a French explorer in the area obtained written evidence that Laing had been waylaid and murdered by robbers on 3rd October 1826, and his body buried with the burnt remains of his belongings. Excavations which turned up bones, bits of iron and scraps of clothing at a site only forty miles or so north of Timbuktu confirmed his fate.

Back in 1824, while Laing was still on his way to England with news of MacCarthy's death, the Asante made no immediate move to follow up their victory at Bonsasu. It later transpired that, in spite of Osei Bonsu's boast, their invasion had been intended only to subdue the Wassa and Denkyira people, and that they had not expected to encounter the British to the west of the Pra. Some negotiations carried out by Ricketts produced a short-lived armistice but in the end, because of Asante determination to secure their dominance of the coastal states, they began to advance on Cape Coast Castle. This was made as difficult as possible by Chisholm and his ever-decreasing number of reliable troops, in a series of short stands and skirmishes, and it was not until the end of May that they were within striking distance of the town.

Shortly before Cape Coast was besieged Lieutenant-Colonel William Sutherland, who had assumed command of the 2nd WIR in 1822, arrived with another small contingent of troops from Sierra Leone and took over from Chisholm. He now received a personal message from Osei Yaw, the new Asantehene (Osei Bonsu, his brother, having died by an odd coincidence on the day MacCarthy was killed) informing him that

> the walls of the Castle were not high enough and should be made higher, and that he ought to land all the guns from the war ships, as he (the King) intended to throw every stone of the Castle into the sea.

This turned out to be an empty threat. Although the Asante made several attempts to take the town in June and July none succeeded. The defenders under Sutherland fought well and suffered many losses, but the besiegers were really beaten by other factors, losing 'thousands of their men from smallpox, dysentery, and want of food'. Those that were left began to retreat on 19th July. After they had retired behind the Pra Sutherland felt free to return to Sierra Leone, and Chisholm once again became the acting governor. He never recovered fully from his experiences earlier in the year and died in 1825, some weeks before MacCarthy's replacement, Major-General Charles Turner, reached Cape Coast. He brought with him from Sierra Leone seven hundred men of the RACC and another two hundred of the 2nd WIR. The latter were not really needed and were soon returned to Freetown. On 14th April all the 2nd WIR, with the exception of one company, sailed for the Bahamas. The company left behind to carry out recruiting for the regiment was joined in August 1826 by a company of the 1st WIR, sent from Trinidad for the same purpose.

On the Gold Coast intermittent hostilities between the Asante and the coastal states continued until 1831 and the signing of a treaty. The Asantehene agreed under the terms of this to give up his claims to the southern states provided Asante traders were allowed unrestricted access to the sea and to the European arms and goods available on the coast. He was then obliged by Turner to deposit 600 ounces of gold at Cape Coast and to deliver his son and a nephew (who were sent to England to be educated) as hostages. The effect of this was to replace the attempted Asante takeover of the coastal states with the beginnings of actual British rule. No formal protectorate was to be declared for another forty-two years, but British influence in the southern provinces increased steadily throughout this period. The gold was returned in 1837 and the two young men, no doubt with Oxford accents, returned from England four years later.

At the same time British rule was also being extended in other parts of West Africa. Trade along the River Gambia, primarily in slaves, had taken place for two hundred years before St Mary's Island, on the south side of the river mouth, was bought by the British in 1816. The town of Bathurst (named after Laing's patron and now the modern Banjul) was established on the island at a site, to quote the English traveller Richard Burton, 'selected for unhealthiness, for proximity to mud, mangrove, miasma, and malaria'. It was protected by Fort Bullen, built at Barra Point on the north side of the river entrance in what was known as the Ceded Mile, a strip of land one mile wide and nearly fifty miles long following the course of the river, which had been ceded to Britain by Brunay, the ruler of the chiefdom of Barra in 1826. Brunay, the most powerful of the chiefs along the lower reaches of the river, had until three years before levied customs duties on all vessels entering the Gambia. In surrendering this right in return for a stipend from the British, and in then surrendering the Ceded Mile, he had also given away much of his authority. The Barra people had become increasingly distressed by their loss of control over the river mouth and by 1831 had had enough. Trading between them and Bathurst was brought to a halt and in August they began demonstrating against white settlers on the north bank. By the end of the month the garrison at Fort Bullen had been forced to withdraw to Bathurst, and Brunay and a large number of his followers were entrenched at Barra Point. At the end of September the Lieutenant-Governor was obliged to appeal to his superior, the Governor of Sierra Leone, for assistance and on 4th October

> a force under Captain Stewart, 1st West India Regiment, consisting of detachments from the recruiting companies of the 1st and 2nd West India Regiments, from the Sierra Leone Militia, and from the Royal African [Colonial] Corps, sailed for the Gambia in H.M. brig Plumper, and the Parmilia transport.

It is not clear why it took so long for the two ships to complete the three hundred mile passage from Freetown, but it was not until 9th November that they reached Bathurst, where they 'found Fort Bullen still in the hands of the natives, who fortunately had confined themselves to making mere demonstrations, instead of falling upon the settlement, which lay entirely at their mercy'.

Two days later Stewart, with a force of about four hundred and fifty men, and under cover of fire from both ships, landed at Barra Point. There were at least two thousand warriors hidden in the dense bush or protected by 'the entrenchments which they had thrown up', and it cost the troops fifty-two casualties and an hour's hard fighting to effect the landing, and to re-occupy Fort Bullen. While they then set about putting the fort's defences back in order, and landing additional guns from the ships, Brunay prudently withdrew to his capital, Essau, a short way inland, and started strengthening his own defences. This activity was not wasted. Stewart marched on the town six days later

> the troops deployed into line, and, the guns having been brought to the front, a heavy fire was opened on the stockade. This was kept up for five hours, and was as vigorously returned by the enemy from their defences, with artillery and small arms. The rockets were brought to bear as soon as possible, and the first one thrown set fire to a house ... but the natives having taken the precaution of removing the thatched roofs of the greater number, the rockets produced but little effect, as they could do no injury to the walls.

The attack, which was getting nowhere, came to an end at midday when 'a very superior force of natives appeared in the bush on the British right, threatening an attack in flank' and another force, equally large, was seen 'making a lengthened detour on the left, apparently with the intention of attacking the British rear'. Having already lost eleven killed and nearly sixty wounded Stewart had little option but to withdraw to the fort and send for reinforcements.

Several hundred men of the RACC arrived from Sierra Leone on 7th December and 'Immediately upon this accession to the British strength, the King of Barra notified his desire to open negotiations'. These duly took place and Brunay acceded to all the British demands, and in a treaty signed in early January reconfirmed their claim to the Ceded Mile. This eroded Brunay's authority even more, and led to a general weakening of the Barra people. This in turn helped to expose the people further up the river to the influence of a Muslim religious and political movement which spread to the region in the middle of the century. During the upheavals which resulted towns and villages such as Essau were not going to escape so lightly from the guns and rockets fired at them, and the West India regiments were going to be caught up in far more bloody encounters than on this occasion.

Stewart's detachment returned to Freetown after an absence of three months, and life for the men of the two recruiting companies resumed its normal uneventful course. For their officers it was perhaps rather less undisturbed. The mortality rate among Europeans in Sierra Leone remained unbelievably high, and army officers were no less susceptible than other white residents to West African diseases. Communication with the regimental headquarters in Trinidad and the Bahamas was intermittent and incredibly slow. When Lieutenant Montgomery of the 1st WIR died 'of fever on April 9th 1833' this left his company 'without an officer of the corps' for almost twenty months before his replacement arrived.

A constant shortage of officers must have thrown more than the usual amount of responsibility onto the NCOs. This seems to be borne out by the fact that it is around this time in the history of the regiments that the first individuals from the other ranks can begin to be identified in connection with the display of more than average initiative, or devotion to duty. Mention has already been made of Dala Modu from Isles de Los (which ceased to belong to Sierra Leone when they were ceded to France in 1904), who was obviously a far from ordinary soldier. Another man who made his mark in the same colony was Sergeant Abraham Potts of the 4th WIR who, five years after his discharge started the first Benefit Society in Sierra Leone. Funds were acquired through monthly subscriptions in order to assist members who sick or in need of support, such as orphans or widows. At a time when government control and administration were still fairly rudimentary the society fulfilled a need, and branches existed in Freetown and six villages by 1827. Potts displayed a bit too much initiative though, and when the society assumed a political and judicial aspect - fining members for misbehaviour and generally acting like an alternative form of administration - it was suppressed. Potts lost his job in the Commissariat as a result, but the Benefit Society movement lived on, under official supervision, for many years afterwards.

Sergeant Buckhardt of the 2nd WIR was in the original detachment sent to the Gambia in 1819. Four years later he was left in sole charge of the settlement on an island in the river about one hundred and sixty miles upstream from Bathurst. Lemani, or MacCarthy Island as it was renamed, was ceded by the local chief and gave Britain a foothold in the upper reaches of the river. This was to be of great importance in the future in establishing British claims to the territory over those of the French. Buckhardt ran the settlement very efficiently, the Governor inspecting it in June 1826 reporting 'the state of the place reflects the greatest credit on the black sergeant'. When he and his detachment of twelve men were relieved the next year it was by an officer and men of the RACC.

The two recruiting companies obtained most of their recruits from among the cargoes of captured slave ships brought into Freetown. Once such a ship was condemned as a lawful prize 'the slaves are adopted as British free subjects, are landed, and conveyed ... to the King's Yard, a large species of prison' where, after a few days, 'freedom visits the captives':

> The men are inspected by a sergeant and officer when conscripts are wanted. The most muscular are drafted at once into the King's service; and are marched in a string, nolentes volentes [willy-nilly], under a strong escort, to the barracks, to learn regimental discipline.

This method of recruitment continued until 1844, by which time the early, brutal ways of instilling discipline had been somewhat abated, and the methods of carrying out basic training considerably improved:

> They soon acquire sufficient knowledge of our language for practical purposes; and the opportunities now afforded in the Garrison Schools for learning to read and write have considerably facilitated their progress.

On completion of their basic training or, at least, their indoctrination into army life, and depending on the availability of transport, the recruits were shipped across the Atlantic to their respective regiments. Whether the means by which most of them had been recruited were altogether reputable or not, at least they left Africa knowing where they were going, what they were going for, and fully aware of what a soldier's life involved. And some may even have been able to read and write.

So successful had recruiting gone for the 1st WIR by 1839 that it was permitted to increase its establishment to thirteen companies. A year later the three supernumerary companies were drafted to Sierra Leone to become part of the RACC. In July 1840 the 'Royal Africans' were re-designated the 3rd WIR, with responsibility for garrisoning all the British possessions in West Africa.

CHAPTER 10
ENLIVENING THE DULNESS

> San Joseph [in Trinidad] is a quiet, healthy spot, frequently serving as a convalescent post for the troops at St James's, and certainly for such a purpose no place could be better chosen. The inhabitants complain of its dulness, for their solitude is no longer enlivened by the band of the 1st W.I. Regt., to which they had been accustomed from 1825, till the chieftain, Donald Stewart, excited his African followers, then his fellow soldiers, (all being alike, enlisted recruits of the 1st W.I. Regt.) to revolt.
>
> **Lieutenant-Colonel Henry Capadose (1845)**

In 1819 when half of the 2nd WIR was sent to Sierra Leone, two of the other five companies remained behind in Nassau, where they continued their peaceful and uneventful garrison duties until the West African contingent returned six years later. The other three, stationed in Belize on correspondingly routine duties, were to find life equally free of military action but otherwise not quite so uneventful. The storm which whistled around the regiment in Belize, beginning at the end of 1819, this time had nothing to do with any misconduct on the part of the troops. On the contrary, it blew up because of a dispute at the opposite end of the military hierarchy concerning, principally, Lieutenant-Colonel George Arthur, the Superintendent and Commandant of the Settlement, and Major Thomas Bradley, the officer in charge of the 2nd WIR detachment.

Arthur was serving as a major in the 7th WIR in Jamaica in 1814 when he was offered the appointment in Belize, with a salary of £500 a year on top of his army pay. He was promoted to lieutenant-colonel in 1815 and, when his regiment was disbanded the following year, he transferred to the 5th WIR. He now became concerned that, as Commandant, if he should lose his army appointment and be put on half-pay he might well find himself subordinate to a serving officer junior to himself. To avoid this possibility when the 5th WIR was disbanded in 1817 he arranged a transfer to the York Chasseurs, only to have this regiment disbanded two years later. He was now a lieutenant-colonel on half-pay, and just what he had feared now took place.

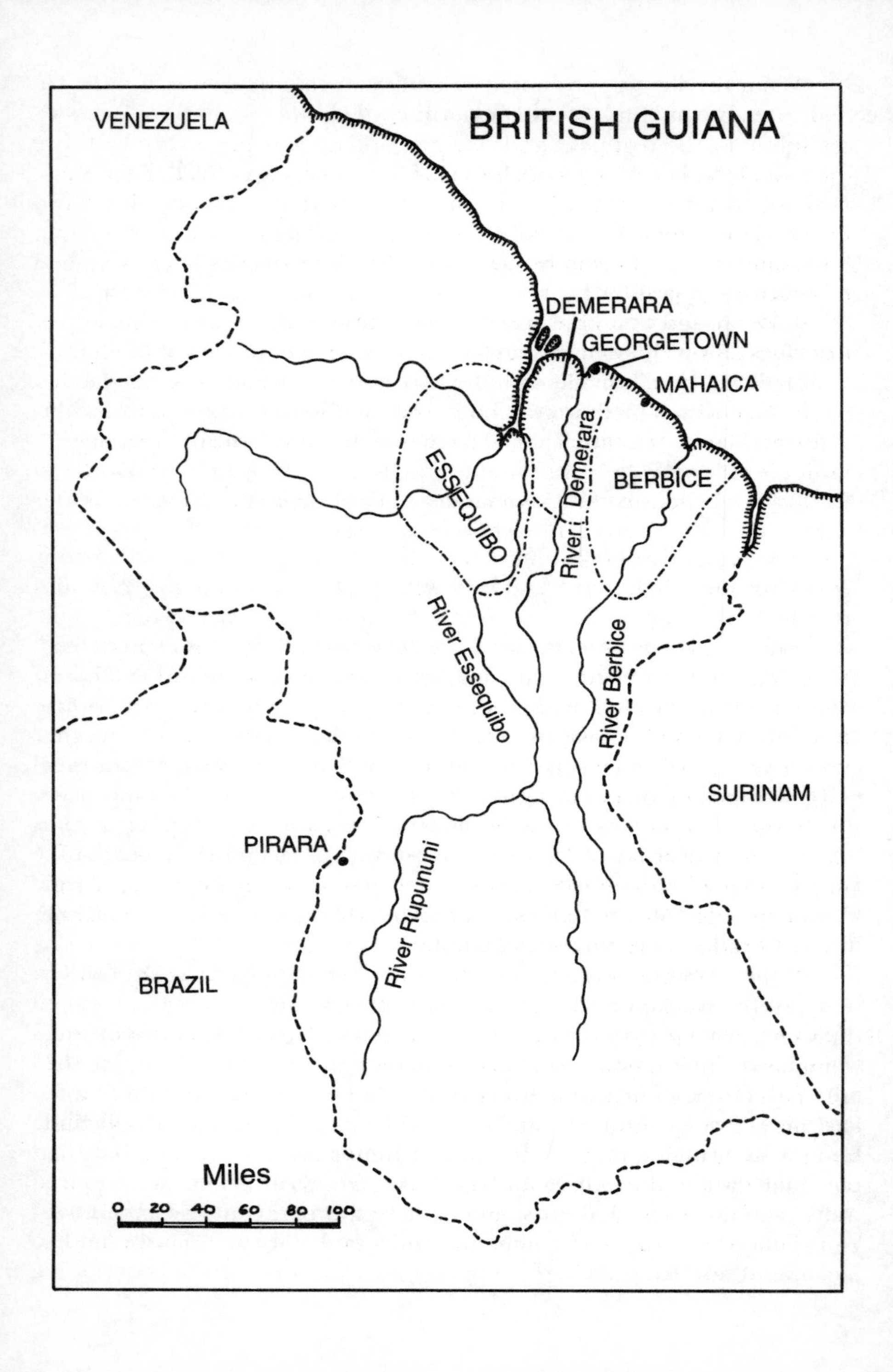
BRITISH GUIANA
VENEZUELA
DEMERARA
GEORGETOWN
MAHAICA
ESSEQUIBO
River Demerara
BERBICE
River Essequibo
River Berbice
SURINAM
PIRARA
River Rupununi
BRAZIL
Miles
0 20 40 60 80 100

Major Bradley was promoted to lieutenant-colonel in March 1820. He had already run foul of the Superintendent over matters to do with discipline in the regiment and duelling and now, being a very bellicose individual, he began to assert his claim - as a serving officer of the same rank as Arthur - to the military command. Matters came to a head two months later when, after Bradley had issued a garrison order announcing his assumption of the command, Arthur had him arrested and examined by a medical board.

It was found that he was not insane but that the 'great irritability of his disposition may have caused a temporary infirmity of mind'. Temporary or not, it made no difference and he remained, as he claimed later, 'a prisoner in that scorching and pestilential climate, from May 1820, to March 1821, making 312 days of suffering and imprisonment', until the affair had been referred to the General Officer Commanding in Jamaica and then to the Commander-in-Chief in London. While under arrest Bradley drew up numerous charges against his second-in-command, Captain Lord, and this created more confusion when Arthur enquired into them, and Lord considered he had been insulted as a result.

In the end both Bradley and Lord, instead of being court-martialled, were allowed to return to England, and presumably, sell their commissions. Both felt aggrieved, but while Lord soon accepted his fate Bradley instigated a process of litigation which continued for another twenty years. Arthur emerged from the imbroglio to continue a successful career as a colonial administrator: he is better remembered today for the notorious penal colony he established at Port Arthur, during his tenure as Lieutenant-Governor of Tasmania which began a year after he quit Belize in 1822. How often in the years he spent there, as the latest bit of legal trumpery from Messrs Dodson & Fogg landed on his desk, he must have wished Bradley were numbered among his charges.

While this feud was upsetting the smooth running of the 2nd WIR in the far west of the Caribbean, the 1st WIR was enjoying a more tranquil existence in the east, with its headquarters in Barbados, and individual companies in Demerara, St Lucia, Dominica and Antigua. In August 1823 the peaceful routine of the detachment in Georgetown was interrupted by 'an alarming insurrection which broke out among the slaves in the district of Mahaica, on the east coast of Demerara'.

Like the Bussa Revolt in Barbados seven years earlier, this was inspired by rumours reaching the colony about the progress of the abolitionist movement in England, and the resistance of the plantocracy to contemplate change. When the implementation of a new law forbidding the flogging of female slaves and the carrying of whips by overseers was deliberately delayed by the planters, calls by a Nonconformist minister for its introduction were misinterpreted by the slaves, who thought the new law referred to emancipation. Rumours to this effect spread throughout the estates to the east of Georgetown, and a revolt broke out on 18th August.

After a futile appeal to some of the slaves by the governor the Militia was called out to patrol the town, while the 1st WIR and a detachment of the 21st Regiment, all under Captain Stewart of the former regiment, marched up the coast towards the seat of the trouble at Mahaica. Martial law was declared the next day when it was realized the revolt had spread to some sixty plantations and involved probably 30,000 slaves. In spite of this there was little damage caused to property and although numbers of white people were seized none received any serious injury. On 20th August, after Stewart had handed over command at Mahaica to Lieutenant-Colonel Leahy of the 21st Foot who had arrived with more troops, 'a body of some 2000 of the better-armed slaves collected together and began to advance on Georgetown'. Leahy read a proclamation issued by the Governor and

> warned them that if they did not disperse [his] men would open fire. After waiting for some time, the order to advance was given, and the slaves at once commenced firing. This was returned by the troops, and after a conflict of a few minutes' duration the rebels fled in all directions.

Again as in Barbados, direct confrontation with the military broke the spirit of the revolt. Although 'constant skirmishing was kept up along the whole line of the coast' for another six weeks or so much of this concerned the search for the ringleaders. This was in the main carried out by the Militia, as always composed of white men only too keen to exact retribution. In addition to slaves who were killed while actively resisting arrest, another sixty were shot out of hand. Later, after the necessary judicial proceedings, fifty more were hanged, and as many again flogged or imprisoned.

Two more companies of the 1st WIR arrived on 26th September but were hardly required; a month later they returned to Barbados, taking Stewart's company with them. After that it was another fourteen years before any of the 1st WIR served in the colony again, by which time it would be known as British Guiana.

In 1825 the headquarters of the 1st WIR moved to Trinidad with four companies to relieve the 3rd WIR (which was then disbanded) and remained there for the next twelve years. The headquarters of the 2nd WIR, having returned from Sierra Leone in 1825, remained in the Bahamas until 1830, and again from 1832 until 1839. During this period, even though both regiments received drafts of recruits at intervals from West Africa, they also continued to enlist men in the Westindies. Slave ships which had managed to escape detection by the West Africa Squadron were still captured from time to time in the Caribbean, and the practice of taking suitable recaptives for the regiments remained in operation. This can hardly have been welcomed by the unfortunate men concerned, although occasionally some seemed quite keen. When such a ship bound for Cuba was captured and brought to Belize in 1836 some forty-five of the men in the cargo 'finding Countrymen amongst the Soldiers of the 2nd W.I. Regt. quartered [there] became desirous of enlisting in that corps', and were duly enrolled. But usually it was quite a different story.

During the 1830s the 1st WIR obtained far more recruits than it needed from this source, even though 'The formality of asking these men whether they were willing to serve was never gone through, [and] many of them did so unwillingly'. In 1837 the regiment laid claim to over three hundred so such men, which the commanding officer, Lieutenant-Colonel William Bush, seems to have seen as an end in itself. At his headquarters in Trinidad he had no clear policy for indoctrinating them into army life, nowhere near enough training staff or resources, and it would appear no notion that they might not be willing to accept their fate too readily. Such was his insouciance that at the end of May, when he had about two hundred and eighty of these recruits in the barracks at St Joseph, he despatched the majority of his other troops to St Lucia and Dominica, leaving behind few other than 'the band, officers' servants, and mess-waiters'.

Three weeks later in the early hours of 18th June, and after much singing and chanting, some of the recruits set fire to the huts in which they were accommodated while others rushed the guardroom. In spite of the noise made beforehand, which had been heard all over the town, none of the officers had been alerted and no extra precautions taken. As the men who had gone to the guardroom 'seized on the muskets and fusees in the racks', four others broke into the storeroom, disposed of the single veteran storekeeper, and collected powder and cartridges. Once these had been passed out the armed men opened fire 'at the long range of white buildings in which Colonel Bush and his officers slept', using up 'so much ammunition on this useless display of fury, that the buildings were completely riddled'. Useless or not, the fury was directed against bricks and mortar, and no attempt was made to harm the occupants directly - something which could have been achieved very easily by a mob of nearly three hundred keyed-up men, if that had been their intention. While this fusillade was in progress most of the officers, 'All young ensigns just arrived from England to join the regiment', escaped from the back of the buildings and seemingly took little further part in the proceedings. Bush, accompanied by the adjutant, Lieutenant Bentley, put on a braver face and in front of the officers' quarters 'commanded the mutineers to lay down their arms'. It is hardly likely that many of the men who heard him could have understood what he was saying and his only answer was 'an irregular discharge of balls, which rattled amongst the leaves of a tree under which he and the adjutant were standing'. Again, in not taking this opportunity to cut down both men where they stood, the mutineers surely showed that their plans to escape from the army did not include the wilful killing of its representatives.

The two officers retired unhurt and after sending Bentley to alert the 89th Regiment at St James's Barracks in Port of Spain Bush went to 'a police-station above the barracks, and got muskets and a few cartridges from a discharged African soldier who was in the police establishment'. He and the policeman, having rounded up a single ensign and one corporal then

> concealed themselves on an eminence above, and as the mutineers (about 100 in number) approached, the fire of muskets opened on them from the little ambush. The little party fired separately, loading as fast as they discharged their pieces; they succeeded in making the mutineers change their route.

As well as being diverted from a route which was intended to take them, not knowing any better, all the way back to Africa, they were also delayed long enough to allow the St Joseph's's Militia to be assembled. This was the beginning of the end; the Militia were just as ruthless here as anywhere else in the Westindies, and very few of the mutineers managed to get through the town. Among those who were captured was the main instigator of the mutiny, a very tall man with 'a singular cast in his eyes, not quite amounting to ... a squint' who had been given the name Donald Stewart when he was drafted into the regiment.

A group of about fifty under another of the ringleaders, Maurice Ogston, made it as far as Arima, ten miles to the east of St Joseph, before being stopped by another band of militiamen. After some negotiation carried out mostly in sign language the Militia's patience ran out:

> A melee commenced, in which 14 mutineers were killed and wounded. The fire of the Africans produced little effect: they soon took to flight amid the woods which flanked the road. Twenty-eight of them were taken, amongst which was Ogston. Six had been killed, and six committed suicide by strangling and hanging themselves in the woods.

With the exception of a single individual who remained at large for a month all the mutineers were recaptured within a week. In that time over forty had been killed, committed suicide (or far more likely had been lynched by the Militia), or died from being wounded. Order was restored in the barracks and in late July the five who had been identified as the ringleaders were court-martialled.

Donald Stewart, Maurice Ogston and Edward Coffin were sentenced to be executed by a firing-squad, William Satchell to 'Be transported beyond seas during the term of his natural life', and the man known to us only as Torrens 'to imprisonment for life'. All five were from that region of West Africa which today is divided by the border between Benin and Nigeria, where the people - like the Asante further to the west - were known for their warlike spirit and fierce independence. It is doubtful if any of them, in spite of their names, spoke more than a few words of English, and an observer who 'attended the whole of the trials of these men' noted 'how difficult it was to make them comprehend any idea which was at all new to them by means of the best interpreters procurable'. Stewart, Ogston and Coffin were shot (not, one hopes, by a firing-squad drawn from the band and mess-waiters) on 16th August.

Afterwards Lieutenant-Colonel Bush remarked that he thought they had mutinied 'mainly owing to the ill-advice of their civil, or, we should rather say, unmilitary countrymen'. What he did not say, nor apparently understand, was that for men like Stewart and Ogston, to be taken into slavery and then forced into becoming a soldier in a country where - as their 'unmilitary countrymen' would have been only too keen to tell them - slavery had been made illegal three years earlier, was not an acceptable fate. As with those Asante who had led the 'mutiny' in the 2nd WIR in Jamaica twenty-nine years earlier, it was better to make some sort of bid for freedom and fail, than to make no bid at all. Although this attempt failed, and at the cost of so many lives, it did produce some lasting result in that 'after this no more wholesale drafting of slaves into the regiment[s] took place'. It had no adverse effect on Bush's career; he remained in command until 1847 when he returned to England to take up a quiet appointment (for which it might be thought he was not totally suitable) as the 'Inspecting Field Officer of a recruiting district'. The regimental headquarters were transferred to St Lucia at the end of 1837 and memories of the mutiny soon faded. Two years afterwards at St Joseph it was observed:

> The barracks were now occupied by two officers and forty men of the 1st W.I. Regt., an officer and twenty men of the 74th Regt., and a staff assistant surgeon, whose office was nearly a sinecure, this year at least, although, he assured me, the previous one had been very unhealthy.

During the time in St Lucia the remaining recruits were transformed into the troops of the three supernumerary companies which, in 1840, were sent to Sierra Leone to become part of the re-raised 3rd WIR. At the end of 1839 the headquarters and two companies were sent to British Guiana 'to relieve the 76th Regiment, which was suffering heavily from the prevailing epidemic of yellow fever'.

They were still in Georgetown three years later when the regiment was called upon to 'expel a party of Brazilians who had for some time encroached on British territory' at Pirara in the far reaches of the country. This was a village on the Ireng River, which formed much of the border between British Guiana and Brazil, about two hundred and fifty miles to the south of Georgetown. This is not an easy journey overland even today: it was almost impossible in 1842, involving crossing a vast area which 'was unexplored and almost unknown'. The only practical route, increasing the distance to travel to nearly three hundred and fifty miles, was via the Essequibo River and its tributary, the Rupununi.

A detachment of three officers and twenty-nine other ranks, under one of the officers, Lieutenant Bingham, embarked in six boats manned by Amerindian guides, on 11th January and set off up the Essequibo. It took four weeks and an immense amount of labour, including some seventy portages, to reach the point on the Rupununi closest to Pirara, and then another day to complete the eleven mile trek from the river to the village. When Bingham entered the village on 13th February he found as expected it was already 'occupied by a detachment of Brazilian troops who had been quietly sent over the border'. He was also able to see that not only were they well supplied food and stores, but they also outnumbered his own troops. A meeting took place between the two commanders: Bingham politely requested the Brazilians to vacate the village and return across the Ireng; the Brazilian commander just a courteously refused to do either.

This left poor Bingham in the unenviable position of being too weak to force a Brazilian withdrawal, and at the same time three hundred and fifty miles up the creek from the nearest reinforcements. His own withdrawal and the consequent British humiliation being unthinkable all he could do was to select a site outside the village for his own camp and send 'Lieutenant Bush ... who had accompanied the party as a volunteer, to Georgetown for further instructions'. It was slightly easier going downstream but Bush (who probably never volunteered for anything again during his military career) was still not able to reach Georgetown before 11th March. As a great deal of diplomatic activity was taking place by this time it was not until 19th April that Bush began his return journey, accompanied by 'a small reinforcement under Ensign Stewart'. They eventually arrived at Pirara on 21st May to find Bingham and his detachment 'all well, but half-starved', suffering both from the ignominy of having had to ask the Brazilians to sell them food and the mortification of having had the request refused. Fortified by the additional troops, and no doubt by the rations they had brought with them, Bingham again asked the Brazilians to leave. The time, more because of the results of what had been taking place between London and Rio de Janeiro than the arrival of Ensign Stewart's reinforcements, their commander 'considered it advisable to withdraw across the frontier'. The whole slightly bizarre incident, as far as the 1st WIR was concerned, was then at an end. After that, 'with the exception of a few occasional night forays made by half-breeds and Indians in the pay of the Brazilians, the detachment met with no further opposition' and eventually returned to Georgetown unharmed.

The year 1843 brought about a major change in policy regarding the deployment of the, by now, three West India regiments. Instead of retaining the 3rd WIR on permanent garrison duties in West Africa, while the 1st and 2nd WIR provided detachments as necessary for the Westindian colonies at the eastern and western ends of the Caribbean respectively, it was decided to introduce a much more flexible arrangement. From then on two companies from each of the regiments would share the burden in West Africa, while the remaining companies of all three would serve as needed in any part of the Caribbean. Under this new arrangement the 1st WIR became part of the garrison of Jamaica for the first time in June 1844. Four years later, because of a chain of events begun by the war between the United States and Mexico which started in 1846, the regiment made its first appearance in Belize.

In 1847 the owners of large estates in the Mexican state of Quintana Roo in the Yucatan formed an army from among the Mayan Indian inhabitants, in order to confront the American forces if the war ever brought them so far south. This did not happen, but once the Indians were armed after being kept in serfdom and near-slavery by the landowners before the war they broke out in a revolt, soon to be called the 'war of the Castes'. As Belize is very much part of the Yucatan peninsula this 'caused much anxiety to the British [Settlement], whose strict neutrality satisfied neither of the contending parties'. This uneasiness was heightened a year later following an Indian attack on the town of Bacalar, about twenty miles from the northern border of the Settlement. Many of the town's inhabitants escaped by fleeing south and crossing the River Hondo which formed the boundary, and in doing so 'spread alarm amongst the colonists'. When raids began to be made by the Indians across the river, in order to attack the refugees near the town of Corozal, the time had come to ask the Governor of Jamaica (who retained the overall responsibility still for the Settlement) for military protection. One company of the 1st WIR, under Major Luke O'Connor, arrived in May 1848 and was sent up to the northern border which was found to be 'a rallying point for both sides'. O'Connor and his men spent the rest of the year along the Hondo, 'continually harassed by alarms and forced marches taken to prevent violation of British territory'. In December they returned to the town of Belize, acting on a rumour that it was about to be attacked by the Indians, but were back at the border again in January after the rumour had proved unfounded. Major O'Conner had a most unenviable task: although in the middle of a 'sanguinary struggle between the Yucatans and Indians' all he and his men could do was watch; 'the most strict orders had been given for the preservation of British neutrality, and nothing could be done'.

Shortly after being sent another company from Jamaica in April, O'Connor 'visited Bacalar to endeavour to make peace, but without success'. Both companies then 'remained stationed on the Hondo, amid the same scenes of horror until February 1852, when they rejoined headquarters at Jamaica'. They were not withdrawn until some semblance of normality had returned to the border region, but the Indians were far from being pacified, and the West India regiments far from finished with the Hondo. After cross-border raids resumed a year or two later men of the regiments were going to spend a lot more time, and see much more action, in the backwoods of the colony.

It was not until 1851, when the regiment's headquarters were transferred from Jamaica to British Guiana, that the 2nd WIR saw any peace time service in the eastern part of the Caribbean, and for the next six years the regiment provided detachments for the smaller islands as needed. In the comfortless surroundings of outdated, crumbling, and soon to be redundant fortifications such as Brimstone Hill in St Kitts, Prince Rupert's in Dominica, or Fort George in Grenada, the various companies whiled away the days in dull, routine garrison duties. Any change was usually brought about by an appeal to provide 'aid to civil power', such as during riots in Grenada in 1851 or in Tortola in 1853, but never amounting to very much. It may have been sheer boredom with life in Georgetown which brought about the composition of a letter sent in early September 1855 by the commanding officer of the 2nd WIR, Lieutenant-Colonel Henry Whitfeild, to the GOC Barbados:

> On the 30th August, after a review order parade, the regiment, with one accord, expressed their wish to be allowed to volunteer for the Crimea ... Having been solicited to make known this loyal feeling on their behalf to his Excellency the Lieut.-General commanding, I have only to add that should they be required, I feel confident this complete regiment to the number of 1,078 bayonets will not be found wanting.

On the other hand, it could just as easily have been that service in the 2nd WIR instilled a more patriotic or possibly a more bloodthirsty spirit: it was, after all, this regiment which in 1809 had volunteered to march three hundred miles to battle in Santo Domingo, or to pay out of their own pockets to be taken there. But whatever the reason it made no difference to the outcome. The letter was forwarded from Barbados to the Horse Guards where, even if the Crimean War was drawing to a close by this time, it surely merited a slightly less elliptical reply than the one sent:

> I have laid before the Field Marshall Commanding-in-Chief your letter of 7th September last, forwarding a copy of a letter from Lieut.-Colonel Whitfeild, commanding 2nd West India Regiment, stating that the Corps wished to be allowed to volunteer for the Crimea or any other active service, and I am directed by his Lordship to request that you [the GOC Barbados] will thank the regiment for their good feeling and patriotic spirit.

The nearest the regiment came to seeing any action was in British Guiana during 1856. Early in the year a half-crazed troublemaker with an anti-Roman Catholic fixation named John Orr began holding public meetings in Georgetown, at which he denounced 'the abuses of Popery and the profligacy of Popes, Bishops, Priests and Nuns'. This incensed the sizeable Portuguese community, who prevailed upon the Roman Catholic bishop to register a complaint with the authorities. Orr's subsequent arrest and imprisonment then led to an outbreak of rioting in Georgetown on 18th February. Although this was soon dealt with by the police with the aid of the 2nd WIR, disturbances soon broke out in the countryside where much Portuguese property was attacked and looted. This created great alarm and within a day or two the Governor, talking about a 'most general rising' and a 'strife of the Races', sent to Barbados for more troops. About two hundred men of the 1st WIR were sent and these, together with the 2nd WIR, the police, special constables, and some auxiliaries from the neighbouring Dutch and French colonies, managed to bring the situation under control and restore order by the end of March. Over a hundred rioters were later fined and jailed, while Orr was given three years' hard labour in a penal settlement.

As for the Crimean War, which ended at very much the same time, the only connection ever made with it by the 2nd WIR was a very tenuous link established after the war had ended, and a year after regimental headquarters had returned to Jamaica. During the Battle of Little Inkerman on 22nd October 1854, Sergeant Ambrose Madden of the 41st Regiment led a small party of men into a quarry where they captured a Russian officer and fourteen soldiers. Madden himself took three prisoners. He was promoted to Sergeant-Major for this deed and three years later, while serving with his regiment in Jamaica, he was presented with the Victoria Cross, an award which had not yet been instituted when he carried out his gallant act. In 1858 he was commissioned as an ensign and shortly afterwards transferred into the 2nd WIR. He served with the regiment in both the Westindies and West Africa before, sadly, dying of yellow fever in Jamaica in January 1863. His medal, which of course had nothing to do with his service in the 2nd WIR, is now in the museum of the Welsh Regiment in Cardiff; the site of his grave, which the 2nd WIR must have had a lot to do with, is regrettably unknown.

Although none of the West India regiments actually served in the Crimean War, a radical change in their appearance can be said to have had its origins in that conflict. A colonial corps of the French army raised in 1831 was recruited solely from a tribe of Berbers living in the mountains near Algiers. The singular dress of these men who were called Zouaves was soon adapted into a uniform which was so distinctive that, twenty years later, it became the official dress of three regiments of French soldiers raised in Algeria, who not unnaturally were then referred to as Zouaves. In 1854, when these regiments were part of the French force sent as Britain's allies to the Crimea, their unorthodox and somewhat oriental appearance created considerable British interest, both on the spot and later in London. Queen Victoria, always one with a keen interest in matters of military dress and decorations, and with an eye for the exotic, was particularly intrigued.

While the war was taking place Major Harry Ord of the Royal Engineers was serving in West Africa as a Commissioner looking into various military matters, and had forwarded a report to London in which he commented on the uniforms worn by the troops. Observing that the costume 'usually worn by the Natives' seemed much better suited to the climate than European dress, he recommended that a more appropriate uniform for the West India regiments and the recently formed Gold Coast Corps (of which more below) would be some sort of robe which 'much resembles a kilt' and sandals. Although sounding like a suggestion to turn the regiments into the Praetorian Guard, it was realized within the newly created War Department that devising a more suitable uniform for troops employed solely in the tropics did make a great deal of sense. The dashing French troops in the Crimea were recalled and as a similar uniform to theirs had already been adopted by *Tirailleurs sénégalais*, the nearest to a French equivalent of the West India regiments, it seemed the latter, instead of being turned into legionaries, would look better dressed as Zouaves.

In accordance with her express wishes about being consulted on all uniform matters, the proposed change was submitted to the Queen for approval towards the end of 1856:

> That the dress of the Gold Coast Corps be more assimilated to that worn by the natives themselves, instead of dressing them in the Uniform worn by the Army generally ...
> It is also submitted to Your Majesty, that the three West India Regiments, which are employed on the coast of Africa and West Indies only, and which are principally composed of Africans, may be clothed in a Uniform similar to that of the Gold Coast Corps, varying only in colour and facings; the Gold Coast Corps being an Artillery Corps and the others Battalions of Infantry.

The new full dress uniform, which was approved by the Queen on 27th October 1856 but was not introduced for another two years, was very colourful and totally different from anything the men had worn before. Together with a red fez wound round with a white turban was an elaborately braided, scarlet, sleeveless jacket, worn over a long-sleeved white waistcoat which had a braided front and twenty brass buttons. The trousers were dark blue, voluminous breeches piped with two yellow stripes on the front and rear of each leg, and were worn, initially with leather leggings and sandals, and later with white stockings, white gaiters and black shoes. Each regiment was distinguished by a different colour for the pointed cuffs of the waistcoat and the large tassel which hung from the fez: white for the 1st WIR, yellow for the 2nd WIR, blue for the 3rd WIR and, when they reappeared later, green for the 4th WIR and scarlet for the 5th WIR. In 'undress' or drill order the turban and over-jacket were not worn, and in action the waistcoat was replaced by a hip-length duck or serge jacket.

The Zouave uniform was issued to all ranks, black or white, below commissioned officer. The suggestion that it also be worn by officers had met with the Queen's disapproval. In November 1856 the Prince Consort, on her behalf, made it quite plain that the uniforms of the officers of both the Gold Coast Artillery Corps and the West India regiments were *not* to be changed. This decision may have met with general approval among those officers serving when the change took place, but it was not always to remain so. On at least two occasions later, the last as late as 1911, moves were made to see if the original decision could be reversed. These never got anywhere, and the officers' full dress uniform remained identical - except for their tropical headgear - to that of the rest of the Line regiments.

At much the same time as the new uniform was being supplied a long overdue change took place in the infantryman's main weapon. The 'Brown Bess' flintlock musket had been replaced during the early 1840s by a percussion-fired model, at much the same time as rifles began to appear. Then in 1854 the short-lived Minie rifle was replaced by the Enfield rifle (named after the place in England where it was manufactured). Although this was still a muzzle-loader, that disadvantage was offset by a rifled barrel sighted to 900 yards and the conical bullet was percussion-fired. It was a marked improvement on anything that had been produced before and was soon brought into service. It was issued to the West India regiments in 1857.

For the men stationed in the Westindies, especially those of the 3rd WIR who had seen no action since arriving from West Africa in 1843, supply of the new weapon probably meant little more than having to carry out extra target practice. On the other hand, for those stationed in West Africa, where they always seemed to be in action in one or other of the colonies, possession of a newer and better firearm than those available to their adversaries frequently meant all the difference between life and death.

CHAPTER 11
TIN-SOLDIERING IT

> When Grandad recited the Tennyson learned at sea,
> I saw companies of redcoats tin-soldiering it
> Through rugged country, picked off one by one.
> By poison-tipped blow darts or arrows from nowhere:
> Their drummers' panicky rattle, their bugler's yelp,
> Musket-clap and popping cannons, smoke everywhere.

Fred D'Aguiar
Papa-T

The scheme adopted in 1843, of using two companies from each of the three West India regiments to provide the garrisons for Sierra Leone and the Gambia, had to be modified almost as soon as it came into effect.

After the signing of the 1831 Treaty with the Asantehene the administration of the Gold Coast settlements was taken away from the governor of Sierra Leone, and put into the hands of a committee of London merchants nominated by the British Government, who in turn appointed their own governor. The Gold Coast Corps (not to be confused with the Gold Coast Artillery Corps mentioned in the previous chapter) was raised locally for the defence of the settlements. When this arrangement ended in 1843, and the British Government again assumed direct responsibility, with the lieutenant-governor once more subordinate to the governor of Sierra Leone, it was decided that the Cape Coast garrison should not only be supplied by the West India regiments, but that it should come out of the six companies already in West Africa. Accordingly, one company of the 1st WIR, consisting of four officers and just over a hundred other ranks, accompanied by six wives and four children, left Freetown for Cape Coast Castle in January 1844.

By this time the judicial authority of the lieutenant-governor had spread far outside the limits of the actual Gold Coast settlements, with the people of the coastal states submitting of their own volition to his rulings. Although not recognised officially in any way, a kind of British 'protectorate' had come into being; extending along the coast from the

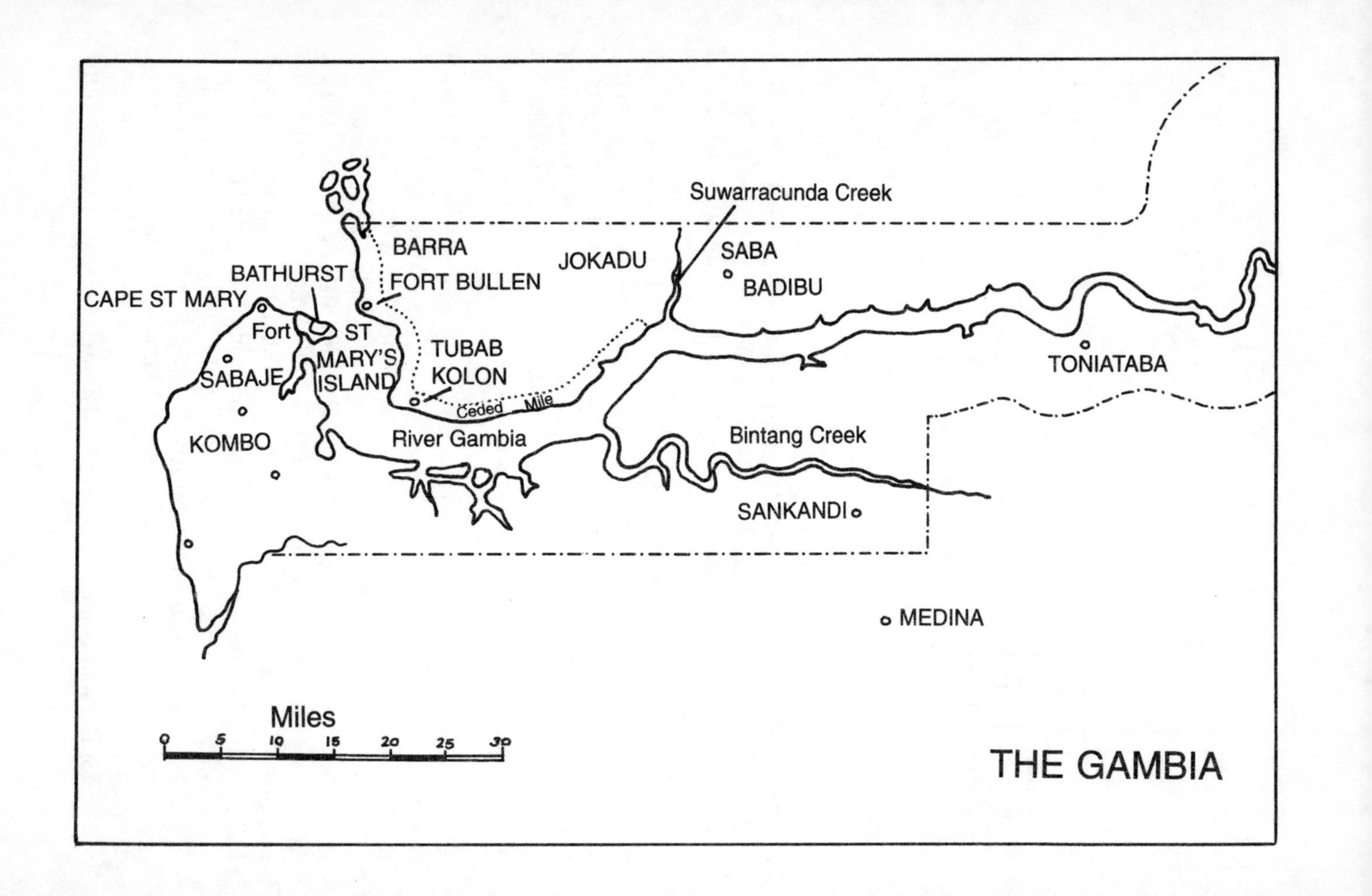
Suwarracunda Creek
BARRA
JOKADU
SABA
BADIBU
BATHURST
FORT BULLEN
CAPE ST MARY
Fort
ST
MARY'S
ISLAND
TUBAB
KOLON
SABAJE
Ceded Mile
TONIATABA
KOMBO
River Gambia
Bintang Creek
SANKANDI
MEDINA
Miles
0
5
10
15
20
25
30
THE GAMBIA

River Tano to the River Volta, some two hundred and fifty miles to the east, and extending inland for an average distance of about forty miles. As one of the most serious offences which could be committed within this area was to 'close the paths', and thus interfere with travellers and trade passing from the coast into the interior, the inhabitants of the 'protectorate' were only too pleased to accept British efforts to prevent this, and to punish offenders when necessary. In 1848, when the ruler of what was then called Apollonia (an area near modern Beyin in western Ghana) 'closed the roads leading to Cape Coast Castle, stopped all trade, and maltreated several British subjects', William Winniett, the lieutenant-governor, raised a force of over four thousand 'native levies' to lead on an expedition to capture and punish the offender and to force his 'principal chiefs ... to make submission'. The very necessary military professionalism was supplied by the 1st WIR company, commanded by the same Lieutenant Bingham who had outfaced the Brazilians at Pirara.

It took a month, with a 'march of more than 120 miles, sometimes through very bad roads, and under the powerful rays of the sun, the crossing of five rivers, and other circumstances of disadvantage', before the errant ruler was caught and brought to Cape Coast. The 1st WIR lost three men in the process, but earned the approbation of Winniett particularly, it would seem from his report of the affair, because 'no complaints were heard, neither was a man seen in a state of intoxication during the campaign'.

Later the same year he led some of the same men on a more peaceful and far more impressive expedition, after the British Government had decided the time had come to establish proper relations with the Asantehene and his people. Having been ordered to pay an official visit to Kumasi, Winniett set out on the one hundred and ten mile-long road between Cape Coast and the Asante capital on 28th September, with an escort consisting of Captain Powell and forty-eight men of the 1st WIR. They travelled along a route which was to become increasingly familiar to the men of the West India regiments as the century progressed. The first stage, as far as Prasu on the River Pra (which here ran parallel to the coast and some fifty miles from it), had already been well traversed in the days of Chisholm and Laing, but Powell's detachment was the first from any of the regiments to cross the river into the Asante kingdom. Ten days after leaving Cape Coast, and four days after crossing the Pra, 'the party halted to prepare for the entry into the capital' then only two miles away.

The Asantehene, Kwaku Dua I (who had succeeded Osei Yaw in 1838), was under no illusions about the British and had laid on an extremely striking reception, which proceeded in carefully managed stages. Winniett and his escort, presumably having stopped in order to put on full uniform and smarten themselves up, were allowed to advance only another mile before 'a party of messengers with gold-handled swords of office, arrived with the king's compliments' and induced another pause. 'After halting for a short time', Powell recorded, 'we proceeded to the entrance of the first street, and then formed in order of procession, the escort leading'. A few minutes later they were stopped again, this time by 'a party of the king's linguists' - no doubt the two English-educated former hostages among them - 'with four large state umbrellas, ensigns of chieftainship, [who] came up to request us to halt for a few minutes under the shade of a large banyan tree'.

Twenty minutes later, after the Asantehene's warriors had fired a salute, they moved on into the main square. This was occupied by the king's 'numerous captains and attendants' forming 'a continuous line about 600 yards in length, and about ten yards in depth' around three sides:

> After we had passed along about three-fourths of the line, we found the king surrounded by about twenty officers of his household, and a large number of messengers with their gold-handled swords and canes of office. Several very large umbrellas, consisting of silk velvet of different colours, shaded him and his suite from the sun. These umbrellas were surmounted by rude images, representing birds and beasts, overlaid with gold; the king's chair was richly decorated with gold; and the display of golden ornaments about his own person and those of his suite was most magnificent. The lumps of gold adorning the wrists of the King's attendants, and many of the principal chiefs, were so large that they must have been quite fatiguing to the wearers.

Later in the day the Asantehene laid on another display which Captain Powell found equally impressive, even if by this time he had become rather more blase about the amount of gold on show:

> we proceeded to an open space at some distance from the market-place, and there took our seats. At 3.15pm the chiefs commenced moving in procession before us, and this lasted until 6pm ... Each chief was preceded by his band of rude music, consisting chiefly of drums and horns, followed by a body of soldiers under arms, and shaded by a large umbrella. The king was preceded by many of the officers of his household, and his messengers with the gold-handled swords, etc. etc. When he came opposite the governor, and received our military salute, he stopped, and approaching him took him cordially by the hand.

After spending nearly three weeks in Kumasi, the lieutenant-governor and his escort returned to Cape Coast. The visit, even though it had certainly put the delicate relationship between the British and the Asante on a better footing, was not a total success. Winniett had been unable to do anything to appease the Asantehene about some parts of the 1831 Treaty which he and his chiefs found increasingly irksome, and their grievances continued to multiply without anyone at Cape Coast taking very much notice. As a result, within fifteen years the Asante and the British would be at war again, and men of the West India regiments would once more be taking the road to Kumasi. In the meantime there was plenty happening in the other West African colonies in which the contemporaries of Powell and his men were involved.

Early in 1849 Richard Macdonald, the governor of the Gambia, also travelled inland but on a different sort of mission from that of Winniett. He went to the river port of Tendaba, about fifty miles upriver from Bathurst, to investigate a robbery supposedly carried out by subjects of the ruler of the surrounding area called Kiang. He very soon returned, having been injured in an affray which arose during his enquiries and, with his *amour propre* probably suffering more than his body, decided to mount an expedition to punish the ruler of Kiang, Farrang Samba. Aware 'that whatever is to be done must be accomplished by the unaided resources of the colony' he assembled a force about 300-strong, consisting of detachments of the 2nd and 3rd WIR, the Gambia Militia, and 'enrolled pensioners' from among the discharged soldiers resident in Bathurst, all under the command of Captain Stephen Hill of the 2nd WIR.

The expedition left Bathurst in two river steamers on 4th May. Two days later, having landed at Tendaba and marched five or six miles inland, punishment was inflicted on Farrang Samba by attacking a number of towns and villages. A field battery of three six-pounders, two three-pounders and a howitzer under Lieutenant Ireland of the 3rd WIR, who had trained up some of his own men as gunners, caused much destruction to begin with: the town of Bambako and several villages were burnt to the ground following bombardment. Kunnong, a more important town which was attacked a day or two later, turned out to be not such a soft target. The inhabitants, who were well armed, put up a strong defence from behind substantial mud walls and stockades, and Ireland's light artillery had little effect. After losing five men killed and another eighteen wounded Hill, perhaps considering enough retribution for MacDonald's wound had been exacted, withdrew to the river and took his force back to Bathurst by 11th May. A month later he gave some of the reasons why 'all the objects of the expedition were not accomplished' in a letter he sent to the *Naval and Military Gazette*:

> We suffered severely from the intense heat of the climate - thermometer 130 - and the scorching air from the burning towns was intolerable. We were constantly engaged for three successive days against an enemy numerically superior at ten to one, and for want of sufficient transport had to take the field without tents, and bivouacked in the open air exposed to the heavy dews of this country.

although he then rather overdid it by claiming:

> The enemy, it has been ascertained as a fact, lost between 3,000 and 4,000 *hors de combat.*

Even if Farrang Samba lost only a tenth of this figure - and Hill's 'fact' surely can only refer to the numbers rendered homeless by indiscriminate burning, rather to those killed and wounded - it was a very high price to pay for what was very little more than the governor's wounded pride.

But, this was the sort of price which had to be paid by many people in West Africa, as British influence and authority continued to spread inland from the original coastal settlements. Even as Captain Hill was penning his letter to the *Naval and Military Gazette* the governor of Sierra Leone

> Found that the state of affairs in Sherbro, a low-lying tract of country some seventy-five miles to the southward of Sierra Leone, imperatively called upon the British to take steps for putting an end to the war which for a long time had been carried on between ... rival chiefs ... and had utterly paralysed trade.

Two ships of the West Africa Squadron, with a transport carrying two officers and ninety men drawn equally from the 1st and 3rd WIR, left Freetown to take the necessary action on 18th June. At the entrance to Cockboro Creek in Yawri Bay, which was the scene of the trouble, the arrival of the force was announced the next day by the shelling and destruction of the village chosen as a landing place. Not surprisingly as a result, after they had landed, the troops had 'difficulty in inducing the chiefs to come in' to discuss means of ending their dispute. It took the detachment ten days of thrashing around the lower reaches of Cockboro Creek before the recalcitrant chiefs could be persuaded to negotiate some kind of peace treaty, and then another week to ensure that normal trading had resumed before they were able to return to Freetown.

As more and more West Africans began to feel the presence of the British so changes were needed in the way the various colonies were administered and defended. In January 1850 the Gold Coast Settlements were separated from Sierra Leone and placed under their own governor. This post was filled the next year by Captain Stephen Hill of the 2nd WIR, beginning a new career in the Colonial Service which would last for twenty-five years and eventually earn him a knighthood. He arrived at Cape Coast to find the garrison consisted of the recently formed Gold Coast Artillery Corps and a single company of the 1st WIR which was well below strength, their combined numbers being well below those he considered necessary for the colony's protection. Nothing was done about this until after February 1852, when Major Luke O'Connor of the 1st WIR was appointed 'Major Commanding the Troops on the Western Coast of Africa' with headquarters in Freetown. He visited Cape Coast in May 'and finding ... that the company on the Gold Coast was reduced by deaths to only 50 rank and file, he recommended that it should be recalled to Sierra Leone, the Gold Coast [Artillery] Corps, then almost completed, being quite sufficient for the garrison'. That in under three years it would found that the GCAC was quite *insufficient* for the garrison could not have been forecast at the time, and the remains of the 1st WIR company were removed to Sierra Leone in March 1853.

By the time this happened O'Connor had been promoted to lieutenant-colonel and appointed governor of the Gambia. Retaining command of all the troops in West Africa, he had been instructed to move military headquarters with him to Bathurst. He took over the administration of the colony at a particularly tense time. During the previous few years a large part of the interior around the headwaters of the Gambia and Senegal rivers had come under the domination of proselytizing Muslims known as Marabouts. Their political and military ascendancy was now rapidly encroaching on areas over which the British, through actions such as that conducted in Kiang, claimed some jurisdiction. By the beginning of 1853 the Marabouts were already carrying their war - a jihad - into Badibu, a chiefdom of the north bank of the Gambia and within a hundred miles of Bathurst; and a Marabout stronghold had been established at Sabaje in Kombo, on the south side of the river entrance, only ten miles from the town. The ruler of Kombo was just as perturbed about the Sabaje Marabouts as the inhabitants of Bathurst, and in May entered into an agreement with O'Connor that 'if the British removed the [Marabout] stockades, the King would cede to them that portion of his territory adjacent to the British settlements.'

The force which O'Connor had gathered together by the end of the month was over six hundred-strong supported by a field battery of seven guns and a promise from the Roman Catholic bishop to provide nuns to care for the sick and wounded. The troops included 463 men of the 1st, 2nd and 3rd WIR, the Gambia Militia, and three dozen 'enrolled pensioners'. A sizeable proportion of the West India troops were drawn from four companies which had arrived in Bathurst on 17th May, as part of the relief for the West Africa companies, and now used as temporary reinforcements for the existing Gambia garrison.

The assault on Sabaje took place on 1st June. The town was over a mile in circumference, well protected by a stockade and ditches, and 'boasted the possession of the largest mosque in that portion of Africa'. O'Connor approached to within about four hundred yards and drew up his troops behind the field battery. Opposite them 'a strong body of the enemy was observed stationed around the mosque, while the stockade was lined with men'. The guns opened fire and

> after a few rounds the roof of the mosque and those of the adjacent houses were in flames. Observing the disorder caused amongst the enemy by the burning of their sacred building, Lieutenant-Colonel O'Connor determined to seize the opportunity, and storm.

Forming into a crescent as they advanced, the troops 'rushed at the stockade at three different points, and clambering over, got at the enemy with the bayonet'. This was enough for most of the defenders who disappeared into the streets and escaped through the rear of the town. Those that held the mosque were of sterner stuff and, having put out the flames on the roof, 'kept up a smart fire upon the troops as they entered the large square in which the mosque stood'. They were only dislodged when rockets were used to set fire to the building again, and then only after many had committed suicide in preference to surrendering.

Even though this brought the fighting to an end, O'Connor was not prepared to show any magnanimity and ordered the destruction of the mosque. This was no simple matter as it

> was a singularly strong building, and for a day and a half resisted every effort to pull it down, being eventually reduced to ruins by blasting the walls with bags of gunpowder. It consisted of a large central hall, with walls made of baked clay, three feet in thickness.

This merely served to strengthen the Marabouts' determination to resist British interference. Soon after the expeditionary forces had left the Marabouts reoccupied the town and began to rebuild both its defences and the mosque. Afterwards they continued with 'their predatory and warlike habits' as 'the dread of the surrounding country', and to the increasing apprehension of the residents of Bathurst. What made such hubris even harder to bear was that after the assault 'by an arrangement with the King of Combo, a portion of that kingdom, including the town of Sabbajee, [had been] ceded to the British'.

The changeover between the incoming and outgoing garrisons was allowed to go ahead once the troops were back in Bathurst. In view of the unsettled state of affairs the Gambia garrison was increased by one company, at the expense of Sierra Leone, for a few months. In October, when all seemed reasonably quiet, one company of the 2nd WIR was transferred to Freetown and each colony then had a garrison made up of one company from each of the three regiments. After that both garrisons remained undisturbed until September 1854, when an urgent appeal for assistance by the governor of the Gold Coast was received in both Freetown and Bathurst.

This had been brought about by a revolt which had broken out around Accra, caused by taxation problems, which had proved too much for the GCAC to handle. At the time help was requested part of the Corps was besieged in Christiansborg Castle near Accra. The response was as swift as mid-Victorian methods of communication allowed, and a detachment of three officers and over a hundred men, drawn from all three companies in Freetown, arrived on 27th October.

> Several small skirmishes had taken place between the Gold Coast artillery and the rebels without either side gaining any material advantage; but, on the arrival of the reinforcement from Sierra Leone, the siege was raised, and the natives retired inland [where] like all undisciplined bodies, they gradually melted away ...

By the time a similar-sized contingent from the Gambia arrived on 7th November the leaders of the revolt, 'finding their followers abandoning them, were compelled to ask for terms'.

Both detachments left the Gold Coast on 12th November in the same ship. When they reached Freetown Stephen Hill, who had recently been promoted to the governorship of Sierra Leone,

> in consequence of the hostile attitude assumed by the chiefs of the [Melakori] and Scarcies Rivers, and the outrages committed by natives ... in those rivers ... decided to detain the contingent which had been sent from the

> Gambia, in order to have sufficient force to overawe the chief of [Maligia], the principal offender, and compel him to sign a treaty of trade.

Although the Melakori River and the town of Maligia on its north bank were over fifty miles from Freetown, and well outside the British settlement (and even today do not form part of Sierra Leone), a four hundred-strong force set out on this mission on 2nd December in two ships of the West Africa Squadron. It comprised troops from all three regiments under the command of Captain Charles Rookes of the 2nd WIR. They landed two days later, surprised the 'chiefs and Marabouts' at prayer in the Maligia mosque, faced down 'from 1800 to 2000 natives armed with firearms, spears, bows and arrows', and entered into negotiations with the senior chief. These ended very abruptly when

> The king ... signified his desire to come to terms, promised to comply with all demands, and to pay one thousand dollars as a fine for his offence. The force accordingly re-embarked, the object of the expedition having been effected without bloodshed ...

Rookes and his men were back in Freetown by 6th December, and the Gambia contingent was allowed to proceed on its way ten days later.

What the ruler of Maligia felt about being so rudely disturbed at his devotions is not known, but he made preparations to make sure it did not happen again, ignored the treaty obligations that had been imposed upon him, made no effort to pay the fine, and carried on in very much the same way as before Rookes and his men had appeared. All might still have been well had not Robert Dougan, the Queen's Advocate, while acting as the governor for a few months in 1855, 'determined to take steps for his punishment'. On 21st May Dougan issued Captain R D Fletcher of the 1st WIR, then in command of the Freetown garrison, with instructions to take a force of one hundred men 'that very day, to burn the town of Malageah, and, if possible, capture the king'. Fletcher very understandably demurred, arguing

> that since a force of 400 men had been deemed necessary to extract a promise from the king, it was, to say the least, injudicious to endeavour to force him to fulfil that promise with only 150 men. He stated that at the last expedition more than 2000 armed natives had been seen [a small exaggeration well justified under the circumstances], and he considered it inadvisable to proceed to actual hostilities without a force proportionate to the duty to be performed.

His reasoning and objections were brushed aside by insinuations that he feared for his personal safety; Dougan issued a peremptory order, and before evening Fletcher with eight other officers and 149 other ranks belonging to the 1st and 3rd WIR had embarked in HMS *Teazer* for passage to the Melakori River. They were accompanied by two commissioners appointed to represent the Sierra Leone administration (and as it turned out act as Dougan's lackeys), Lieutenant-Commander Nicolas of the *Teazer*, and Mr Dillet, the acting governor's private secretary.

Arriving off Maligia the next morning to find a flag of truce flying over the town, the commissioners 'determined to depart from their instructions, and make an attempt to settle the affair without having recourse to force'. The troops disembarked and a message was sent into the town, informing the ruler that if he paid the fine within an hour no further action would be taken, otherwise Maligia would be razed. Two hours later, when no money and no reply had been received, HMS *Teazer* opened fire and Fletcher ordered an advance into the town. It was found to be deserted. Once in the main square the troops 'set fire to the mosque, the king's house, and other principal buildings; and ultimately the whole town appeared to be in flames'. Eventually, when the fire had really taken hold, the intense heat forced a withdrawal to the river bank, where the troops re-embarked in the ship's boats As they pulled away from the shore 'a volley was poured into the boats from the dense bush which grew close to the edge of the water; and the ambushed enemy then commenced firing rapidly'. Fortunately their aim was so poor, or perhaps the seamen at the oars pulled so lustily, that only five men were wounded before the boats drew out of range.

Towards sunset back on board the *Teazer*, and to the dismay of the two commissioners, it was seen that the flames ashore had subsided 'leaving a considerable portion of the town still unconsumed'. On being told that this would mean the troops would have to complete the job the next morning Fletcher objected angrily, 'pointing out that the whole country was now alarmed', that reinforcements were bound to appear from further up the river, and 'that quite enough had been done to punish the king'. Nicolas and Dillet, like many other officials before and since more concerned with their own careers and prospects than with the lives of mere soldiers, blandly stated 'that their orders were so peremptory that they could not, without the risk of censure, leave the river until the entire town had been destroyed', and that the landing must take place.

Both commissioners were so anxious to avoid blame that they landed with the troops early the following morning in order 'to point out which houses it was most important to thoroughly destroy'. They were to regret this almost as soon as they stepped ashore. Fletcher and his men had barely left the river bank

> when they were received with a murderous discharge of musketry from the enemy concealed in the bush. Almost the whole of the advanced party were shot down in this one volley, twenty men being killed on the spot, and Lieutenant-Commander Nicolas and Mr Dillet severely wounded.

Fletcher and the main body, although under heavy fire which caused many losses, managed to prevent the two commissioners from being captured and had them taken back to one of the boats. As soon as this boat had pulled away the rearguard was attacked by another enemy force which had moved along the river bank, and which was only driven off in the end with a bayonet charge. Within an hour or so of the landing the force had lost a third of its strength and was all but cut off from the only line of retreat.

As the short distance to the river's edge was being 'contested inch by inch' Company Sergeant-Major Scanlan of the 3rd WIR was shot and mortally wounded. He fell to the ground

> his chest riddled with bullets, when the chief fetish priest of the place, to encourage the natives to make further efforts, sprang upon a ruined wall in front of him, and began dancing an uncouth dance, accompanying it with savage yells and significant gestures to the dying man. He paid dearly for his rashness, however, for Scanlan, collecting his strength for a last supreme effort, seized his loaded rifle, which was fortunately lying within reach, and discharged it at the gesticulating savage, who threw up his arms and fell dead.

While poor Scanlan was then being finished off 'by a horde of infuriated barbarians' the rest of the troops still standing reached the edge of the river, where they found themselves in an even worse situation. They had landed in two boats. One had been sent back the ship with the wounded commissioners; the other now lay high and dry, 'separated by an expanse of reeking mud from the shore', having been grounded by the ebb tide. Panic set in as some men, 'seeing their last chance of safety cut off, threw themselves into the mud ... sank and were no more seen', while others who reached the boat found it 'so riddled with bullets, that she filled and sank almost immediately'.

Fletcher with three other officers and about thirty men attempted to make a stand on 'a small islet of mud and sand', but with no natural protection it was a hopeless gesture. When over half of them had been mowed down the survivors had no alternative but to dive into the river, and attempt to swim to the *Teazer* while still being shot at from the river bank.

> As the last of the survivors [including Fletcher] gained the vessel, the natives, between two and three thousand in number, lined the banks of the river, brandishing their weapons and uttering shouts of defiance; and the heads of several of the killed, horribly mutilated, were held out towards the ship on spears, amidst cries of exultation.

The humiliation was made complete by the knowledge that the *Teazer*, which had been poorly prepared for the expedition, had used up all her ammunition during the previous day's shelling of Maligia, and no retaliation whatsoever could be offered to the gesticulating hordes along the shore as she weighed anchor and crept out of the river.

The remains of the expeditionary force stumbled ashore in Freetown the next day. Of the one hundred and forty-nine men who had left three days earlier only sixty-five returned and eleven of those were wounded. Given the ancestry of most of those killed, there is no comfort to be gained from the knowledge that the man responsible, Robert Dougan, was what a modern historian of Sierra Leone calls 'an Afro-West Indian' or, as Ellis sneeringly preferred in his history of the 1st WIR, 'a gentleman of colour'. In November Dougan lost his post as Queen's Advocate and his seat on the governing council for having

> without authority, and upon insufficient grounds, sent an expedition ... beyond the Colony, with orders to burn or destroy the town of Malageah, planned without foresight or judgment, disastrous in its termination, and disgraceful to the British power.

It took almost a year for drafts to make up the severely depleted companies of the 1st and 3rd WIR to arrive in Freetown, making it just as well that the services of the garrison were not needed on any more expeditions during this time. The same could not be said for the Gambia garrison, which in the middle of 1855 found itself in action against the Marabouts of Sabaje once again. By then the inhabitants of the town had long since recovered from the British depredations of two years earlier, and in June 'an influential Mohammedan' named Fodi Osumanu felt confident enough to send an armed party into British territory 'to seize a woman, whose husband he had already placed in confinement in

Sabbajee itself'. A small detachment of the 2nd WIR which was sent with the police on 16th July to arrest the perpetrator of this 'outrage' was attacked, and only managed to escape from the town by forming a square. Once outside they were forced to retreat all the way to a fort at Cape St Mary in the very north of the British settlement, while Fodi Osumanu's Marabout supporters pillaged behind them.

This kind of behaviour was more than Governor O'Connor could tolerate and he 'at once called out all the available force of the Colony' and 'marched the same day'. His force consisted of one hundred and twenty men in total from the three West India regiments, a similar number of the Royal Gambia Militia, and the usual little band of 'enrolled pensioners' - this time only twenty-six in number. They all spent the night at the fort on Cape St Mary and marched on Sabaje the next morning. All went well until the route entered thick forest at Bakau, 'a jungle of dense tropical vegetation, only traversable by a single path some five feet in breadth'. Fortunately O'Connor had gained enough experience during his years on the coast to order rockets to be fired into the trees on either side of the track before sending his men along it:

> Hardly had the first rocket fallen than the wood appeared alive with men, who, from every bush and tree, opened a destructive fire upon the British.

This was returned by the men in the van and within a few minutes all the men of the West India regiments were in action. The Militia in the rear, as soon as they came under fire, 'fell back hurriedly in great confusion', ignored O'Connor's orders and 'retired upon Cape St Mary, abandoning their wounded'. Even though the regular troops (plus one hopes the enrolled pensioners) were still able to hold their own it soon became clear that they could never force a passage through the forest unaided, and O'Connor was obliged to order a retreat. Total casualties amounted to twenty-three dead and fifty-three wounded, the governor himself being among the latter with severe injuries to his right arm and left shoulder.

Back in Bathurst, harassed by his wounds and the consternation of the town's inhabitants, O'Connor was now in a quandary: the militia had proved unreliable, the garrison had been reduced by the action at Bakau, and the nearest other troops in Freetown were still recovering from the Maligia fiasco. All he could do was appeal for aid from the neighbouring French colony of Goree (now part of Dakar in Senegal) which was only a hundred miles away. The French governor responded promptly and a ship carrying some eighty marines and three twelve-pounder guns reached Bathurst before the end of the month.

A few days later, on 4th August, O'Connor marched on Sabaje once again. His force this time consisted of men of the 1st and 2nd WIR, French seamen and marines, a field battery under a French lieutenant, and 'an irregular contingent of some 600 loyal natives'. At the entrance to Bakau forest, where the enemy were waiting as before, it took two hours of artillery fire, rocket-fire and 'obstinate fighting' with four bayonet charges, before a passage could be forced. Once through the forest, the next obstacle was the stockade around Sabaje now in places made up of tree trunks eighteen feet high. After a bombardment lasting an hour-and-a-half, during which the men of the 1st and 2nd WIR had to beat off an attack by a 'large body of natives from the disaffected and neighbouring town of Burnfut' brandishing scimitars, the defences had still not been breached. As the ammunition began to run out, and another retreat being unthinkable, O'Connor ordered the 1st and 2nd WIR, supported on either flank by the French marines, 'to carry the stockade by storm'. They advanced 'in the face of a tremendous fire of musketry that was opened throughout the entire length of the loop-holed stockade', and those that made it then set to at the foot of the barricade. After some extremely bloody fighting, with men from both sides firing and stabbing at each other through the loop-holes, an entrance was eventually effected. The Marabout defenders still left alive were quick to try to escape, but as they left through the rear of the town 'they were pursued and shot down by the irregular contingent'. Out of the two hundred or so men making up the combined force of regular troops, British and French, a total of seventeen were killed and thirty-one were wounded. The Marabout losses were not enumerated, but were heavy enough to deter any further incursions from Sabaje; the next time they gave any trouble it would be on the opposite side of the River Gambia.

Early in 1857 yet another change was made to the composition of the West African garrisons, when it was decided that all six of the companies needed should be provided by each of the three regiments in turn. Additional companies of the 1st WIR left the Caribbean in January and by the end of February the regiment had assumed sole responsibility for the garrisons of Sierra Leone and the Gambia. The three companies in each colony settled down for a tour of duty which was to last for four years, during which they would have plenty of time to grow accustomed to the new Zouave uniform when it was issued, and to master the use of the new Enfield rifle as supplies became available. In 1859 the governor of the Gambia, Luke O'Connor, was promoted to colonel and soon afterwards relieved as governor. Although his promotion removed him from the 1st WIR, it did not mark the end of his association with it: he was going to have a lot more to do with the regiment in the years to come on the other side of the Atlantic.

The governorship of the Gambia was taken over by Lieutenant-Colonel George Abbas Koolie D'Arcy of the 3rd WIR. He assumed the post in the middle of a yellow fever epidemic, but had the good fortune to survive both this and, as will be seen, a much closer brush with death seven years later. Once the epidemic had passed and he was able to concentrate on wider issues, D'Arcy found that trade in the colony was being badly affected by various quarrels and feuds between rival chiefs along the upper stretches of the river. Much of the unrest had been brought about by clashes between the Soninke, who had long dominated trade in the interior, and the Marabouts who were intent on founding new Islamic states in place of the traditional chiefdoms. Their hostilities had brought about disruption in trade with Bathurst, and many of the settlement's traders had had their up-river warehouses or 'factories' plundered. Compensation had been exacted in most cases, but in Badibu on the north side of the river about fifty miles from the capital, the ruler refused to pay. This sort of refractoriness among subject peoples was calculated to drive colonial officials to distraction and normally, as will be all too familiar by now, led to the inevitable punitive expedition. D'Arcy decided to try something different, and to enforce payment of whatever compensation was owed by closing down the Badibu river ports, and to prevent the state from receiving any imports by means of a blockade. This was established in the middle of October 1860, using a number of river craft, each carrying a small detachment of the 1st WIR. This cannot have been the most popular of duties, particularly as the regiment was now very close to the end of its four-year stint in West Africa, and anxiously awaiting the arrival of the relief which by then was already well on its way.

Six companies of the 2nd WIR, comprising sixteen officers and five-hundred and eighty-eight other ranks with 'the usual number of women and children', had left the Westindies in September in HMS *Perserverance.* The passage across the Atlantic was entirely uneventful until the ship reached the Cape Verde Islands, where it ran aground at full speed off Maio on 21st October. Whether or not the ship's company had been celebrating the anniversary of the Battle of Trafalgar a little too heartily it is, of course, impossible to say, but the ship ended up hard and fast on a reef and the passengers and crew were forced to take to the boats. For the second time in its history the 2nd WIR had been shipwrecked. There was no loss of life, as there had been none when HMS *Dromedary* sank in 1800, but this time the survivors 'had to abandon their clothes, arms, and accoutrements' and when they pulled ashore on Maio ' officers, men, women and children had nothing except what they stood in'. As the Cape Verde Islands contained an important coaling station several other vessels were soon found to transport the regiment onwards to West Africa, but the correct distribution of three companies at Freetown, and three at Bathurst, was not sorted out until towards the end of November. The considerable distress among both officers and men was not helped by the parsimony of the War Office, which allowed only titular amounts of compensation for much of what they had lost, and nothing at all for the families, there being 'no provision in the regulations authorising it'. The officers were especially aggrieved to find all they were given to cover the lost mess kit and wine stock was £50, when the wine alone had been worth five times that amount.

The loss of the *Perserverance* delayed the departure of the 1st WIR until the news reached London and another vessel could be sent to transfer them to the Westindies. Unfortunately for the men now longing to be quit of the place, by the time the hired transport *Avon* arrived in Bathurst in January 1861, the problem of Badibu and the outstanding compensation had still not been resolved, and

> as ... the blockade had manifestly failed in its object of inducing the King of Baddiboo to indemnify the plundered merchants, Governor D'Arcy determined to take advantage of the presence of an unusual number of regular troops to organize a formidable expedition.

As the six companies he already had in Bathurst were not enough for his purposes, he took passage in the *Avon* to Freetown and returned on 2nd February not only with the other three companies of the 1st WIR, but also with one company of the 2nd WIR. Two weeks later, with a force made up of six companies of the 1st WIR under Lieutenant-Colonel Augustus Murray (who also commanded the whole expedition), four companies of the 2nd WIR under Major William Hill, a howitzer battery commanded by Captain Rokeby Jones of the 2nd WIR and, for what they were worth, the Gambia Militia, the governor set off to deal with the recalcitrant ruler of Badibu.

Using HMS *Torch* and three river craft as transport the force moved up-river and anchored off the entrance to Suwarracunda Creek on the north bank in the evening of 15 February. The next morning the earthworks at the landing place, less than two hundred yards from the *Torch's* anchorage, were swarming with armed men 'who shouted and brandished their weapons, amid a tremendous beating of war drums'. After an appeal for their surrender had been ignored the *Torch* and troops lined up along her deck opened fire on the earthworks, keeping it up for two hours before the defenders showed any signs of backing down. Once this movement was seen, and believing it was the start of a general withdrawal, D'Arcy ordered the troops ashore. The ships' boats had already been prepared and were soon loaded, but as they approached the shore

> some eight-hundred natives, who had occupied the extreme right of the earthworks, which had not suffered from our fire as much as the other portions, rushed down to oppose them.

It was a shock, but the troops were well-trained, competently led for a change, and determined. A fierce struggle broke out around each boat as it reached the bank, and the landing was turned into a wild mÍlÈe. As this hand to hand conflict reached its height with all the troops ashore, a shrill cry was heard above the din and the Badibu defenders suddenly broke off the fighting to allow a charge by about three-hundred armed horsemen who had been hidden among the trees. Again, discipline and training came to the fore, and the majority of the troops formed squares just in time to prevent the horsemen from being able to do much more than gallop around, shouting and stabbing ineffectually with their spears. Three men of the 1st WIR and two from the 2nd WIR were caught outside the squares; standing back to back they managed to shoot or bayonet eleven of the horsemen before they themselves were ridden down and killed. This was all the Badibu cavalry could achieve and fighting ended for the day when they withdrew. Having posted pickets, buried the dead and attended to the wounded, the force then made camp of a sort on the river bank. The miserably uncomfortable night which followed probably put the men in just the right frame of mind for the next day's operations - carrying out the task which by now was an integral part of any expedition into the West African hinterland.

Led by Lieutenant-Colonel Murray (D'Arcy, as honorary Colonel of the Gambia Militia, having placed himself under Murray's orders) the force moved inland on 17th February to the village of Kerewan, drove off some halfhearted defenders, and burnt it to the ground before moving on to the town of Suwarracunda and repeating the exercise. Much encouraged by the disappearance of the enemy and the arrival of reinforcements in the form of a contingent of seamen and marines, Murray decided more destruction was in order and to 'advance into the interior, and strike a blow that would bring the war to a conclusion'.

Two more towns, Saba and Kinti Kunda, had been destroyed by 20th February, and plans were being made to attack a third - 'the king's town' - when Murray was informed 'that the king's warriors, having been largely reinforced', had returned to the ruins of Saba and erected a stockade. This certainly could not be permitted and 'although it did not suit Lieut-Colonel Murray's plans to return to Sabba, he did not consider it advisable to leave this unexpected challenge unanswered', and so marched back there the following day. This time the town, or what was left of it, was well defended. A double stockade had been erected 'which appeared to be full of armed men', and a lot more warriors and horsemen were to be seen in the offing as the force approached. Captain Jones was ordered to bring his howitzers into play while the troops skirmished on either flank, and the naval party was told to prepare to storm the town as soon as a breach had been made.

The bombardment began as the troops went into action against the prowling warriors and the Badibu cavalry, but it quickly became 'apparent that this would be a work of some time' as the stockade was so strongly built. Murray grew impatient after a few rounds and gave the order to storm. The naval contingent went at this with a will and effected a breach sooner than anyone had expected. The marines and bluejackets then set about the defenders 'with the bayonet, [and] soon carried the place'. At the same time the 1st WIR charged the warriors they had been firing at and 'cutting them off from the stockade, killed or wounded the entire force', one officer and twenty-two men suffering severe wounds in the process. A similar action was carried out by the 2nd WIR on the opposite flank but with no casualties. The Navy suffered worst of all, with four killed and twenty-two wounded.

No sooner had Saba been reduced to ashes for the second time than messengers came to Murray from the ruler of Jokadu, the small chiefdom immediately to the west of Badibu. Obviously concerned about the devastation and carnage taking place on his doorstep, he offered - if D'Arcy and Murray would declare a short armistice - to mediate with the various chiefs of Badibu and get them to agree some acceptable peace settlement. The armistice was duly arranged, and on 26th February a treaty was signed by the ruler of Badibu, in which he agreed to pay a large indemnity, to refer all future disputes between his people and those of the British colony to the governor for arbitration, and to provide hostages as a guarantee of his word. The expeditionary force then returned to Bathurst where the Avon was still waiting, and the 1st WIR finally set out for the Caribbean on 3rd March. Eight days later the company of the 2nd

WIR borrowed from the Sierra Leone garrison arrived in Freetown just as another conflict was getting underway.

This had been brought about by the slow buildup of resentment between the Temne who inhabited Koya, the area immediately adjoining the colony, and the British settlers and traders who were constantly encroaching on their land. An incident early in 1861 had been used by Stephen Hill, the governor, as an excuse to force the ruler of Koya, Bai Kunta, to cede a strip of land which extended the colony some ten miles further to the east, but this did not solve the problem. Instead it became worse. Inter-tribal conflicts which previously had been of little concern in this area, because they now took place in 'British Koya' were seen as threatening the peace of the colony. The villages of Waterloo and Campbell, founded by discharged soldiers of the West India regiments forty years earlier, were on the border with the ceded strip and considered particularly vulnerable to any disturbances. In May a small detachment of the 2nd WIR was stationed in Waterloo to provide the settlers with better security, and to deal with any further signs of unrest among the Temne. In late November the officer in charge of the detachment, learning of more disturbances inside the ceded area, decided to march through it in order to restore peace, and impress upon those involved that this part of Koya was under British rule. All went well for a few days, but on 27th November the column came under attack by a sizeable contingent of Temne and was forced to return to Waterloo, having lost one soldier killed and had one officer and several men wounded.

This was precisely the sort of 'outrage' which could not go unpunished, and as soon as the governor was informed orders were issued for an expeditionary force to be assembled. The officer in command of the garrison, Major William Hill, who was just as much of a fire-eater as his father, Stephen Hill, wasted no time and set off for Waterloo with the 2nd WIR and three companies of Militia on 2nd December.

On arrival there work began on improving, and in some parts constructing, the road across 'British Koya' to the town of Songo on its eastern border. This was carried out by 'a large gang of natives' under the protection on alternate days of the 2nd WIR and the Militia. This work created even more ill-feeling among the Temne, who began making forays against the road-builders from the stockaded village of Madonkia. Because progress on the road was slowed down as a result Major Hill decided on retaliation. On 19th December he attacked the village with a force of about one hundred and fifty men, mostly of the 2nd WIR, together with a single howitzer and two rocket tubes to deal with its substantial stockade.

> Outside the stockade and about six feet from it was a war fence, which had to be got through before the stockade was reached; this fence was made of poles about four inches in diameter, and about 16 or 18 feet high, let in to the ground about three feet, and bound together with country rope in three different places.
> The stockade was made of strong beams of wood, and trees about one foot in diameter, crossed obliquely with the same and loopholed. There was also a small tower built in the front of the stockade, about twenty feet high, big enough for two or three men to sit in.

From a safe distance away from the war fence the artillery was brought into action. The rocket tubes, which it will be all too obvious by now the West India regiments hardly ever went into action without, were simple portable pieces of equipment which by this time had been in use by the army for over fifty years. The rockets that were fired could not be aimed with any precision, and in any case were erratic in performance. Their psychological effect was often much greater than their destructive power - as here, where after a few had been set off and a number of howitzer shells had burst inside the village, 'the enemy began moving out in small parties'. As these were being shot down Major Hill was hit in the shoulder by a musket ball and had to hand over command to Captain Rokeby Jones, who straight away ordered the stockade to be stormed. This was carried out very rapidly as 'the enemy precipitately retreated', but at the expense of one sergeant killed and four other soldiers seriously wounded. Modonkia was then put to the torch in the, by now, normal manner.

Later in the month Captain Jones led a two-hundred strong column on another trek through the ceded territory. They returned to Waterloo on 29th December having 'marched in ... two days ... not short of fifty miles', burning and destroying as they went, but with four more casualties from the intermittent resistance they had met. Jones was now so adept at this sort of work that in January he and his detachment were ordered about thirty miles up the Ribi River to raze two fortified villages belonging to 'a chief who had been hostile'.

Having been taken by ship to the river mouth they transferred to armed boats for the passage up-river. On arrival off the first village, well outside 'British Koya', they 'opened fire with shell, case and rockets, making some excellent practice', after which they landed and 'thoroughly destroyed the town'. The exercise was repeated further upstream, but only after the boats had been fired on along the way. Although this resulted in casualties among the troops and the boats' crews of three dead and fourteen wounded, the remainder of the force under Jones still landed and made sure the second village, too, was 'totally destroyed'.

Shortly after Jones and his detachment had returned to Freetown the governor ordered the 2nd WIR to stand down as 'the chiefs and headmen had sent in to sue for peace'. A peace treaty was signed on 1st February, under the terms of which the Koya strip became unequivocally British, and the ruler of Koya (who had not been responsible in any way for the Temne resistance) was forbidden to live there. A few days later Governor Hill complemented Major Hill and the regiment for

> their courage and endurance during the late war in [Koya], which has been brought to a satisfactory conclusion by their distinguished conduct and contempt of danger and difficulties under very trying circumstances.

One hundred and thirty-odd years later it is difficult to think of the wanton acts of destruction carried out under his, Stephen Hill's, orders as anything approaching a 'war' or to believe that what the men of the 2nd WIR were asked to do in any way justified the lives lost or the wounds received. But, they did what they were told to do, which is normally all that is required of a soldier; and both Major Hill and Captain Jones received brevet promotion for their services. Stephen Hill had to wait a little for his reward, but it came not too long afterwards: in 1863 he was given the far more congenial post of Governor-in-Chief of the Leeward Islands and returned, after an absence of fifteen years, to the Westindies.

CHAPTER 12
WAR DOWN A MORANT BAY

War down a Monkland! War down a Morant Bay!
War down a Chiggerfoot - The Queen never know!
War, War, War oh!
War oh! Heavy war oh!
Soldiers from Newcastle come down a Monkland,
With gun and sword fe kill sinner oh!
War, War, War oh!
War oh! Heavy war oh!

Jamaican folksong (1865)

The six companies of the 1st WIR, whose departure from West Africa had been so long delayed by the loss of the *Perserverance* and Governor D'Arcy's campaign against Badibu in the Gambia, returned to the Westindies in April 1861. Two went to St Lucia, two to British Guiana, one to Trinidad, and one joined up with the rest of the regiment in Barbados. In their absence significant changes to the way the British possessions in the Caribbean were defended had taken place in the aftermath of the Crimean War. The number of garrisons had been reduced and the impressive military installations in islands such as Antigua, St Kitts, Dominica and St Vincent had been abandoned. A more telling change was in the number of British regiments it was now felt necessary to maintain in the remaining garrisons. Before the war white troops in detachments of varying sizes had been scattered throughout the Westindies: now they were only to be found in Jamaica, Barbados and Trinidad.

At the time when the troops fresh from West Africa were taking up their new posts, the only place in the Caribbean where any men of the West India regiments were in action was in Belize, where disturbances along the northern border had resumed three years earlier. These were men of the 3rd WIR, which had its headquarters in Jamaica. This island was reasonably peaceful, but had not been so for very long, and was not going to be again within a few years. Serious riots had taken place in different parts of the island in 1859, which had involved the 2nd WIR in

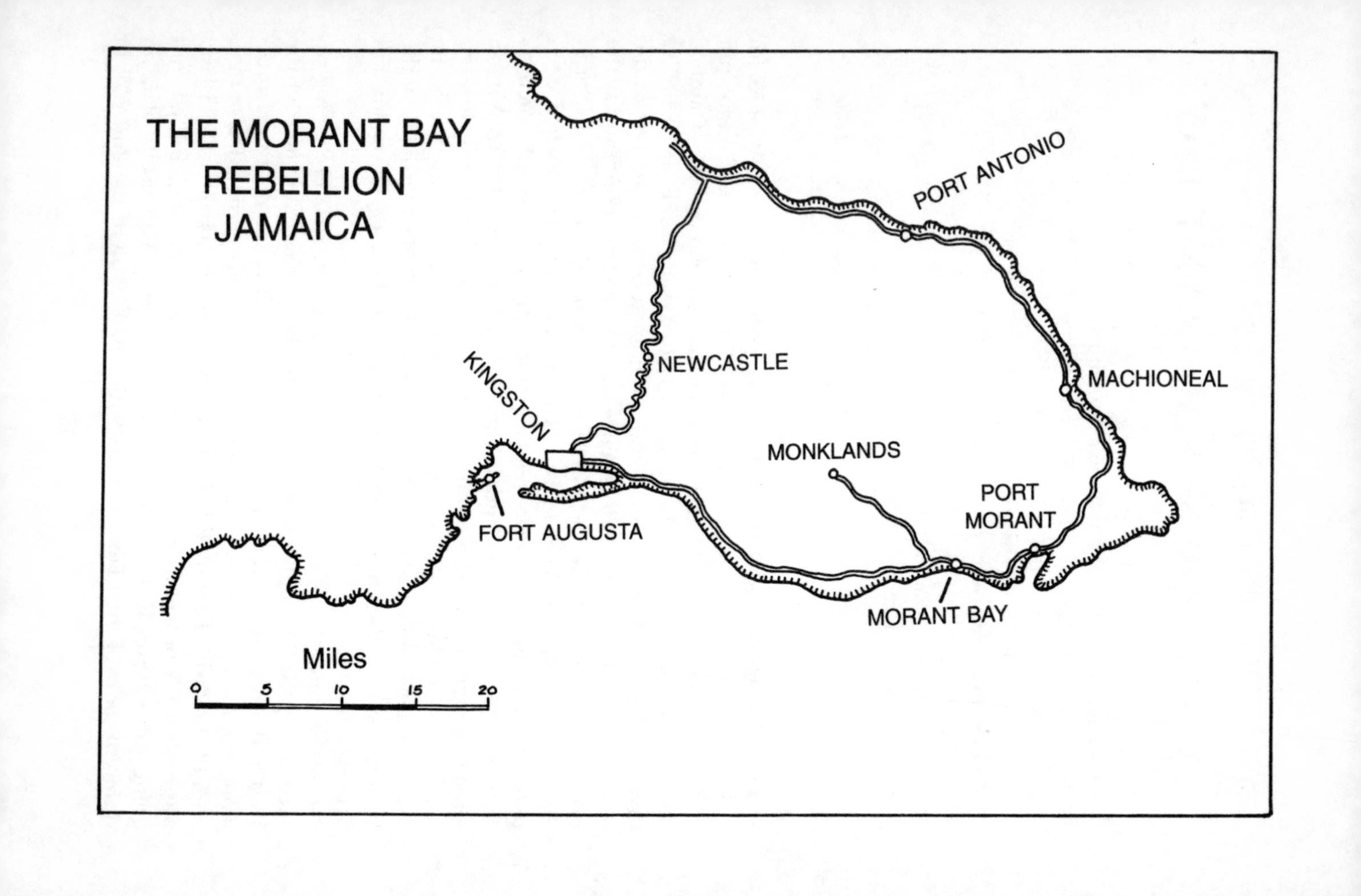
THE MORANT BAY
REBELLION
JAMAICA
PORT ANTONIO
NEWCASTLE
KINGSTON
MACHIONEAL
MONKLANDS
PORT
MORANT
FORT AUGUSTA
MORANT BAY
Miles
0
5
10
15
20

providing aid to the police in the parishes of Westmoreland and Trelawney for over eight months. The 2nd WIR's headquarters had by May been transferred to the Bahamas, where there was no dissension involving the military - and nor had there been for as long as anyone could remember.

Of all the places in which the regiments served, Nassau must have been far and away the cushiest number, or whatever was the equivalent in the Westindian soldier's slang of the day. The tedium of garrison duties was relieved only very rarely by incidents such as the 'alarming fire' in Fort Charlotte, at the western end of the town, which broke out in January 1860. The men of the 1st WIR who were providing the garrison at the time rallied around smartly when 'danger of an explosion from the proximity of the flames to the magazine was imminent'. Company Sergeant-Major Mason and four men in particular were most courageous, actually climbing onto the burning roof of the magazine to put out the flames with wet blankets. Had the magazine exploded the citizens of Nassau might well have been more startled than they already had been when witnessing the regiment on ceremonial parade.

Lieutenant-Colonel Henry O'Halloran, a tall thin man 'with piercing eyes set in an unusually small head, covered with a profuse growth of hair and flowing beard', assumed command of the 1st WIR in March 1858. He was 'a most popular and able Commanding Officer' who combined a kind and well-disposed nature with keen professionalism; he was also an eccentric and the only officer known to have disobeyed the Prince Consort's order about the wearing of the Zouave uniform. This he wore only on special occasions when, 'with hunting-boots, Mameluke spurs and stirrups', he made in the words of Major William Ross (who had been a company commander at the time) 'a most picturesque Commanding Officer':

> The Regiment would be drawn up in line, awaiting him on the town square at Nassau, when he would suddenly appear at a gallop to receive the salute, - bearing a strong resemblance to 'Don Quixote' charging the windmills; and if by chance he spotted a soldier presenting arms incorrectly, he would jump off his horse and, taking the delinquent's rifle, would proceed to show the man his mistake.

One might have thought that, in a place like Nassau which even then had begun to attract winter visitors from North America, the value to the colony's economy, not to mention to the army's reputation, of such bravura displays would have outweighed any criticism of them. But no, there was little room for eccentrics in the army so soon after the Crimean War (in which, to many observers, the top brass on the British side had appeared to be composed of nothing else) and the dashing colonel had to go. O'Halloran was forced into retirement in March 1860, and replaced by the more staid Augustus Murray, then serving in West Africa. His departure was 'much deplored' by the regiment as Major Ross recalled:

> At his farewell tea-party, he expressed sorrow at his recall, and said that he had never treated anyone unfairly, during his long period of service, and I don't believe he did.

He remained just as idiosyncratic in retirement and was seen some years later 'sitting on a rail at the second international Exhibition, at the Crystal Palace' waiting to be awarded 'a prize, - honorary mention - for a patent knapsack of his own invention'.

In November 1862 the 4th WIR was re-raised, following a decision in London to base an entire regiment in West Africa instead of just six companies, and to reduce its tour of duty there to three years. Each of the existing regiments was ordered to reduce from ten to eight companies, sending the redundant pair to form the nucleus of the fourth. At the same time, each was given an establishment of officers sufficient to run ten companies, in an attempt to offset the sort of losses suffered by the 1st WIR during its last tour in West Africa, when five officers had 'fallen victim to the fatal ... climate' in under three years. Lieutenant-Colonel Edward Conran, who up until his appointment had been in command of the 3rd WIR detachment in Belize, became the first commanding officer of the 4th WIR. The decision to re-raise his regiment was very opportune, but even while it was forming in the Westindies events in West Africa indicated that more than just one regiment of eight companies was going to be needed in order to provide adequate protection for all the British possessions on the coast.

During 1863 the locally-raised defence forces of both the Gold Coast and the newly-acquired island of Lagos (the embryo of the future colony of Nigeria, which had been ceded to Britain in August 1861) were found seriously wanting, and created the need for the West India regiments to provide two more garrisons in addition to those in Sierra Leone and the Gambia. To meet the demand two companies of the 3rd WIR were sent out ahead of the 4th WIR, which did not arrive in West Africa until August, and two companies of the 2nd WIR - which was being relieved -

were retained on the coast for an extra year. The events which then took place there, some of which having an effect on the regiments in the Caribbean, are described in the next chapter.

Early in 1863 the 1st WIR was required to provide three companies for duty in what by then had become the colony of British Honduras, and to take over from the 3rd WIR on the northern border, still plagued by the internecine warfare between rival Indian groups from Quintana Roo. Later in the year the headquarters of the 1st and 2nd WIR were switched between Barbados and the Bahamas, the men of the four companies accompanying the former to Nassau probably rejoicing at the change. If so, the happiness for the members of B Company did not last for more than a few weeks. In December they were shipped, via British Honduras where they were joined by two more companies, to the Gold Coast as reinforcements in the war then being fought against the Asante. It was nine months later before they returned, together with the two companies of the 2nd WIR retained in West Africa for an extra year. The latter had been relieved by companies of the 3rd WIR, and it was to take the place of this regiment in Jamaica that most of the 1st WIR was sent in early September 1864.

The regiment reached the island at a particularly low point in the history of the Jamaican people. A chain of events, beginning with unrest created by a widespread religious revival in 1860, followed by the effects of the American Civil War on the price of imported foodstuffs and an associated fall in the price of the main export, sugar, and ending with floods followed by a drought had, by the time the 1st WIR arrived, reduced a great many people to virtual starvation. The acting Governor, Edward Eyre, who was out of sympathy with the members of the House of Assembly and whom he refused to consult, thought all the fault lay in the laziness of those who were suffering. His views prevailed with the British Government when a petition was sent to the Queen for assistance at the beginning of 1865, and a cold and unsympathetic reply refusing to help reached the island in July. The great resentment this added to the already deep despair had its inevitable consequences three months later.

In the morning of 11th October Eyre received a letter from the chief magistrate or Custos of Morant Bay, a town in the southeast of the island. This informed him that a riot had taken place the day before, after several days of unrest connected with the proceedings of the Court of Petty Sessions. Attempts by the police to control the situation had failed, and the assistance of troops was now needed. Details were passed to the officer commanding the troops, who was none other than the previous commanding officer of the 1st WIR, now Major-General Luke O'Connor, who issued orders for a company of his old regiment to be sent by sea to Morant Bay. A warship, HMS *Wolverine*, was in Kingston Harbour and sailed with Captain William Ross and his company as dawn broke the next morning. Later that day news reached Kingston that the riots had turned into a revolt with many people killed or injured, the court house had been burnt down, and the countryside around Morant Bay was in an uproar. General O'Connor, who later confessed to being sceptical about reports of a rebellion and thought it more a 'disturbance, magnified into an insurrection', despatched another company of the 1st WIR, under Captain Henry Luke, using the gunboat HMS *Onyx* as transport.

The *Wolverine* reached Morant Bay around midday on 12th October. Ross and his men landed to find the town quiet, deserted by all the white inhabitants but one, and to discover a number of bodies lying in and around the ruined courthouse. The rebels were reported to be at Stony Gut, a village a little way inland, or heading towards Manchioneal on the east coast. When the *Onyx* arrived the next day Captain Luke found Morant Bay picketed, the dead had been buried, the roads in and out were being patrolled, and Captain Ross awaiting further orders. Luke, being senior, assumed command of the whole detachment and moved inland with the troops to restore order where needed and to escort to safety any white inhabitants who were found.

Martial law throughout the whole of the eastern part of the island had been declared that same morning, the 13th October; troops of the Second Battalion of the 6th Regiment stationed at Newcastle had been ordered into the troubled area; and Eyre himself with various officials and more troops arrived at Port Morant, a few miles from Morant Bay, late that night. Within a few hours of landing the acting Governor, now beside himself with rage, had 'personally arranged for and supervised the first operation under martial law'. Some poor fellow, accused only of threatening behaviour, was hauled out of bed, given a drumhead court-martial, sentenced to be hanged and then casually shot when the rope broke, all within a couple of hours, and all in Eyre's presence. This had a marked effect on everyone in his entourage, and through them on the conduct of everybody involved in restoring order, including most regrettably the officers and men of the 1st WIR.

By 15th October all the roads out of the area had been sealed off. Ross' company had been taken by sea to Port Antonio on the north coast, from where part of it joined up with a detachment of the 6th Regiment and began to march along the coast towards Manchioneal. More of the

6th Regiment had occupied Monklands, a village in the mountains to the northwest of Morant Bay. Luke and his company were retained in the vicinity of Port Morant. Elsewhere, gangs of Maroons, 'volunteers' and 'irregulars' were allowed to operate more or less where and how they pleased. During the last two weeks of the month these forces, operating mostly independently, occasionally in concert, and almost always out of proper control, carried out a campaign of terror throughout the disaffected part of the island. While it is impossible today to accept that this was in any way justified, it is just as difficult to understand how it could have been allowed to go on for so long without Eyre, O'Connor or anyone else in a position of authority attempting to bring it under control. It is even harder to understand knowing that regular troops were involved, and both the 1st WIR and the 6th Regiment committed acts of savagery which outdid anything the former may have seen or experienced in West Africa; Lieutenant-Colonel Thomas Hobbs of the latter even felt called upon to boast of his exploits:

> I ... adopted a plan which struck immense terror into these wretched men, FAR more than death, which is, I caused them to hang each other. They entreat to be shot to avoid this.

In all, when the rebellion had been put down, some 430 people had been killed or executed, 600 men and women had been flogged, and over 1000 houses had been destroyed. The tenor of the whole horrific operation is well caught in a letter, written from the field, by the white Jamaican roughneck in command (if that is the right word) of a gang he called the 'St Thomas in the East Irregular Troop', in which he proudly recounts:

> On our march from Morant Bay we shot two prisoners and catted five or six and released them, as these latter were only charged with being concerned in plundering, not murder. This morning we made a raid with thirty men, all mounted, and got back to headquarters at 4pm bringing in a few prisoners, and having flogged nine men and burned three negro houses, we then had a court martial on the prisoners, who amounted to about fifty or sixty. Several were flogged without court martial, from a simple examination; nine were convicted by court martial, one to a hundred lashes, which he got at once, the other eight, hanged or shot. We quarter on the enemy as much as possible; small stock, turkeys, etc ... we take *ad libitum*; we press all the horses and saddles we can find ...

But such inhumanity and theft was not confined to his own men:

> ... the black troops are more successful than ours in catching horses - nearly all of them are mounted. They shot about 160 people on their march from Port Antonio to Manchioneal, hanged seven in Manchioneal and shot three on their way here. This is a picture of martial law. The soldiers enjoy it - the inhabitants have to dread it. If they run on our approach they are shot for running away.

The infamous march to Manchioneal to which the writer refers was carried out by sixty men of the 1st WIR together with forty from the 6th Regiment, all under the command of Captain Hole of the latter. His second-in-command was Lieutenant Cullen of the 1st WIR. This detachment, along with all the other regular troops who had taken part in the suppression of the revolt, were praised afterwards by Major-General O'Connor for having 'highly distinguished themselves by their patience, perserverance, and general good conduct'. It is not difficult to see why O'Connor felt the need to exercise his imagination in this way; he was after all ultimately responsible for the way his troops had behaved; and it was very soon in his, and Eyre's, interest for the outside world to believe the troops had saved Jamaica from an 'Island-wide conspiracy for rebellion, arson and murder'. The enormous row which developed in Britain once the scale of the amount of death and destruction wrought by those dealing with the revolt became known is well outside the scope of this book, but it did have its repercussions in Jamaica. The formation of a committee in England, determined to seek some redress for the suffering inflicted on the peasantry, eventually forced charges to be brought against some of the officers who had been involved, and in October 1866 a general court martial was convened in Kingston.

Among those charged were Lieutenant Cullen, and the Assistant Surgeon who had accompanied the 1st WIR in the field. The former was accused of having three men 'wantonly shot', while the doctor was accused with the actual shooting of a fourth man. With everyone in the military in Jamaica, from O'Connor downwards, with something to hide it is hardly surprising that both men were acquitted. But even if they were innocent of those particular crimes there can be little doubt that both, along with Luke, Ross and many other officers, were guilty of the most culpable negligence. Even if martial law was in force it was hardly the duty of these officers to permit their troops to commit random murder, torture, arson and looting, while charging around on stolen horses behaving, in the words of Captain Luke, like 'the best Bashi-bazouks in the West Indies'. Such actions denote either an almost total loss of military discipline, or equally complete condonation of such behaviour by those who were supposed to be in charge. A time-honoured, proven maxim of the British Army is there are no bad men - only bad officers. During the field operations which followed the Morant Bay Uprising (which was not the widespread planned and organised rebellion Eyre took it to be, but rather a wild outburst among people living in desperate poverty and frustrated beyond endurance), the truth of this saying was made only too apparent. If it was equally apparent in the aftermath of the revolt, it was ignored. A history of the 1st WIR written less than twenty years later gives no hint of criticism, and can only record praise for 'the fidelity of the black soldiers ... [who] were required to hang, capture, and destroy the habitations of not only their countrymen and friends, but, in many instances, of their near relatives', By the time the book was published the officers of the regiment had long since spent the £100 which they had been voted by the Jamaican House of Assembly 'to be expended in plate' in recognition of 'the valuable and efficient services' they had rendered at the time.

The 2nd WIR was also involved, but only marginally. The headquarters and four companies were summoned from Barbados at the end of October to maintain order in the western part of the island. There, in places such as Lucea, Falmouth and Montego Bay, all they did for the next five months was to suffer

> considerable hardships, owing to the absence of all proper accommodation, being supplied with one blanket only, having to put up in sheds, barns, etc., exposed to the heavy rains usual at that time of the year.

When they were withdrawn in 1866 half the regiment moved with the headquarters to Nassau; the other half going to West Africa, where it was joined later in the year by the whole of the 1st WIR, and where together they relieved the 3rd and 4th for service in the Westindies.

Two companies of the 4th WIR were required straight away in British Honduras, where by now the northern reaches had been in more or less constant turmoil for the previous eighteen years. At this time, encouraged by the Mexican Government's claim to part of the colony, the Icaiche Indians were proving 'very troublesome' to the gangs of timber cutters working anywhere near the border, both to the north and to the west of Belize town. During 1866 they turned from making irregular demands for 'rent' from the logging firms, to kidnapping and the extortion of ransom money; and towards the end of the year to the seizure of an entire village.

San Pedro, about ten miles from the border almost due west of Belize, was occupied by '300 Indians and half castes' under an Icaiche chief named Marcos Canul - a man who was to make a great nuisance of himself to the colony for the next six years. His taking over of San Pedro was more than the lieutenant-governor was prepared to tolerate, and a commissioner, Edward Rhys, was appointed to go to the village and negotiate Canul's withdrawal from British territory. His escort for the mission was provided by one hundred and forty-two men of the 4th WIR under Major Angus MacKay.

Leaving Belize on 12th December the commissioner and his escort travelled up the Belize River by boat and arrived at the settlement of Orange Walk, the nearest river landing to San Pedro, eight days later. In order to surprise the Icaiche interlopers at daybreak the following day MacKay decided on an overnight march to the village. The distance was only twelve miles or so, but:

> The route was by an abandoned truck-path, crossed by enormous creeks and knee-deep in mud, the season being the wet one. The men were soon exhausted, and the loaded mules 'bogged' at every creek.

The going became harder and harder and, shortly after ten o'clock the next morning, by which time there was still a mile to go and many of the troops had lost their shoes in the trail's glutinous mud, 'the head of the column was suddenly attacked by a party of Indians'. Although thoroughly tired out and taken completely by surprise, the men rallied quickly and were soon putting up a good defence. Twenty minutes later, just as the troops sensed the Indians had had enough and were beginning to pull pack, MacKay 'showed a lamentable lack of firmness and judgement' and ordered the bugler to sound the retire. What ought then to have been, under proper leadership, an orderly covered retreat quickly turned into a rout. Many of the men were reluctant to obey the order to begin with

> 'but as the three combatant officers, the gallant major at their head, nobly led the strategic movement to the rear, the retreat soon became a stampede back along the line of the previous night's march, during which the black troops threw away everything but their rifles and pouches.'

And who was to blame them? They left behind four dead and were having to help along sixteen of their fellows who had been wounded. They also left behind poor Mr Rhys, who had disappeared when the column was ambushed, and who was never seen again.

After collecting his wits together with his bedraggled, mostly shoeless and close to mutinous troops at Orange Walk, MacKay set off for Belize to face the music.

> 'The news of the disaster preceded the troops to Belize, where the greatest excitement and apprehension prevailed. The volunteers were kept on duty day and night, the Indians being looked for either ahead of, or in the immediate wake of MacKay and his routed Zouaves ... the inhabitants, Governor Austin's family, at least, included, if not himself, were all packed up ready to take to the shipping.'

In the event the lieutenant-governor did not flee, but sent off a request to Jamaica for assistance. This was answered in January with the arrival of Lieutenant-Colonel Robert Harley and three hundred men of the 3rd WIR. Before the end of the month, at the head of the 270-strong 'British Honduras Field Force' containing men of the 3rd WIR, the 4th WIR and the Royal Artillery, he set off for Orange Walk 'and the district of the recent disaster'. Although the Field Force scoured the area for two months 'without the foe being encountered, or greater military achievements accomplished than the burning of ... San Pedro ... and other Indian villages', this did calm the fears of the citizens of Belize and bring about a temporary halt to the Icaiche incursions.

Major MacKay was not included in the Field Force as he was being examined by a Court of Enquiry in Jamaica. The findings of the court were mixed, but as one or two cast veiled criticism on the lieutenant-governor no-one wanted the matter to go any further, and MacKay 'was leniently allowed to sell out'. In this he was fortunate: his commission was worth at least £3000 at the time; a few years later, after the buying and selling of commissions was abolished in 1871, it would have been worth nothing, One officer who did find a place in the Field Force was a twenty-year-old ensign named Jaheel Brenton Carey, who had joined the 3rd WIR just two years earlier. It was perhaps fortunate for his regiment (with officers like Cullen and MacKay in two of the others) that, during the six years he spent in it there arose no hint of the apparent defect in his character which was to lead to his future notoriety.

After his service with the 3rd WIR ended in 1870, Carey spent some time in the 81st Regiment before transferring in 1873 to the 98th Regiment. Six years later during the Zulu War in South Africa, because he spoke fluent French and was on the staff of the commander-in-chief, he became friendly with Louis Napoleon, the Prince Imperial and heir-apparent to the French Empire, who happened to be serving as a humble lieutenant in the British Army. Disaster struck them both on 1st June 1879, when their small patrol was surprised by a large party of Zulus. In the panic which resulted Carey and the troopers rode off and left the Prince to be speared to death. The incident became a *cause célèbre*, involving French accusations of assassination, to be followed by Carey's court martial, dismissal, and reinstatement following a public outcry. His subsequent banishment to a regiment in India, where he was shunned by his fellow officers, ended when he was kicked to death by a horse in 1883.

The reason why Carey left the 3rd WIR in 1870 was because the regiment was disbanded in March of that year, only eleven months after the 4th WIR had gone the same way. With Marcos Canul back on the Mexican side of the border with British Honduras, Jamaica back to normal after the Morant Bay affair, the Bahamas still slumbering peacefully; and with the West African colonies free for a while from the crackle and smell of burning villages; it was felt that two regiments only would be enough to meet all future commitments. From then on the headquarters of both the 1st and 2nd WIR were to remain in the Westindies, while each in turn provided the West Africa garrisons which were now required in Sierra Leone and the Gold Coast only. To make sure they would be able to cope each regiment was given an establishment of nine companies.

All the necessary changes had taken place by the beginning of October 1870. The 1st WIR was back in the Bahamas and British Honduras. The 2nd WIR had its headquarters and three companies in British Guiana, with the remaining companies divided equally between Barbados, Sierra Leone and the Gold Coast. This regiment, the 2nd WIR, was now commanded by Lieutenant-Colonel Harley, who had transferred within two months of the 3rd WIR being disbanded. Obviously a man with an eye for the main chance, after three years and like Stephen Hill before him he would begin a new career as a colonial governor.

Harley's opposite number in the 1st WIR for much of the time, Lieutenant-Colonel John McAuley, although about the same age was a very different sort of officer in background, but with an eye for advancement no less keen than Harley's. He had joined the army as a private in a line regiment and transferred to the 1st WIR as a quartermaster-sergeant in 1855. Having been given an ensign's commission the same year it took him until 1866 to reach the rank of captain, by which time he was thirty-five-years old and stationed in Jamaica. There his fortunes changed dramatically

when he met and married 'a rich West Indian lady'. Within six months of becoming a captain his wife gave him the means to purchase a major's commission, and four years later he was in command of the regiment as a lieutenant-colonel. He enjoyed this position for only two years before ill-health forced him to retire, and he died in 1877 - while Harley was still going strong as a colonial administrator, and well on the way to the knighthood he was awarded in 1883.

The relative peace which Harley's Field Force had brought to British Honduras in 1867 lasted for about three years before Marcos Canul and his men once again began harassing the inhabitants of the northern districts. This led to the establishment of several military outposts in the area, including one at the small town of Orange Walk on the New River (not to be confused with the village of the same name on the Belize River which featured in the MacKay escapade of 1866). This consisted of a group of six fairly basic buildings more or less in the middle of the town and about fifty yards from the river's edge. The largest building, which provided the troops' accommodation, was of a decidedly basic construction, the walls being

> constructed of pimentos, or round straight sticks, varying from half-an-inch to three inches in diameter, driven firmly into the ground, in an upright position, as close together as possible, and held in their place by pine-wood battens. The roof was composed of palm-leaves , or 'fan-thatch'. The floor was boarded.

The rest of the outpost consisted of the officers' quarters, a kitchen and storerooms. In the middle of 1872 it was manned by thirty-eight men of the 1st WIR under Lieutenant Joseph Smith, who was the only officer other than a doctor, Staff-Assistant-Surgeon Edge.

At about eight o'clock in the morning of Sunday, 1st September, the outpost came under attack from two directions by large groups of Icaiche Indians led by Canul, as more of his men began to destroy houses and stores in the town. There had been no warning of their approach and the little garrison was caught, literally in the case of Smith and Edge, with its trousers down. Both officers were engaged in their morning ablutions as the attack began, 'while the first notice the men in the barrack had of the approach of the enemy, was the shower of lead which rattled on the building'. Smith managed to haul on his trousers before dashing to the barrack building, one end of which was partitioned off as the guardroom, but Edge who followed on his heels remained 'in a state of nudity'. By the time they had burst into the troops' quarters

> the enemy had taken up their respective positions, and were pouring in unceasing discharges of ball, which penetrated the pimento sticks and raked the building from end to end.

The only men able to return the fire were the members of the guard, using the small amount of ammunition in their pouches. As this began to run out Lieutenant Smith was faced with two major problems: the outpost's ammunition supply was in a portable magazine in the guardroom which could not be entered from the barrack-room; and the key to the magazine was still in the quarters he just vacated. He had no option but to return. Accompanied by his senior NCO, Sergeant Edward Belizario, he ran back to his room, found the key, and returned to the barracks. This hair-raising double journey was made through another 'unceasing shower of lead', but Indian marksmanship was so poor that both men returned unscathed. Belizario now had his blood up and immediately went back outside, to run to the guardroom and bring out the magazine. This was so heavy and awkward that he was only able to drag it 'outside the guardroom and a little way along the wall' before having to unlock it, and pass the contents packet by packet 'between the thatched roof and the top of the pimento wall' to the men inside.

> This done, he returned to the barrack-room. He seemed to have borne a charmed life, for he was untouched, while the portable magazine was starred with the white splashes of leaden bullets.

With ammunition available, and by lying on the floor using the heads of their iron cots for protection, the troops were now able to give as good as they got. Smith received a serious shoulder wound about half an hour later, and from then on had to rely on Sergeant Belizario and the doctor (who presumably by this time was clad in a pair of Zouave breeches at least) to direct the defence and rally the men as needed. Before long

> The Indians, impatient at the delay caused by the obstinate resistance of the soldiers, now vacated the houses ... opposite the southern end of the barracks, and set fire to the thatched roofs, hoping to involve the barracks in a general conflagration. The houses burned fiercely, and the flames spreading across the road, caught a small kitchen situated not ten yards from the barracks. The Indians raised yells of triumph, for they considered it certain that their foes would now be driven from their shelter and then easily overpowered by force of numbers.

Their rejoicing was premature. The flames miraculously failed to reach the barrack building, the destruction of the houses deprived the attackers of any cover but for some stacks of timber, and the razing of the kitchen opened up the defenders' field of fire. The fight continued until about half past nine when the Indians behind the timber stacks were themselves attacked by two Americans (veterans of the Civil War) from a nearby ranch, who had come into town to find out what all the shooting was about. Their appearance caused so much confusion that, during the lull in the action which followed, both men were able to join the troops unharmed in the by now very splintered barracks.

The building was in even worse condition by two o'clock in the afternoon when the attack ended:

> For some time no one stirred, it being suspected that the cessation of the attack was only an Indian ruse; but after a quarter of an hour had elapsed, Sergeant Belizario was sent out with a party to reconnoitre.

They returned to confirm that the Indians had indeed given up, although it was not known until later that the reason was because Canul had been badly wounded, so badly in fact that he died before he could be carried across the River Hondo into Mexico. It was just as well that the attack ended when it did; Lieutenant Smith was by then 'incapable of further action, and out of the detachment of thirty-eight men, two had been killed and fourteen severely wounded'. The number of enemy dead was estimated at fifty, there being no-one left in a fit state, or sufficiently interested, to carry out a proper count. How many wounded they took away with them is also unknown, but the number might well have run into three figures. After three more very trying days, during which they had to stand on guard for a possible renewed attack, the survivors were relieved late in the night of 4th September.

Their action, if not quite in the same league as that of the 24th Regiment at Rorke's Drift seven years later, and even if it is now almost entirely forgotten, was no less heroic. Recognition of this at the time came in various forms: Smith was given immediate promotion to captain; Sergeant Belizario was awarded the Distinguished Conduct Medal with an annuity of £10; Lance-Corporals Spencer and Stirling were also each awarded the Distinguished Conduct Medal, but with no annuity; Edge was informed he would be promoted to the rank of Surgeon 'as soon as he qualified for the higher position'; and six other men who were commended had to be content with their commanding officer being 'requested to record their claims, and give such recognition of them regimentally as may be possible from time to time'. It is possible to argue that Belizario, who showed remarkable courage throughout and, because of Smith's wounding, was in effective command for the most of the time, deserved something better. Unfortunately for him, his colour prevented him from being promoted above the rank of sergeant, and his actions did not quite merit the award of the only higher decoration available to him - the Victoria Cross. This was, and remains, a medal awarded very sparingly and only for acts of conspicuous bravery or devotion to duty. The only member of any of the West India regiments to have won one by this time, had been presented with it in Belize five years earlier shortly before he died, and one year after he had earned it in West Africa.

PART FOUR

AVOIDABLE WARS IN FOREIGN PLACES

We were the bolt,
the incredible, willing jackpot,
gunned down through the years.
We were the black question-box.
We were slotted into all the avoidable wars,
in foreign places.

Knolly S La Fortune
Breaklight

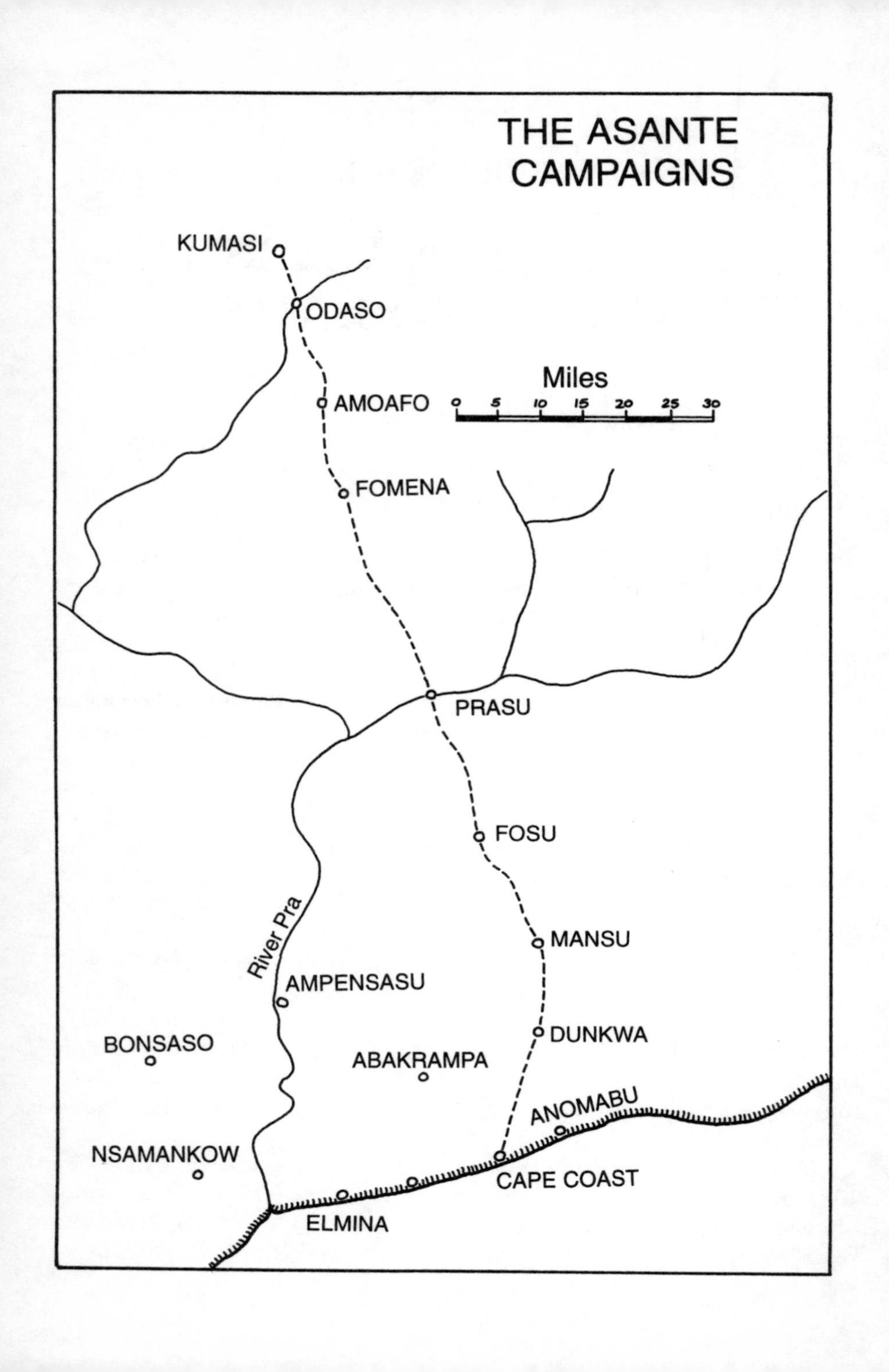
THE ASANTE CAMPAIGNS
KUMASI
ODASO
Miles
0 5 10 15 20 25 30
AMOAFO
FOMENA
PRASU
FOSU
River Pra
MANSU
AMPENSASU
DUNKWA
BONSASO
ABAKRAMPA
ANOMABU
NSAMANKOW
CAPE COAST
ELMINA

CHAPTER 13
CANNONS TO THE FOREST

The white man brings his cannons to the forest,
but the bush is stronger than the cannons.

Kwaku Dua I (1863)

In the early part of 1863, a few months after the 4th WIR had been re-raised in the Westindies, an attempt was made to raise a fifth regiment purely for service in West Africa, with recruitment confined to Africans, and in particular to the Hausas of the Lagos hinterland. The defence of Lagos, since it had become a British possession two years earlier, had been in the hands of a local force known, variously, as Glover's Hausas, the Hausa Militia or the Lagos Constabulary, and it was hoped the Hausa tribesmen who formed this would also provide recruits for the 5th WIR. This proved to be far from the case: service in the West India regiments had become highly unpopular among most West Africans by this time, and few were enlisted. Officers were a different matter; sixteen, including Lieutenant-Colonel William MacBean who was given the command, came from the disbanded St Helen Regiment in June; and another thirteen were obtained in August when the Gold Coast Artillery Corps was disbanded after it had mutinied. Here was one West India Regiment without the perennial problem of a shortage of officers, and it is quite possible that at one stage they outnumbered the other ranks on the strength. A proposal to recruit in a part of Canada where 'a black population originally emigrating from the United States [was] located' was considered in the middle of 1864, but sensibly not pursued. In February of the following year all further attempts at recruiting were abandoned and for the second and last time the 5th WIR was disbanded. During the time it was in existence the only active service recorded was by four officers and ten other ranks who joined an expeditionary force assembled on the Gold Coast in April 1864.

In the same way that the invasion of the Gold Coast 'Protectorate' in 1823 by the Asante had its origins in what, in their eyes, was a serious offence committed by one individual, so did that which took place forty years later. In 1862 one of the Asantehene's subjects found a gold nugget and, instead of turning it over to the Asantehene as Asante law required, fled with it to Cape Coast. The governor's refusal to send him back to Kumasi to stand trial was considered by the Asantehene, Kwaku Dua, to be a 'gross injustice'. Taken in conjunction with Asante objections to certain provisions in the 1831 Treaty it provided sufficient cause for them to invade the 'Protectorate' in March 1863.

This was carried out by three columns of warriors: one marching into the country to the west of the River Pra; another heading directly for Cape Coast along the road from Prasu, the main river crossing; and the third and largest sweeping through the region to the east of Cape Coast. The defence organised by Richard Pine, the governor, consisted of a hastily raised force of about 15,000 Fante and other African levies, stiffened by two companies of the 2nd WIR and the two-hundred and fifty-strong Gold Coast Artillery Corps. The resistance they put up was easily overcome, and by the beginning of June the Asante forces were within thirty miles of Cape Coast. Fortunately for Pine the rainy season had begun and the Asantehene, recalling the epidemics which had afflicted the Asante the last time they had besieged Cape Coast Castle during this season, wisely withdrew over the Pra. This left the governor with the problem of finding a way of deterring their return, other than by handing over the wretch mainly responsible for their coming in the first place. In addition to asking for more troops he decided that a military outpost at Prasu would sufficiently impress the Asante to keep them on their own side of the river.

The arrival of the newly-formed 4th WIR under Lieutenant-Colonel Conran in August was so welcome that Pine 'and the Civil Establishments of Government' vacated the castle 'to afford room for this large reinforcement' and 'took up residence in the town'. A detachment of the 3rd WIR sent from Sierra Leone, and the two 2nd WIR companies (already well overdue for relief), were accommodated a few miles away at Anomabu. The Gold Coast Artillery Corps, 'apart from having mutinied, had given a great deal of trouble for some time past and was considered quite useless and unreliable'. So useless, in fact, that within a week of his arrival Conran had it disbanded.

In January, while yet more troops were being assembled in the Caribbean ready for shipping to Cape Coast, the next stage of the governor's plan of deterrence was put into effect. The troops under Conran began moving up to the Pra and by 8th February, when Pine received halfhearted permission from London for them to enter Asante territory if it was considered this would assist in 'the purpose of obtaining reparation and securing the peace of the Protectorate', they were all at

Prasu. A camp was constructed inside a stockade near the ford and supplies were brought up from the coast. These included rations for six weeks for twelve hundred men, and two hundred rounds of ammunition for each man. Two twelve-pound howitzers and the inevitable rocket tubes and rockets came a little later. All went well while the troops were kept active and the dry season lasted, but

> when the rains set in early in March and the men, camped on low swampy ground, were more or less confined to their tents and huts, the climate and exposure, combined with their enforced idleness, soon began to tell [and] fever and dysentery broke out.

The long-awaited reinforcements, in the form of the remainder of the 4th WIR and three companies of the 1st WIR, amounting to about seven hundred in all, arrived on 9th April. With the titular detachment of the four officers and ten men of the 5th WIR, this gave Conran a total force of about fifteen hundred, drawn from all five regiments - but on paper only. At least a quarter of all the men at Prasu were already incapacitated by sickness, and with conditions as they were on the river there was no possibility of crossing into the Asante kingdom until the next dry season. All that could be done was to maintain the outpost throughout the rainy season, and towards the end of April the 1st WIR was 'detailed for the fatal duty of relieving the detachment then encamped at Prahsu'. The two companies given this task, since their arrival from the Westindies, had been living outside Cape Coast where 'owing to the insanitary condition of the site and the want of proper shelter, [they] had already begun to suffer from the effects of the climate'. They now exchanged these foul conditions for the discomfort of a seventy-mile march 'amidst continuous torrents of rain' which got them to Prasu by the end of the month.

> Here in the midst of a primeval forest, on the banks of a pestilential stream, without proper shelter or proper food, they remained for nearly three months. The sickness that ensued was almost unparalleled. Before they had been a month encamped, four officers and 102 men were sick out of seven officers and 214 men who had marched out of Cape Coast; and the hospital accommodation was so bad that the men had to lie on the wet ground with pools of water under them.

Conditions in the almost incessant rain were truly appalling and called for incredible stoicism when

> it was impossible to light fires for cooking purposes except under flimsy sheds of palm branches; and night after night officers and men turned into their wretched and dripping tents hungry and drenched to the skin.

Hunger and sickness were made worse by the almost complete lack of any other activity but that of burying the dead, and the growing feeling that they were 'forgotten and neglected by the rest of the world'. This was not quite the case; one company was withdrawn in early June, and when reports of what was happening were read in London orders were sent out to bring a halt to the whole sorry business. Terrible as the conditions at Prasu undoubtedly were it is hard to believe that the officers, by exercising more initiative and genuine leadership, could not have improved conditions and done more to make sure their men - who after all had access to rations and accommodation for five times their number - were at least kept dry and well-fed. As it was they displayed no more gumption than the miserable trio from the 2nd WIR had shown under similar circumstances in the Isles de Los all those years earlier. But then, if the officers were prepared to go to bed wet and hungry themselves, what hope was there for the shilling-a-day privates?

The preparations to break camp which now took place at least gave those that could still stand something to do:

> The stores that had been carried up to the Pra at such trouble and expense now had to be disposed of, for it was out of the question to bring them back to the coast ... Much of the ammunition was considered useless ... and was thrown into the river, and the guns were spiked and buried secretly.

This caused Kwaku Dua, who had been kept well informed of all the British activities, to remark with some perspicacity that 'the white man brings his cannons to the forest, but the bush is stronger than the cannons'. Once the outpost had been evacuated he was more convinced than ever that the British troops could only put up a fight under the shelter of the coastal forts, and that in the bush his warriors would always win. Although his successor ten years later would find out that this was not altogether true, it was going to take until the end of the century to convince the whole of the Asante nation otherwise.

Having destroyed or disposed of anything of any value the remaining company of the 1st WIR 'marched out of the deadly camp' on 12th July. Of the thirty-one dead of both companies they left behind, not one had been killed in action or, indeed, ever laid eyes on any of the 'enemy'. For the company commander, Captain Alexander Bravo, the after-effects of all he had seen and experienced since landing at Cape Coast in April were to remain with him for the rest of his life. By the 1870's, when he was serving in Freetown, he had developed such a phobia about disease and such a distrust of doctors, that he devoted most of his energies to matters of public sanitation. When faced with returning to the River Pra during the next Asante campaign his health broke down and he was forced to leave the service. At Cape Coast in early September his company embarked with the rest of the 1st WIR detachment, and the two long-suffering companies of the 2nd WIR, and were transported back to the Westindies before the end of the month.

They were able to depart because the Asantehene did not pursue the matter of the fugitive and his gold nugget, being content with what his invasion of the previous year had achieved. His warriors 'had, in a short time, reduced the country from the most satisfactory and prosperous condition it had ever been in to the opposite extreme', and a general state of unrest was to prevail in the Gold Coast and its still unofficial 'Protectorate' for the next decade. Such unrest involved the West India regiments only marginally, something which was not the case in the Gambia, where trouble with the Marabouts still rumbled on, reaching another crisis point in the middle of 1866.

The Marabouts by this time had strengthened their hold over more of the chiefdoms bordering the river. Four years earlier they had even threatened the villages in the Ceded Mile on the north bank before Governor D'Arcy, with his small 2nd WIR garrison, had faced down about five hundred of their warriors near Fort Bullen. The peace treaty which followed maintained the integrity of the Ceded Mile, but one of the Marabout leaders, Amer Faal, who was not a signatory to the treaty, persisted in creating trouble for the headmen appointed by D'Arcy. By July 1866 the governor had had enough and decided to deal with Amer Faal using the by now traditional punitive expedition. The 4th WIR was providing the garrison, and some two hundred and seventy officers and men, led by D'Arcy himself, were taken up-river by two ships on 26th July. After landing without opposition at Albreda, about thirty miles from Bathurst, they were joined by about five hundred Soninke 'irregulars' and marched on Amer Faal's stockaded village of Tubab Kolon.

As usual the artillery carried into the field was too light to do much damage to the stockade when the village was attacked on 30th July. After the initial bombardment had failed to make much impression D'Arcy, impatient to get the job done, called for volunteers to assist him in creating a breach by hand. Two officers and fifteen men answered his call and, as soon as the necessary axes had been issued, all set off in the face of very heavy fire towards the stockade. The two officers were killed almost instantly, and only D'Arcy and two of the soldiers avoided being wounded before the rest of the party reached the high, wooden fence. Privates Hodge and Boswell were then the only two able to set to work with their axes, although still under intense close-range fire, and make the required hole. As soon as it was big enough for them to pass through Boswell was shot dead. Hodge followed D'Arcy through the gap, and was then shot and badly wounded just as he hacked open the gate fastenings. The governor remained unscathed and was able to direct the fighting which then took place as the remainder of the troops poured in through the open gates. The defenders put up a fierce resistance, not giving up the village until they had suffered several hundred casualties. The 4th WIR's losses amounted to two officers and four men killed, and close to sixty wounded. Among the latter of course was Private Hodge, whom D'Arcy warmly praised in front of the rest of his force before they put Tubab Kolon to the torch, and whom he subsequently recommended for the award of the Victoria Cross.

Samuel Hodge was born in Tortola in the British Virgin Islands, and was twenty-six years old at the time of this action. The award of the Victoria Cross was gazetted in January of the following year, by which time he was a lance-corporal and serving in British Honduras. He was presented with the medal on 24th June and, because he never fully recovered from his wounds, died less than seven months later. He was the first black soldier to win the medal, and only the second man of African descent to be so honoured (the first being Able Seaman William Hall of the Royal Navy). Had posthumous awards been made at this time there is no doubt that Private Boswell would have been the third.

The usual change-round of regiments took place in the latter part of 1866, and for the next three years the garrisons in Sierra Leone, the Gambia, the Gold Coast and Lagos were provided by the whole of the 1st WIR and four companies of the 2nd WIR. Except for one or two minor peacekeeping tasks carried out by the former in Sierra Leone, and the latter in the Gold Coast, the tour was one of the quietest yet experienced by either regiment. Most of their time was spent in the usual round of garrison duties, and in trying to avoid the epidemics which sprang up from time to time. The 1st WIR detachment in the Gambia lost eighteen men in an outbreak of cholera in May 1869, nearly ten per cent of its strength; but this compared well with the losses incurred by the population of Bathurst as a whole, which amounted to more than fifteen-hundred of the five-thousand residents. But if this period marked a high point in the utilization of the West India regiments in these colonies, with over twelve hundred troops divided between them, it was also a turning point in the development of a defence policy for the West African possessions.

Although the British Government at this stage was reluctant to increase its commitments in West Africa, the area over which each of the four colonies exercised control was gradually increasing. This resulted from the interventions made into the affairs of neighbouring states, brought about by pressure on the colonial authorities from merchants, missionaries and traders, anxious to keep the coastal areas free from attacks from the hinterland. As regular 'Imperial' troops such as the West India regiments could not be used outside the colonies without reference to London, many colonial officials would have preferred their particular garrisons to be composed of locally-raised troops under their own immediate control. Added to this, amongst the same officials, there was growing dislike of the West India regiments for their own sake: the troops were black; they were paid too much; their conditions of service were too good for them; and if ever used in conjunction with local troops were likely to make the latter think themselves entitled to the same treatment.

The colonial authorities were assisted in their cause by a report sent to the Secretary of State for War in June 1864. This had been written by Captain Andrew Clarke of the Royal Engineers, one of four staff officers sent to the Gold Coast the previous year, and someone who had spent his entire career before this in Tasmania, New Zealand and Australia. In his report, when it came to describing the composition of the various West African garrisons Clarke, who before 1863 had never set eyes on an African or a Westindian, felt free to draw both on hearsay and some of the more durable racial prejudices. The men of the West India regiments, he maintained

> suffer almost as much, if not more, when taken to Western Africa, than would white men who were ordinarily sober and steady.
>
> Their powers of endurance, or of extra exertion, altogether fail when continuous exercise is called for.
>
> They require the same, and in some cases more transport and aid than British soldiers, and they have not those moral qualities which the latter possess to sustain them in times of pressure, difficulty, and disaster. They cannot move with the same rapidity, and if broken or separated from their officers, they are said to be wholly unable to act for themselves.

After having compared them unfavourably with white troops for courage and devotion to their officers, he then asserted that 'they are not so feared by their own race as are the white men', before adding the comment which, if he could have read it, would surely have brought a smile to the face of Kwaku Dua:

> To come into collision with [white men] is the negro's dread, nor has he become free from a certain awe which deters him from even threatening his [the white man's] life.

All this led him towards the conclusion of his report to state what was increasingly becoming the view of many of the colonial officials:

> Two-hundred white soldiers would be more than equal to the work that could be expected from the present number of about fifteen-hundred West Indian men, bearing in mind that the performance of the police duties, now carried out by the troops and which ought not to devolve upon them, would not be continued by the Europeans.

Although the replacement of the West India regiments with white troops was never contemplated, most of Clarke's report met with a very favourable response. By the time the next triennial relief of the garrisons was due the policy with regard to their future composition had changed once again. As a result in 1870 the twelve-hundred or so men of the 1st and 2nd WIR went back to the Westindies, the Lagos Constabulary resumed sole responsibility for the defence of Lagos,a police corps was formed in Bathurst to defend the Gambia, and the four companies of the 2nd WIR who had spent the previous three years in the Caribbean now found themselves divided between Freetown and Cape Coast. The 3rd and 4th WIR had of course been disbanded.

All went well until January 1873, when the Asante invaded the Gold Coast 'Protectorate' yet again. The reasons for this are many and varied, some dating back to long before the previous invasion ten years earlier, but none of particular relevance to the story of the West India regiments. All that needs to be recorded is that Kofi Karikari, who when he succeeded Kwaku Dua I as Asantehene in 1867 is reported to have stated "my business shall be war", was at last turning his words into action.

The invasion was made in the by now familiar manner, with the main army heading directly for Cape Coast, while smaller forces marched in parallel at some distance on either flank. News of the crossing of the Pra reached Cape Coast on 31st January, four days after the last of the twenty-thousand strong main force had entered the 'Protectorate'. Colonel Robert Harley, who on leaving command of the 2nd WIR the previous year had become the administrator, was unable to believe that the Asante meant to go to war, but soon changed his mind as their advance proceeded. The forces of some of the more important states which made up the 'Protectorate' did their best to slow down the advance, but could not prevent the Asante reaching Dunkwa, less than twenty miles from Cape Coast, by the beginning of April. After a major battle there, and another in June at Jukwa further to the west, the states' forces faded away, leaving the defence of Cape Coast to the regular and other organised forces at Harley's disposal. These consisted of three companies of the 2nd WIR (one company having been sent from Freetown in March), about two-hundred and sixty men of the Hausa Constabulary sent from Lagos, and a similar number of Cape Coast Volunteers.

What could have been a desperate situation now turned into a stalemate. The Asante, camped to the west of Cape Coast, had again been caught by the rainy season and soon many were afflicted by dysentery and smallpox, making any further fighting out of the question. Harley, with the few troops he could muster, and with the town overflowing with refugees he was quite unable to feed, was in no position to take advantage; even the arrival on 6th July of another three-hundred and sixty men of the 2nd WIR from the Westindies, made little difference. The substantial reinforcements needed to drive the Asante back over the border, and the drastic action required to prevent their return, could only be supplied from Britain. Fortunately, plans for an expedition to carry out precisely the sort of action needed already existed. They had been drawn up in May at the War Office by the Assistant Adjutant-General, Major-General Sir Garnet Wolseley.

Wolseley, a fiercely ambitious man, saw in such an expedition an excellent opportunity to further his own career and, as a protégé of the Secretary of State for War, had no difficulty in getting himself appointed to its command. Although a fine soldier, an excellent general and a keen army reformer, he betrayed his humble origins as a shopkeeper's son in his retention of a shopkeeper's racial prejudices; a belief that India was populated by 'niggers', and that Africans were 'so many monkeys'. These views were apparent throughout the campaign he now left England to lead, and very much influenced the demand he made before leaving that several battalions of British troops should be put on stand-by in England in case he should need them. He arrived at Cape Coast on 2nd October and, the British government having decided to 'unite the chief civil and military command' , was sworn in as administrator. Colonel Harley, whom he replaced, left the colony under something of a cloud but one which had no lasting affect on his career as a colonial official: he soon found himself back in the Westindies and all set for the inevitable knighthood which came his way ten years later.

The new administrator made some attempt to raise enough troops locally for his campaign, but when this produced less than nine-hundred levies, divided between formations known as Russell's and Wood's regiments, together with about two-thousand five-hundred irregulars, he quickly turned to the alternative. On 13th October he wrote to the War Office

> to request that the troops which, before my departure from England, I requested might be held in readiness for service in the Ashanti Expedition, may be despatched to this station at the earliest possible date.

In the rest of his long submission, justifying the request, he gave cogent reasons for not relying on 'native troops alone to pursue the war', but was less convincing when it came to arguing why the West India regiments were also not suitable:

> In the first place, the moral effect of their presence upon the Ashantis is not to be compared with that which a similar number of Europeans would exert; and, in the next place, they are not physically by any means as capable of withstanding the climate, still less exertion and fatigue.

As if this calumny, flying in the face of the very reason the regiments were formed in the first place and had been serving in Africa for the past half century, was not enough, Wolseley backed it up by resorting to hearsay and the 'well-known fact here that Europeans suffer from the climate less than black men from other localities'. Although the letter was greatly delayed and did not reach its destination before 17th November, the War Office responded swiftly, and within a few days most of the troops asked for, the 23rd Regiment and the Second Battalion of the Rifle Brigade, together with detachments of the Royal Artillery, the Royal Engineers and various auxiliary services, were on their way. The 42nd Regiment followed on 3rd December.

Long before this, however, the Asante forces, 'too dispirited, too broken by disease and disaster, to have any wish beyond the absorbing desire to get back to their own country', had begun to retreat. Their intention was to leave by the same route they had come, but a number of well-prepared outposts had been established along the main road which they would either have to attack or bypass. After failing to take the post at Abakrampa, about ten miles inland from Cape Coast, where they were fought off by the 2nd WIR, they had no option but to leave the road and begin hacking their way northward through the bush. Twenty miles further on, and many days later, they rejoined the road north of the last British-held position and headed for Prasu and the river crossing. A small force made up of men from the 2nd WIR and Wood's Regiment, which had harassed the Asante rear from time to time, was beaten off at a village called Fosu on 26th November, and from then on all contact was lost.

When General Wolseley arrived at Fosu in early December his call for volunteers to go forward to find out if the Asante had yet crossed the Pra was answered by two men of the 2nd WIR, Privates R Fagan and J Lewis. These two then made their way 'through the lonely and irksome forests, with the knowledge that at any moment some body of Ashantis who had lingered behind the rest might spring out upon them', some twenty-five miles to the river.

> They found large numbers of dead lay by the path along its whole distance, and that at [Prasu] there were very many dead. The survivors had all crossed.

Fagan and Lewis had been in the army long enough to know that a private's word did not count for very much, and with Wolseley a black private's word counted hardly at all, so before leaving the river they wrote their names on a piece of paper and fastened it to a tree to prove they had been there. They then 'fired their rifles in derision across the stream' and set out on the twenty-five mile, extremely noisome, hike back to Fosu with the news. They both returned safely; six day later their piece of paper was recovered by an advance party; and at the end of the campaign both were awarded the Distinguished Conduct Medal.

The ships carrying the first contingent of troops from England had arrived by the time Wolseley returned to Cape Coast but, as his meticulous preparations for the campaign were not yet complete, and he wanted to preserve the health of the troops, 'the ships were ordered to sea, to cruise until the last day of the year'. The 42nd Regiment, which was intended to be kept 'as a reserve in case of need', arrived some days later and about two weeks before the 1st WIR which had been summoned from the Westindies. This gave Wolseley an opportunity to revise his plans: 'I had intended to take into Ashanti territory', he wrote to the War Office on 15th December,

> only the two English battalions originally asked for, together with the 1st and 2d West India Regiments, and Russell's and Wood's Regiments of native levies. But ... when so splendid a battalion as the 42d is ready to my hand,

> [and] when I see the martial spirit which animates both officers and men ... I don't think I should be acting wisely in keeping the 42d regiment at sea while employing in the field the 1st West India Regiment ...

The reason he gave for thinking so, while hardly couched in shopkeeper's language, again betrayed something of a shopkeeper's mentality, for

> however excellent their officers and men, [it] must, from the very nature of their material, be inferior to a regiment with such traditions and in so fine a state of discipline as Her Majesty's 42d Highlanders.

The 1st WIR duly arrived on 27th December and 'was encamped on ... two heights overlooking the town of Cape Coast' while the commanding officer, Lieutenant-Colonel James Maxwell, 'assumed command of the garrison in the Castle'.

The campaign got underway on 1st January when the British troops returned from their 'cruise', during which they had had plenty of time to study the notes for their 'information and guidance' which Wolseley had had printed and distributed in the ships. These began with much practical advice about matters of health and bush fighting, but continued with some less discerning words of wisdom:

> It must never be forgotten ... that Providence has implanted in the heart of every native of Africa a superstitious awe and dread of the white man that prevents the negro from daring to meet us face to face in combat ... Although when at a distance, and even under a heavy fire, the Ashantis seem brave enough ... they will not stand against the advance of the white man ...

before concluding in true Wolseleyan style:

> Soldiers and sailors, remember that the black man holds you in superstitious awe; be cool; fire low, fire slow, and charge home: and the more numerous your enemy the greater will be the loss inflicted upon him, and the greater your honour in defeating him.

The plan called for an advance into the Asante kingdom in four columns, the largest under Wolseley himself moving directly on Kumasi along the main road and over the river at Prasu, while being supported by the others marching in parallel, one to the west and two to the east. As the three flanking columns consisted of local forces under the command, respectively, of a naval officer and two officers of captain's rank, it is not hard to work out what value the Major-General placed on them, and their part in the campaign may be ignored. The main column, half a battalion with its attendant train of carriers at a time, began moving up to Prasu on the first day of the year. All went smoothly for four days and then the supply of carriers ran out. As soon as this happened, and as had happened so often in the past when they were used in conjunction with white troops, the West India regiments were instantly relegated to the role which officers like Wolseley assumed was all they were good for:

> Sir Garnet Wolseley in this emergency called upon the West India regiments for assistance, saying that the fate of the expedition was hanging in the balance; and in response to his appeal, they volunteered to carry supplies, in addition to their arms, accoutrements, and ammunition.

As the 2nd WIR was based at Mansu, about halfway between Cape Coast and the Pra, at this time the 'volunteering' of both regiments to hump supplies in this way was most fortuitous. The next week was spent by the 1st WIR in transferring fifty-pound loads from the coast to Mansu, and by the 2nd WIR in carrying the loads on to Prasu. With his supplies coming forward again and with his line of communication with Cape Coast secure, Wolseley was now able to cross the Pra, using a bridge built by the Royal Engineers, and continue the advance on Kumasi.

The column now consisted of the 42nd Regiment, the Rifle Brigade battalion, a small naval brigade, and one company of the 23rd Regiment. The rest of the 23rd, mourning the death of the regimental goat which had found 'his first day on shore ... apparently too much for his constitution', had been re-embarked owing to the general shortage of carriers. Why the fate of the expedition did not depend on their volunteering to do what the West India regiments were doing, and carry their own supplies upcountry, is neither here nor there. The 23rd Regiment later came ashore again and were employed *escorting* supply convoys up to Prasu - not quite the same thing.

As the column wound its way completely unopposed towards Fomena, a town halfway between the Pra and Kumasi, it was followed by two companies of the 2nd WIR, for whom

> This was a most trying march, as in addition to their kits, 3 day's rations, 70 rounds of ammunition, and blankets, each section of five men had to carry one box of ammunition and one *tente d'abri*.

A day or two behind several companies of the 1st WIR struggled along with similar loads. Neither regiment had any active part in the one major battle of the campaign which took place on 31st January at Amoafo, about twenty miles south of Kumasi; nor in the engagement three days later at Odaso only a few miles outside the capital; but neither could have been fought without their labours. This was not recognised by Wolseley who, when he entered Kumasi with his victorious column on 4th February, made quite sure the single company of the 23rd Regiment was present, but ordered the West India regiments to remain at Amoafo. This was a deliberate slight, felt by the men of both but especially by the 2nd WIR:

> Great was the disappointment felt at [Amoafo] when the news arrived that Coomassie had fallen, and that the regiment which had borne the brunt of the campaign for over eight months, were not allowed to participate in the honour of entering it.

The One Hundred Years' History of the regiment, from which this extract is taken, was written by one of its commanding officers, Lieutenant-Colonel James Caulfeild, who had been a lieutenant at Amoafo in 1874. He was still sufficiently upset over twenty years later to add the comment 'the regiment deserved better treatment than it got on this occasion'. As by the time the book was published Field Marshal Viscount Wolseley was Commander-in-Chief of the Army, he might well have read insubordination into such a remark. But then, as he never had much time for any of the West India regiments, it is hardly likely he would ever have bothered to read a history of one of them, and Caulfeild retired with his pension intact. By that time, too, some amends had been made the by the inclusion of both regiments in the list of those awarded the Battle Honour 'Ashantee 1873-74', the first for the 1st WIR since that of Guadeloupe in 1810, and the first ever for the 2nd WIR.

The entry into Kumasi marked the end of the campaign, but it did not end the war. Kofi Karikari (much mocked by all and sundry at the time as 'King Coffee') was not found, none of the demands which had been sent to him early in January had been met, and most of the population disappeared overnight into the surrounding countryside. Wolseley, anxious to get his sick and wounded to safety and to stick to his self-imposed timetable for completion of the campaign, waited one day to see if any word would be heard from the Asantehene. When nothing was forthcoming, he issued orders for the palace to be blown up and the town to be set on fire, and departed for the coast on 6th February. A week later the Asantehene's envoys caught up with him at Fomena with assurances that the British demands would be met.

They turned over a thousand ounces of gold as a sign of good faith and were given a draft peace treaty in exchange. This called for the Asante to pay an indemnity of fifty-thousand ounces of gold, renounce all claims to the Fante kingdoms, withdraw all armed warriors from what is the present-day western region of Ghana, promise to keep the road from Prasu to Kumasi open to legitimate trade, and to check the carrying-out of human sacrifice 'with a view to hereafter putting an end to it altogether, as the practice is repugnant to the feelings of all Christian nations'.

The Treaty of Fomena, ratified on 14th March, replaced the 1831 Treaty as the basis of relations between Britain and the Asante, but proved to be equally unbinding on the latter. Within an incredibly short time it was as if Wolseley's campaign had never taken place. By the time the treaty was signed the great man himself was well on his way back to England, where he was to be appointed knight-commander of the Bath as well as knight grand cross of St Michael and St George, and collect £25,000 voted him by Parliament - undoubtedly, as *The Pirates of Penzance* was going to proclaim before very long, 'the very model of a modern Major-General'.

After Wolseley's departure Lieutenant-Colonel Maxwell took over the administration of the Gold Coast, but lasted only a few weeks before being invalided and dying on his way back to England. Kofi Karikari became involved in a scandal and was deposed in September. The 1st WIR took over garrison duties at Cape Coast, and in the following year at Freetown as well. The 2nd WIR embarked for the Westindies on 19th March in an old tub named the *Nebraska*, and spent a month floating around off Cape Coast and then Freetown, waiting for orders from England before they could leave the coast. As a result, 'Twenty-three men, two women, and two children died of pneumonia during the fortnight they lay off Sierra Leone, the ship was overcrowded and badly fitted for the tropics'. A sad ending to a very sorry period in the regiment's history, but then the 2nd WIR never did have much luck with ships.

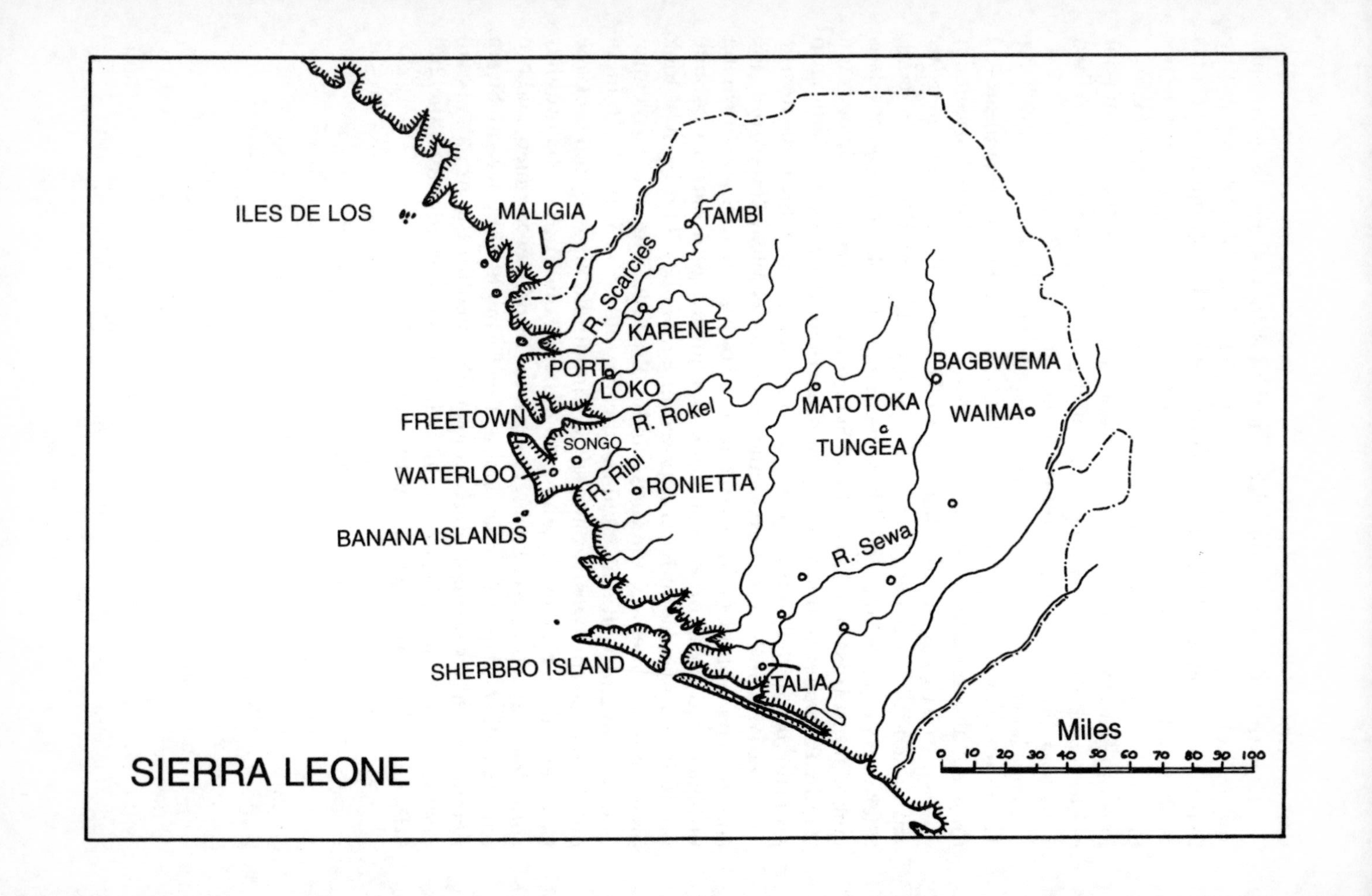

ILES DE LOS
MALIGIA
TAMBI
R. Scarcies
KARENE
PORT
LOKO
FREETOWN
R. Rokel
SONGO
WATERLOO
R. Ribi
RONIETTA
BANANA ISLANDS
MATOTOKA
TUNGEA
BAGBWEMA
WAIMA
R. Sewa
SHERBRO ISLAND
TALIA
Miles
0 10 20 30 40 50 60 70 80 90 100
SIERRA LEONE

CHAPTER 14
JUNGLE MARCHES

These jungle marches
sickle us, parch us like madmen for a sea
so blue it stains.

Derek Walcott
Homage to Gregorias

Early in January 1883 the hired transport, *Bolivar*, embarked three companies of the 2nd WIR at Bridgetown in Barbados and sailed for Sierra Leone, where the troops were to relieve the 1st WIR. Less than two hours after leaving port, and in attempting to take its departure for the transatlantic passage from the most easterly point of the island, the ship ran aground on Cobbler Reef, which extends about a mile offshore in that area. No lives were lost, but once again in true Jonah-like fashion the regiment consigned another complete cargo of baggage and equipment to Davy Jones's locker, and the three companies had to return to St Anne's Garrison to be refitted.

This incident, which caused an upset in the smooth relief of the West African garrisons following a by now well-established triennial routine, can be seen as a portent of things to come. For the previous ten years in the Westindies, a decade of increasing economic depression and increasing neglect by the British government, neither regiment had had much to do other than provide occasional assistance to the civil authorities. Rescuing a woman abducted by Indians in British Honduras in 1874, helping to quell a riot in Barbados in 1876, fighting a fire in Kingston in 1882, and a few similar happenings were all that broke the routine of garrison life. In the future they were going to have even less to do, and fewer places in which to do it: the garrisons in Trinidad, British Honduras, British Guiana and the Bahamas were all withdrawn during the next ten years.

In West Africa it had been much the same story since the end of the Asante campaign of 1874. Apart from a scare at the end of 1880, caused by the 'threatening attitude of the Ashantis', and which had brought the 2nd WIR out to reinforce the 1st WIR on the Gold Coast for three months, life had been equally uneventful. A few more towns in Sierra Leone had been burned down in 1875 as punishment for what were taken as 'outrages', but otherwise garrison life had pursued its normal dull and unhealthy course at Freetown and Accra (which had become the capital of the Gold Coast in 1876).

This was soon to change. Although the term was not coined until 1884 the 'Scramble for Africa' among the European powers was already well underway before the *Bolivar* sank. The international conference held in Berlin in November of that year, and attended by delegates from fifteen nations, was convened to ease tension caused by competing claims in West and Central Africa. In the space of twenty years, beginning in 1875 when only about ten per cent of Africa was under European domination, events were to move so rapidly that by 1895 only ten per cent of the continent would remain uncolonised. The changes this brought about among the British West African colonies also had their affect on their garrisons, beginning as soon as the freshly kitted-out companies of the 2nd WIR arrived on the coast, with one at Accra and two at Freetown, at the start of April 1883. Things had been so quiet in recent years that these three were all that were intended to relieve six companies of the 1st WIR but, almost before they had had time to settle in, events in both Sierra Leone and the Gold Coast indicated they were not going to be enough.

In February Mensa Bonsu, who had taken over as Asantehene after Kofi Karikari's deposal, was himself deposed. This had thrown the Asante kingdom into a state of anarchy, and was now drawing the Gold Coast administration into the confusion surrounding the selection of a successor. At much the same time the governor of Sierra Leone had been instructed to 'annex a considerable tract of territory extending ... to within a few miles of the Republic of Liberia' in the southeast. Although the reason for this was supposedly to prevent trade in the hinterland of Sherbro Island from being 'affected by the continued lawlessness and squabbles going on among the natives', it had just as much, if not more, to do with keeping the French out of the area. The annexation did little to stop the 'squabbles' and the governor soon realised the colony's police force and just two companies of troops were not enough to impose law and order. At the beginning of May the decision to keep only three companies of a West India regiment on the coast was rescinded, and the headquarters and three more companies of the 2nd WIR sailed for West Africa at the end of the month.

The garrison at Freetown, under the command of Lieutenant-Colonel Thomas Talbot, was in action before these reinforcements could arrive. The police had proved so ineffectual in dealing with a 'marauding chief and his war-boys' who had 'carried their depredations into territory which was clearly within the boundaries of the colony' in the Sherbro region, that in mid-May Talbot was ordered to mount the inevitable punitive expedition. His force of 165 officers and men of the 2nd WIR and 200 from the Sierra Leone Police, with a rocket battery and two howitzers, was ready to leave by 18th May. The colony's steamer, *Prince of Wales*, was used to transport the expedition in relays to Sherbro Island, about a hundred miles south of Freetown, where a base was established on the east coast. Using a flotilla of boats to move up and down the various rivers and creeks behind the island, a number of stockaded villages - the anathema of all such expeditions - were attacked and burned in the next few days. On 25th May an assault was mounted on Talia, 'the principal stronghold ... of the hostile tribes', about thirty miles east of Sherbro.

After a two-hour early morning march from the nearest river landing, during which they brushed aside two attempts at an ambush, the force sighted the village in the middle of a huge clearing nearly a mile in diameter. It was surrounded by no less than three stockades, the outer of which was twelve feet high, and inside it was estimated there were about two thousand warriors, 'the most trusty and bravest' of whom 'had been tied to the rear gate, and furnished with musket and sword, with orders to shoot any who tried to escape'.

Two thousand strong or not, the defenders stood little chance against the attack which Talbot then ordered:

> To most of them the huge twenty-five pounder rockets, with their fierce lurid light, flying zig-zag from side to side, and then bursting into thousands of fragments, were a horrid revelation. The shells, too, exploding in the thick of the closely-packed horde, shedding carnage all round, were enough to dismay the stoutest heart, and the wretched fellows, in their newborn fright, endeavoured to protect themselves from these missiles by putting iron pots and pans on their heads.

The attempt to storm the village which followed was held off for some considerable time, but eventually the defenders, including presumably the brave soul who had been tied to the rear gate, could take no more and began to flee. Their chief 'narrowly escaped capture, and was hotly pursued, throwing away in his flight his silver snuffbox, his sword, and whip, and even his embroidered gown'.

The defence of Talia had lasted for more than three hours. By the time the troops entered to set about its final destruction they encountered scenes which even Hieronymus Bosch might have had difficulty putting on canvas:

> Inside the town the sight was ghastly in the extreme. In a small space one officer counted eighty-two dead; in another part twenty-three bodies were lying huddled together, evidently the work of a single shell; and here and there were scattered groups of threes and fours, while a single corpse supported by a fence, stood up, grim in death, grasping the rusty musket which in life he was in the act of loading.

Even if the chief who had escaped, leaving behind his snuffbox and other impedimenta, had indeed made himself 'the terror of the Sherbro country' by plunder and murder, it is difficult to believe that retribution on this scale was necessary or justified. But this is a thought for today; a century or more ago it was nothing more than 'a salutary lesson' intended to 'have a most beneficial effect', and a job carried out 'with completeness and thoroughness deserving of the highest commendation'. Some weeks later, back in Freetown, Talbot received letters from the Commander-in-Chief at Horse Guards, the Secretary of State for War, and the Secretary of State for the Colonies, all expressing the writers' approval of his actions and their appreciation of 'the excellent service rendered by the troops' under his command.

The Sherbro expedition had the desired effect, 'for the peaceable natives returned to their work, while those who had been living by plunder and murder realised that they were not safe from punishment, as they had supposed, even in the depths of these fever-stricken rivers and creeks'. Even so, the effect did not last all that long, and it was restricted to one small part of Sierra Leone; there was plenty of scope elsewhere in the colony for 'peaceable natives' to be kept from their work. There were no more serious disturbances for the 2nd WIR to deal with during the remainder of their tour, but this did not prevent the headquarters and three companies from being retained in Freetown for a month after being relieved by the 1st WIR at the beginning of 1886, because of trouble brewing in the interior.

Throughout the nineteenth century a struggle had taken place between the Yoni, a people living in a region centred about sixty miles inland of Freetown, and their neighbours in an effort to secure unimpeded access for Yoni traders to the tide-water trading centres on the Rokel, Ribi and Bumpe rivers, which were all outside their control. Because of this perpetual strife trade had gradually moved southwards into the Sherbro region, an area which included the lower reaches of the Ribi and Bumpe, as well as Sherbro Island itself. Yoni interests had moved with the trade, but their warlike activities produced little reaction among the authorities in Freetown, other than a marked dislike of the Yoni warriors, until Sherbro became part of the colony. Then, of course, it was altogether different: the Yoni were now carrying war into British territory.

A truce between the Yoni and their Mende neighbours, arranged by the governor in 1886, lasted for less than a year. It was broken in January of the following year when the Mende attacked and plundered the Yoni town of Ronietta 'in revenge for former raids'. The Yoni waited until the approach of the dry season before retaliating and then in early October destroyed Senehun and several other Mende villages along the Bumpe river. Animated by this they moved on the nearby town of Rotifunk, but before launching their attack mutilated one of their captives and sent him to tell the governor that, once they reached Freetown, all the white residents would lose an ear, a hand and a thumb in the same way.

Telegrams instantly flew back and forth between Freetown and London and War Office approval to respond to this threat with military action was received by the governor on 11th October. It was accompanied by information that an officer would be sent out from England to take charge of the operation. The man chosen was Colonel Sir Francis de Winton who was nominated on 18th October, received his instructions three days later, and arrived in Freetown on 9th November. During this time the Yoni had raided and destroyed more villages in the Ribi and Bumpe districts, accused the governor of bad faith, and returned to their own country with their plunder and captives to prepare for what they were soon to term the 'Whiteman's War'. Robari, about forty miles east of Freetown, became their main stronghold.

Colonel de Winton's plan called for an attack on the Yoni to be delivered from a base at Mafengbe, which was at the highest navigable point on the Ribi, and about twelve miles from Robari. Within a week of his arrival in the colony he had the base set up, and had assembled there an expeditionary force made up of two hundred and fifty men of the 1st WIR, fifty members of the Sierra Leone Police, a small naval detachment, and about four hundred 'irregulars', supported by five hundred carriers and another two hundred men to cut a road through the bush. In addition to a seven-pounder RML (rifled, muzzle-loading) field gun and a Maxim machine gun, which were to be worked by the seamen, the 1st WIR had the usual rockets and rocket-tubes and each man was armed with a Martini-Henry rifle. This breech-loading, single-shot weapon, with its great range and high accuracy, had been issued ten years earlier. Although it had already been made obsolescent by the development of the Lee-Metford magazine rifle (which would not be issued to the West India regiments for another six years) it was much superior to anything with which the Yoni were likely to be armed.

The road cutters went to work on 17th November and three days later the entire force had moved up to within four miles of Robari. On the way it had been joined by about a thousand so-called 'friendlies', much to the disgust of de Winton who reported, 'they cling to the rear of the column and their only object is plunder and the capture of slaves'. All went well with the final stage of the advance on 21st November until the column ran into an ambush two miles from its destination, after which it took nearly five hours of continuous fighting in dense bush to clear the remainder of the route. The rockets which were used to great effect during this engagement proved to be even more useful once the troops reached the town. Four rockets and four rounds from the field gun were enough to cause 'the whole of the defenders of the town to stampede', and the battle for Robari was over before it had properly begun. The crowds of 'friendlies' saw their chance and, before any of the troops could prevent it, rushed in to begin looting and burning and a major part of the town went up in smoke.

During the next four days several other Yoni towns were destroyed by de Winton's force, while the 'friendlies' - now out of all control - went on the rampage among the smaller villages. The Yoni offered little resistance and in December their leaders were only too willing to discuss a peace agreement with the governor and Colonel de Winton. It was made clear to the Yoni that their country was 'now to be considered the Queen's by conquest', and both men took part in the process of selecting a new principal chief who would be amenable to British authority. All the expeditionary force, with the exception of a small detachment of the 1st WIR left at Robari, was back in Freetown by 15th January and de Winton left for England six days later. The 1st WIR was later awarded the Battle Honour 'West Africa 1887' for its part in the campaign; although whether the words 'battle' or 'honour' are quite appropriate in connection with the operations involved is perhaps open to question.

Just as the officers and men of the garrison were settling back into the routine of Freetown barrack life they were distressed to learn that a decision had been made to amalgamate the two West India regiments, and that this would take place before the triennial change-over between them was made at the end of the year. It was news that was equally unwelcome with the 2nd WIR in the Westindies for, as was observed at the time:

> Oddly enough, the two regiments rather dislike one another [perhaps there was something to the 'men' versus 'gentlemen' business after all ...], and if

you happen to say anything to a fellow in the 1st West about the 2nd, he snorts and speaks of it with ineffable disdain, while his brother officer in the 2nd will say, "Poor chap, I don't envy him being in that regiment, I can tell you - rum lot the 1st."

Distressing or not, the news could hardly have been unexpected by either regiment. Seven years earlier a major reorganisation of the army had taken place, when eighty-two infantry regiments had been amalgamated by pairs to create forty-one new regiments, each of two battalions and with a new title. This had taken place amid much opposition, and had created great resentment among the officers and many of the longer-serving other ranks in regiments joined in some of the more unlikely combinations. At least the two West India regiments had everything in common, which was more than could be said of some of those paired in 1881: the Shropshire Regiment and the Bucks Volunteers; the Dorsetshire Regiment and the West Norfolk Regiment; even the Durham Regiment and the Bombay Light Infantry.

The amalgamation took place on 1st October 1888, with the 1st and 2nd WIR becoming, respectively, the First and Second Battalions of the West India Regiment. Each battalion was made up of eight companies, the ninth company of each of the old regiments being used to create the regimental depot in Kingston. The white facings and tassel of the Zouave uniform worn by the 1st WIR were now adopted by the whole regiment, with the exception of the bands and drummers who wore yellow tassels. The running of the new regiment was not affected in any way by any lingering animosity between the battalions; for the next twenty years they would always be serving on opposite sides of the Atlantic.

The relief of the West African garrisons began a month after the amalgamation. Leaving one company behind in British Guiana, the 2nd Battalion had taken over in Freetown and Accra by March 1889. In Sierra Leone, although de Winton's expedition had put paid to Yoni militarism and brought about an end to the trade wars, it was still felt necessary to retain an outpost at Robari, where a wooden blockhouse had been built to accommodate a small detachment of troops. Command of this post was a job for a subaltern, and among the 2nd Battalion's junior officers in Freetown was one who saw immediately he arrived the opportunities such an independent command could offer.

Lieutenant Edward Lendy, who had joined the regiment from Sandhurst four years earlier, 'begged hard to go, and was sent'. His boyish enthusiasm and somewhat exaggerated thirst for glory may have irritated other members of the officers' mess, but

> He soon showed a capacity for handling men and a rare judgement and pluck in dealing with native chiefs. Had he stayed idly at his command, he would never have been known; but from the moment he arrived at the post he started off with an independence and self-reliance that soon won the respect of the authorities.

With a remit to keep order in the general vicinity of Robari, and the nearest officer senior to himself some forty miles away, 'he treated the red tape and narrow orders of the Home Government with a breezy contempt' and set about suppressing the traffic in slaves:

> He asked no one to share his responsibility and took no one's advice; but if he heard of a slave capture, he would start off with a handful of men ... and would attack the scoundrelly convoy.

Towards the end of the year he tracked one such convoy to Fula Town, about fifteen miles south of Robari, where he and his handful of troops entered into a pitched battle with the slave traders. For this, and the subsequent release of eighty slaves who had been brought down from the interior, Lendy became one of the first recipients of the Distinguished Service Order, the DSO, an award which had been instituted only three years earlier. Unfortunately his enterprise and intrepidity, not to mention his alerting the world to the continuance of slavery on British soil, eventually caused dissension between the War Office and the Colonial Office. Arguments which arose, about whether such operations as Lendy conducted were offensive (in which case they had to be sanctioned by the former) or defensive (in which case they could be authorised by the governor of the colony), ended with the 2nd Battalion being ordered to withdraw the Robari detachment in March 1891, and to turn over the outpost to the newly-formed Sierra Leone Frontier Police. This body had been formed out of the existing police force, but along much more military lines, primarily to deal with interior and border problems. As this sort of work was obviously Lendy's *métier*, and the new force needed officers, he immediately volunteered for secondment. Within a few months he was back upcountry, with the rank of captain and holding the position of Inspector-General of the SLFP.

In July, because 'of an uneasy feeling with regard to the native tribes', a detachment of two officers and fifty men of the 2nd Battalion WIR was sent to the Gambia. The administration of the colony had been separated from that of Sierra Leone in 1888, and a year later a boundary agreement had been signed with France which restricted British territory to a narrow strip on either side of the river for about two hundred miles inland. A joint Anglo-French Boundary Commission began work on delimitation of the boundary early in 1891. By the time the WIR detachment arrived the Commission, which had begun work on the southern side of the lower reaches of the river, was encountering much hostility from some of the local tribesmen. Those led by Fodi Kabba, operating from a base at Marige about fifty miles inland from Bathurst, were particularly troublesome. In December, as by this time neither the presence of the WIR nor the stationing of three gunboats in the river had had any affect on Fodi Kabba's behaviour, the administrator decided stronger measures were needed.

Another four officers and one hundred and twenty men of the 2nd Battalion were brought from Freetown on 29th December, and four days later a joint naval and military force began an advance into the area under Fodi Kabba's suzerainty. Four of five towns, including Marige, were destroyed in the usual manner, but Fodi Kabba himself managed to avoid capture by crossing into French territory. The expedition ended in early February when the troops had to return to Bathurst in preparation for their return to the Westindies. The 1st Battalion had already begun to arrive, and a detachment under Major George Madden took over the colony's peacekeeping duties.

In March Madden and a dozen men were sent about eighty miles upriver to Toniataba, in order to bring one of Fodi Kabba's henchmen, Suleman Santu, to Bathurst where he was required to acknowledge the authority of the administrator. They arrived on 13th March to find the village surrounded by the inevitable stockade, the gates firmly barred, and no-one willing to given them entry. As there were no armed men in sight and no apparent danger, Madden decided to force his way through the gates; a suitable length of timber was found and brought into use as a battering ram. While he watched this being wielded, a number of loopholes were opened in the stockade, and several musket muzzles were aimed at his back. Very fortunately, the movement was spotted by Lance-Corporal William Gordon who was directing the battering operations. Acting instinctively he threw himself at the major as he yelled out a warning, and both men fell to the ground as the muskets fired. Gordon was hit and badly wounded in the chest, but his action undoubtedly saved Madden's life. It also so impressed or alarmed the invisible musketeers that no more shooting took place and the party was allowed to withdraw without further incident. For his gallant action Gordon, a twenty-eight-year-old Jamaican, was awarded the Victoria Cross nine months later. He never fully recovered from his wound, but still rose to the rank of sergeant before discharged on medical grounds in 1902. After some time with the Kingston Militia he was found employment at the regimental headquarters at Up Park Camp, where he was always treated with great respect and remained much-esteemed until his death in 1922.

The affray at Toniataba could not go unpunished and towards the end of April a force of three hundred men from the Freetown garrison, under the battalion's commanding officer, Lieutenant-Colonel Alfred Ellis, stormed the village, burnt it to the ground, and killed the recalcitrant Suleman Santu in the process. The reason for the delay in carrying out the attack was because more pressing events in Sierra Leone had prevented Ellis and his men from leaving the colony any sooner.

Since 1889, because of events taking place outside Sierra Leone where the French were busy 'scrambling' in what was soon to become French West Africa, the people living between the middle reaches of the Great and Small Scarcies rivers to the northeast of Freetown had been plagued by a horde of dispossessed marauders, under a man named Karimu. These operated from a number of fortified 'war camps', of which the strongest was at Tambi on the west bank of the Small Scarcies, about eighty miles from its mouth. When an attempt by the SLFP to destroy this camp and capture Karimu failed on 14th March, the governor was obliged to ask for the help of the WIR. Lieutenant-Colonel Ellis rushed back from Bathurst, where he had just gone to discuss the Toniataba problem, and by 28th March was ready to set off for Tambi with a force of four hundred and fifty men of the WIR and one hundred and thirty of the SLFP, with three seven-pounder RML guns and two rocket tubes.

Over the next two days they were taken by sea to the Great Scarcies and landed at Robat, about twenty miles upstream. From there the force trekked eastward through thick forest into Kasse, a state on the banks of the Small Scarcies whose inhabitants were among those most afflicted by Karimu and his raiders. On 6th April at Kamasassa, abut twelve miles from Tambi, Ellis was joined by about four hundred Temne warriors under Kebelai, their chief - a man better known to history by his official title, Bai Bureh.

On the following day the entire force advanced on Tambi, taking over four hours to cover the final six miles 'owing to the dense bush and the necessity of searching for ambuscades'. These precautions paid off and no opposition was encountered, nor later while Tambi was being reconnoitred:

> It was defended by a strong stockade with two war fences round it, distant 12 and 30 feet respectively from the stockade. At intervals there were watchtowers, with their upper parts made of bullet-proof logs; but the loopholes for firing had not been cut in such a way that the defenders could bring their fire to bear on anyone close at hand.

This was enough for Ellis, who ordered two of the field-guns to be run up to within fifty feet of the stockade where the gunners were out of danger. Within minutes the gates had been blown apart with a few rounds at point-blank range, the breach widened with demolition charges, and the troops sent it. Even though the defenders numbered about fifteen hundred they stood no chance with muskets, spears and swords against disciplined and well-led troops armed with rifles, and within an hour or so they gave up the fight. Total casualties among the WIR and the SLFP amounted to nine wounded. Bai Bureh's men, who took no part in the actual storming, were responsible for most of the two hundred enemy dead, caught as they tried to flee from the stockade, but themselves suffered over thirty dead and wounded. Once the remains of Tambi had been cleared of everything of any value what was left was put to the torch, and the expeditionary force began the long trek back to Robat, accompanid by a large black goat. This animal, given the name Tambi, subsequently became the regimental mascot. The Temne returned to their villages bearing their wounded along with their loot. Bai Bureh himself carried back something even more valuable than plunder; he had now seen how the British, as represented by the WIR and the Frontier Police, fought and dealt with stockades; and this was knowledge he would put to good use when he became their enemy a few years later.

After dealing with Karimu at Tambi, and immediately afterwards with Suleman Santu at Tonitaba in the Gambia, the 1st Battalion was able to settle down in Freetown in May to a more routine existence for the next eighteen months. Outside the British colonies however the French continued with their empire-building at the expense of the people inhabiting what are today Senegal and Guinea, and it was this which eventually brought an end to this peaceful interlude.

During the 1870s a Malinké leader named Samori Toure had created his own empire in the Guinea highlands, based on his capital at Bissandugu, nearly three hundred miles inland of Freetown. The conquest of the various states making up his empire had been carried out by a well-trained army of about thirty thousand men known, because many of them were mounted, as Sofas ('horse fathers'). They were armed with modern weapons purchased mainly through traders in Sierra Leone, and paid for in gold, ivory and, indirectly, slaves. Their activities, which ran counter to those of the French, had resulted in a long series of engagements with French troops, and the general unrest so created had gradually spread into the border areas of Sierra Leone. By 1892 Samori had had enough, and began moving to the east with his army to carve out a new empire well away, he hoped, from European interference. This merely aggravated the situation. The rivalry created by the frantic 'Scramble for Africa', which was now approaching its apogee, caused the French to begin to believe that Samori was being supported by the British; the British to start seeing the growing discontent in the east of Sierra Leone as French-inspired; and Samori and his lieutenants to see everything as an Anglo-French plot against them.

In February 1893 the French occupied the Sofa town of Heremakono, just a few miles from the most northeasterly part of Sierra Leone's boundary, and this quickly resulted in fresh disturbances inside the colony. By August it was reported that Sofas had crossed the border and a number of villages, particularly in the east, had been occupied. Much of this information was gathered by the SLFP and Captain Lendy, still as keen as ever for action and personal glory, painted as black a picture as possible while pressing for an expedition to restore order. He found a ready ally in Ellis who, using the experience gained during the previous year's operations, had spent a lot of time training the battalion in the art of bush warfare, and now wanted to put it to good use. The governor who perhaps had a wider view of what was taking place was not so enthusiastic, as he informed the legislative council:

> it behoves us to feel perfectly sure that we do not have recourse to hostile measures without sufficient cause. For my part, I should like to feel better satisfied as to what the actual state of the country is, and what the Sofas are really doing before such measures are taken.

The matter was referred to London and on 25th November, still against the governor's better judgement, the War Office sanctioned the mounting of an expedition under Ellis to restore order in the eastern region of the colony.

Plans had already been drawn up and on the following day two officers and half a company of the 1st Battalion were sent up the River Rokel, to organise a supply column of carriers at the police post at Matotoka in the middle of the country. It was also hoped by this to deceive the Sofas as to the true movement of the expeditionary force, four hundred-strong, which was shipped to Bendu near Sherbro Island over the next three days.

> From this point began a march which is in itself a remarkable achievement in respect of the natural obstacles to be surmounted. A road in Africa means something like a beast's path through grass: throughout the whole expedition the column marched in single file. The jungle, sometimes of shrub, sometimes of cane-grass, is as impenetrable to the eye as a thick laurel hedge: it thins slightly at the top, so that a man's head can occasionally be seen four or five yards. The country is full of water, and of the endless rivers that had to be crossed some were 200 yards broad and upwards.

On 16th December, after having marched nearly two hundred miles in twelve days, and having been joined three days earlier by Lendy and four dozen Frontier Police, the force established a forward base at Kommendi, close to the eastern boundary of the colony. Here Ellis formed a two hundred and seventy-strong flying column, made up from his own troops and some of the police, and set off with it on 19th December to hunt down the Sofas. They soon came across evidence that they were dealing with a particularly brutal enemy: 'Outside one of the towns was a mass of corpses, many beheaded, all with their hands tied', and all along the route 'the troops on their march would find here a leg, there a hand, or it might be a baby with its head hacked off'. Such gruesome sights had their effect on the soldiers:

> Previously they had been grumbling at the weight of their rifles. From [then on] at every halt men would be seen polishing them with any bit of grease available, and nursing them like babies ... An old sergeant came up to an officer and told him how in another expedition "he had sowed the seed of the Word with bullets and ploughed in faith with the bayonet," and meant to do the same among the Sofas.

For the next three days Ellis pushed northwards towards the village of Waima, stopping along the way to burn villages belonging to the Kono, who had allied themselves with the Sofas. As a result the column suffered repeated attacks, usually on the rear, from Kono fighters armed mostly with cheap and unreliable 'trade guns (sold at 7s 6d each)', but these were easily driven off. The march was not entirely one of unrelieved tension and horror, and one private at least managed to provide a diversion when, during a brief halt, he came across an orange tree in full fruit. Having devoured as many as he could before the march resumed he soon began to feel uncomfortable, and at the next halt

> came to the doctor [Surgeon-Major Morgan] with a tragic tale. "His belly cut him bad". The doctor upbraided him with oranges, but he denied it indignantly: "Swah, sah; not touch one, sah." The doctor said nothing, but administered a strong emetic, and, amid the jeers of his comrades, the unfortunate effectively confuted himself; and, once he was partially recovered, took to his heels and fled. "Dat man dam liar, sah; see him eat two dozen oranges."

Later, during one of the Kono attacks, Morgan came across the same man 'groaning and abject' and taking no part in the fighting, and accused him of cowardice.

> This rankled in his soul, and for the rest of the march he established his honour by hanging behind in the rear when the enemy were attacking, waiting at corners of the path, and discharging his Martini into a whole line of them. In the evening he would come and call upon his traducer to recant.

During the three-day march 'Numerous wounds were received, but happily none very serious'. This was due in part to the aggression of the repentant, self-appointed rearguard, moreso to the poor quality of the enemy's weapons, but most of all to the training Ellis had given his men:

> The orders were, that when firing began a halt should be called - the men to sit down facing alternately right and left: it was in the discretion of officers to pour volleys into the bush or let the men reply to individual shots. The lower part of the bush was so thick that neither party could see the other, and the steadier men remained longest in their position. When there were barricades, the procedure was to wait for the natives to fire, then fire a volley, and charge before they had time to reload.

By using such tactics the column reached Waima in the afternoon of 21st December with no more than fifteen men on the casualty list, and none of them in any serious condition.

Earlier in the month Ellis had sent messages to the nearest French outposts, warning them of his approach, but had no way of knowing which if any had been received. During the march he had gathered enough intelligence to know that a sizeable French force was active somewhere in the same area, and that it too had been in action. At Waima he now found a letter giving him more details of this force, and the name of its commander, Lieutenant Gaston Maritz of the *114ieme Regiment d'Infanterie.*

Maritz, with a detachment of about thirty *Tirailleurs sénégalais,* had been sent from the outpost at Kisidugu in November to reconnoitre the area around Waima, and to make treaties with the local chiefs in order to forestall the British in a region where there was as yet no fixed boundary. Before the arrival of Ellis and his force, whose exact whereabouts were unknown to him, he had entered into an agreement with a number of chiefs and, as part of the protection offered to them by France, attacked their Sofa enemies as and where he found them. On 22nd December, having been informed by his allies - who now supplied him with an additional force of over one thousand irregulars - that Waima had been occupied by a large group of Sofas, he decided to mount an attack the next morning before daybreak.

And so the inglorious 'Waima incident' took place. Ellis's sentries and Maritz's scouts probably opened fire on each other at the same moment, each side shooting at suspicious noises or vague movements in the dark. Within a few minutes the rest of the startled British force had joined in, convinced the encampment was under attack by Sofas. Although both sides soon began to have doubts about the identity of their opponents, the rate and type of fire and the quality of marksmanship being inconsistent with what they knew of the Sofas, the battle continued for forty minutes before dawn allowed them to see what was happening. By the time it was over the fight had cost the WIR two officers, a sergeant-major and nine privates killed, and another sergeant-major and nine men severely wounded. The SLFP who were not so well disciplined or trained had responded badly when the attack began. The new recruits among them had panicked in the initial confusion, and had shot and killed not only two of their own number but also their commanding officer. Poor Captain Lendy, so hellbent on fame and glory, shot down by his own men in the back of beyond before he was even twenty-five years old. The French fared just as badly: Lieutenant Maritz was so badly wounded that he died within an hour of being found by a scouting party sent out by Ellis, and the bodies of ten of his *Tirailleurs* were discovered. All the dead, French and British, were buried together just outside the village.

The shattered column resumed its march on 26th December, following the trail of the Sofas who had moved further into the colony and established themselves at Bagbwema on the River Sewa. Considerably hampered by the injured and a general shortage of rations, it took the column nearly a week to traverse about forty miles through country which had been totally laid to waste. During the march Ellis exposed an aspect of his character which until then may not have been apparent to the men under his command. As they approached Bagbwema they

> saw proofs of tenderness in him which seemed almost inconsistent with that hard and stern nature. He was very fond of children; and at two or three points little black babies, deserted by their mothers, were found along the path. Colonel Ellis picked up the little creatures and carried them along himself, trying to keep life in them till some native woman was found to take them in charge.

Such sights only made the troops even more determined to exact revenge on the Sofas when the opportunity arose, and it came when they reached Bagbwema on 1st January. Over seven hundred warriors had barricaded themselves in with the usual stockade, but had made no proper arrangements for its defence, and were oblivious of danger. Having disposed his forces, Ellis attacked before sunrise the next day, taking the stronghold completely by surprise. A few Sofas offered some resistance as troops broke in, but the majority tried to bolt into the surrounding bush only to find more troops waiting for them. Over two hundred were killed, and another eighty were taken prisoner, while the remainder headed back towards French territory.

Once the town had been cleared some four or five hundred of the Sofas' captives, mostly women and children waiting to be sold into slavery, were released - only to become 'a frightful addition to the troubles already existing'. Hardly any food was found and, as his men were already on half-rations, Ellis had nothing to spare for them or for his Sofa prisoners. He was left with little alternative but to head for the nearest SLFP outpost, about twenty five miles to the south at Tungea.

> Messengers were immediately sent out to order up provisions to this place, but the three days' march thither was a matter of terrible trial, and the nature of the bush which the hospital party had to hack through increased the labour ... The route lay through marshy ground, the worst met in the whole expedition, and the weather was rainy. From Waima to Tungea, except while halted [for three days] at Bagbwema, the men slept in the open, and on four nights under tropical rain.

This foretaste of purgatory ended when they reached the police post on 8th January. A day or two later, after being reprovisioned and after turning over the Sofa prisoners to a local chief 'to do as he pleased with', the column resumed its march to the west. This time its destination was Matotoka, the outpost still occupied by the detachment of troops Ellis had sent there at the very beginning of the expedition. There is no record of what took place when the column met up with this detachment, but it requires no effort to envisage the scene, nor to guess at the kind of remarks passed between the men of Ellis's bedraggled cavalcade and the well-fed, neatly uniformed fellows lined up to greet them.

The campaign ended on 21st January with the return of the force to Freetown. In spite of the losses incurred, not to mention the unfortunate affair at Waima, it had achieved its objective. Samori and his Sofas were never again a serious threat to the colony; instead they concentrated their efforts further inland against the French, whom they fought until Samori was captured and sent into exile in 1898.

Within a month of his return to Freetown Colonel Ellis's exertions in the field caught up with him, and he had to be invalided to the Canary Islands. His death there on 5th March deprived him of the knighthood for which he had been recommended, and the regiment of one of its finest commanding officers. Although superficially a typical, rather arrogant Victorian army officer, he had interests and a sensibility which enabled him to, if not completely overcome, at least greatly modify, many of the prejudices which were common among his contemporaries both in the services and in civilian life. For a professional soldier who was only forty-two years old when he died he was a prolific author, and six out of his seven books deal with West African subjects (the seventh was his *History of the First West India Regiment*). While some of these volumes contain a great deal of ridicule and abuse directed at Africans, 'noble savages', 'black gentlemen' and all the rest, they contain just as much about colonial officials, traders, naval officers and missionaries: his sardonic sense of humour was far-reaching and, for his day and age, surprisingly colour-blind. If today he would be accused of paternalism in his dealings with the troops under his command, his interest in their welfare, appreciation of their individuality, and ready praise for their achievements in the field, were not sentiments expressed by too many other WIR officers at the time, or come to that, at any other time. Although it was physical ailments, brought on by the Sofa expedition, which ended Ellis's life, there were several disturbances to his peace of mind in Freetown during February which probably assisted in hastening his end. The start of a long series of recriminations about the Waima incident was one; the outbreak of more trouble in the Gambia was another.

Following the destruction of Toniataba in 1892 one company of the WIR had remained in the colony to back up the Gambia police in the event of more disturbances. Their services were not needed until the beginning of 1894 when traders passing through Kombo, the state on the southern side of the Gambia River entrance, began to be stopped and robbed on the orders of a local chief, Fodi Silla. His ignoring of the administrator's demands in early February for this to stop had the inevitable result: the organising of an expedition to destroy his four principal towns. This was mounted by the Royal Navy with only nominal WIR assistance, and proved entirely unsuccessful. One town was destroyed, but the attack on one of the others failed with the loss of thirteen dead and forty wounded, and ended in an ignominious withdrawal.

A second attempt was made on 1st March, after the arrival from Freetown of another three hundred men of the 1st Battalion WIR, accompanied by two seven-pounders, a Maxim machine-gun and a supply of rockets, by a force under the command of Major Fairtlough of the Royal Artillery (Ellis having been invalided by this time). Within a week all four towns had been destroyed and Fodi Silla driven over the border into French territory to avoid being captured. Kombo was afterwards incorporated into the colony.

The remainder of the 1st Battalion's tour of duty in West Africa passed without incident, but the troops must have been relieved in more than one sense when the 2nd Battalion, under Lieutenant-Colonel James Caulfeild, took over in February 1895. The early death of Colonel Ellis had brought about a similar sort of change-round among the regiment's senior officers prior to this. At the time of Ellis's death the 1st Battalion's second lieutenant-colonel, Charles Dale, was junior to his opposite number in the 2nd Battalion, Arthur Bosworth, so it was the latter who was appointed in Ellis's place. The vacancy for a lieutenant-colonel this then created in the 2nd Battalion was filled by Major George Madden from the 1st Battalion. These changes may have had the beneficial effect of creating a more united regiment, but both officers were singularly ill-fated: Madden was to be put on half-pay due to ill-health in 1895, and Bosworth was to die in the field three years later.

CHAPTER 15
THE INFLUENCE OF THE BRITISH FLAG

> Thus ended the [Ijebu] campaign. In five days a force of several thousand men had been routed, a walled town of four miles in circumference, containing a population of at least 15,000, had been captured, and a thickly-populated territory of 8,000 square miles had been brought under the influence of the British flag. All this had been accomplished by a force of little over four hundred native troops (including auxiliaries) led by sixteen Europeans.
>
> **Lieutenant F J Davies (1892)**

Lieutenant-Colonel George Madden's premature retirement for reasons of ill-health in 1895 was brought about largely through his exertions during his last tour of duty with the 1st Battalion. After having had his life saved by Lance-Corporal Gordon in the Gambia in March 1892 he had returned to Sierra Leone just in time to be sent on another expedition on a quite different part of the coast.

Lagos, which had been a separate Crown Colony since 1886, had by this time been increased in size by the addition of the Oil Rivers Protectorate around the delta of the River Niger. This was connected to the island of Lagos by a narrow strip of land between the sea and an extensive lagoon, which historically was part of Ijebu, the large and ancient state which controlled the trade routes from the coast to the interior. In 1892, after the Ijebu had closed these routes and then 'insulted' the acting governor of Lagos by refusing to discuss their reopening, approval was obtained from London for military action to exact retribution and to enforce free trade.

As the only force available in Lagos was the five hundred-strong Royal Niger Company Constabulary, commonly called the Lagos Hausas, of whom barely a third could be spared for an expedition, approval was also given for reinforcements to be obtained from the other West African colonies. In April the Lagos Hausas were joined by one hundred and fifty men of the Gold Coast Constabulary and about a hundred Ibadans, a traditional enemy of the Ijebu, who were armed and enrolled as auxiliaries. Command of the expedition was given to Colonel Francis Scott, the inspector-general of the Gold Coast Constabulary, because he was senior to the officer holding a similar appointment with the Lagos Hausas. On 20th April Scott was joined by seven special service officers who had been rushed out from England to provide him with a staff, and three days later several of these began to reconnoitre landing places on the north shore of the lagoon, By the time Major Madden with three more officers and one company of the 1st Battalion WIR arrived on 9th May to complete the force, all the necessary preparations had been made.

The entire force, complete with three seven-pounders, three machine-guns and two rocket troughs, embarked in a collection of small vessels on 12th May, to be transported through the lagoon to the chosen landing place at Epe. That this town was more or less due south of the Ijebu capital, Ijebu Ode, was about all the intelligence available to Colonel Scott as he stepped ashore the next day. 'The immediate task', one of the special service officers, Lieutenant Davies of the Grenadier Guards, wrote later

> was the occupation of Jebu Ode and, if possible, the capture of the King. Of several roads leading from the shore of the lagoon ... that from Epe had been selected because it was a 'fetish' or sacred road along which no white man had ever been allowed to pass ... It was difficult to ascertain the exact distance from Epe to Jebu Ode. The road was known to pass through bush throughout its length, and to cross several streams. Guides were obtained at Lagos and Epe.
>
> Opinions differed as to the active opposition that might be offered, but the Jebus were not supposed to be a fighting race.

At Epe, after more carriers had been obtained to increase the total to well over five hundred, Madden was ordered to leave part of the WIR contingent, one officer and a dozen men, in the town to secure that end of the expedition's line of communication. As a colonial official Scott was anxious to prove that the Gold Coast and Lagos police were fully capable of taking on the job by themselves; and as an officer who had served under Wolseley against the Asante in 1874 and imbibed many of the great man's opinions, he had very little time for the WIR. One way of showing it was to reduce a section to mundane guard duties at Epe. Another was to make sure the rest of Madden's company were given no chance to upstage the Hausas who formed both his own and the Lagos constabularies. When the force moved out on 16th May the men of the

WIR were stuck firmly in the main body along with the artillery, 'ammunition reserve, stretcher, baggage, [and] cattle', while the Gold Coast and Lagos Hausas alternated daily as the advance and rear guard. The Ibadan irregulars were employed as scouts.

After climbing to the top of the bluff above the town the force 'entered an almost impenetrable jungle, from which we never emerged until the gates of the Jebu capital [were] reached' some five days later. The track they followed was so narrow, in places 'worn down by generations of feet until it [had] become triangular in section, entailing a straddling position in marching', that it was impossible to proceed in anything other than single file in a column two miles long. Before midday, and while the rearguard was still only a mile or two out of Epe, it was discovered that the martial character of the Ijebu had been seriously underestimated. As the head of the column approached the village of Pobo it came under heavy fire from the surrounding bush, and nine men were wounded before the attackers withdrew. This then became the pattern for the rest of the march, with such attacks becoming heavier and more prolonged the closer the column came to the capital. At the Yemoyi River, about five miles south of Ijebu Ode, which was reached on 19th May, the Ijebu made their most determined effort to prevent the advance continuing:

> At the ford itself the river was nearly forty yards in width, and in some places four feet in depth; above and below it the stream narrowed, and disappeared into the thick bush, impenetrable to anyone but a born bushman, and strongly held by the Jebus, who were able to fire from a distance of fifteen to twenty yards without showing themselves. The Jebu position had been admirably chosen for their purpose; the thick bush on either bank of the stream completely screened their movements from view, and at the same time made it impossible for the column to deploy so as to bring a sufficiently heavy fire to bear; for nearly half-an-hour the fight was at a standstill ...

It continued until one of the machine-guns was able to be manoeuvred along the track, past a single line of soldiers unable to move in any direction more than a pace or two, and to be brought into action from the river bank. Under its covering fire the advance guard of Lagos Hausas started to wade across the river, only to waver as the hidden enemy opened fire on them, and then to fall into disarray as the officer leading them was shot dead. Sensing the possibility of a debacle Colonel Scott waded out himself and yelled for the WIR, who by now had been able to move up to the edge of the river, to take over and force the crossing. A few minutes later Madden and his men were up to their waists in water and working their way across the ford. Their example, as they continued in the face of heavy sniping until they reached the far bank, undoubtedly saved the day. The Hausas rallied and once they, too, had forded the river they joined the WIR in clearing the exit, helped belatedly by rocket and shellfire over their heads from the south bank. Attacks were made on the rear of the column as the rest of the force moved up to the river, but these were beaten off and by early afternoon the crossing was complete. The advance continued for another half mile to the village of Imagbon where, after the Ijebu had been driven out, Scott ordered a halt in order to attend to the wounded and to make final preparations for the assault on Ijebu Ode. Since leaving Epe the force had had 56 men killed and another thirty wounded. The Ijebu, at the river crossing alone, had lost about seven hundred men, but as their total force was estimated to be between five and eight thousand, this still left a considerable number to be defeated before the capital could be taken.

It was with some surprise therefore, the next morning as the column resumed its advance, that 'the word was passed from the advanced guard that a party of Jebus had come in with a flag of truce':

> Their message was soon delivered; the King, they stated, thanked the colonel for coming; by doing so he had proved him to be right when he said that the white man was too strong. The Jebus had been defeated; they were "no fit for fight with white man", and he implored the colonel to kill no more of them, and to burn no more villages, and offered his complete submission.

A few hours later Scott entered the capital, informed the ruler that 'he must consider himself a prisoner', turned the palace into the officers' mess, and appropriated all the surrounding buildings for use as quarters for the troops. Within a few days a flying column had been sent north to reopen the trade routes between Ibadan and the Ijebu kingdom, and at the end of the month Madden and the WIR were sent to open the routes to the southwest on their way back to Lagos.

Although the total casualty figure for the expeditionary force was high, the financial cost was derisory: as calculated by the Colonial Office the Ijebu campaign was conducted for a little over £4,600. In return the Lagos colony acquired what from the following year was known as the Niger Coast Protectorate, extending over much of what today is southern Nigeria. In September, long after had and his men had returned to Sierra Leone, Major Madden was awarded a well-deserved DSO. For his part, the expedition's commander returned to the Gold Coast as Colonel Sir

Francis Scott KCMG. Three years later his services in a similar capacity were needed once again; this time to lead an expedition against the Gold Coast's perennial foe, the Asante.

During the twenty years since Wolseley's campaign of 1874 the policy of the Gold Coast authorities with respect to the Asante had been largely self-defeating. On one hand the Asantehene was expected to be strong enough to keep the various tribes making up his kingdom in order, but on the other hand not powerful enough to pose any further threat to the colony. These contradictory aims had by the end of the 1880s produced a situation bordering on chaos. Instead of maintaining the integrity of the border along the Pra, the Accra government permitted refugees from Asante to settle in the colony, and took no steps to prevent dissidents based in the colony from raiding Asante territory. The Asantehene was then blamed for the subsequent unrest by the Gold Coast authorities, whose policies were the very ones undermining his power and prestige. Matters were made worse after 1883 when difficulty over the choice of a new Asantehene produced a state of civil war, which did not end even when a new ruler, the sixteen-year-old Kwaku Dua III, more commonly known by his nickname Prempeh ('Tubby'), was installed in 1888. Five years later the British government proposed he accept a British resident in Kumasi to assist him in running his kingdom, but Prempeh merely vacillated and the general state of unrest became even worse. Eventually, at the end of October 1895 and on expiry of an ultimatum, the Secretary of State for the Colonies authorised the formation of an expeditionary force to bring the Asante under British control.

Colonel Scott was the obvious man for the job, in spite of being over sixty years of age, but it was realised that he would be unable to take on the Asante as he had the Ijebu with just a handful of troops, and arrangements were made to supply him with a much larger force. The four-hundred fittest men of the 2nd Battalion of the West Yorkshire Regiment, on their way home after seventeen years in India, were hauled off their transport at Gibraltar and sent to Cape Coast. A Special Service Corps of picked men, drawn from twenty different regiments and corps, was sent out from England, and sizeable contingents of the Royal Niger Constabulary and the Sierra Leone Frontier Police were despatched from their respective colonies. Major Robert Baden-Powell, the future founder of the Boy Scout movement, was given the task of recruiting and training a large force of local levies. And finally, four companies of the 2nd Battalion WIR were sent from Freetown. By mid-December Scott had at

Cape Coast over two thousand two hundred troops, and was busy assembling the six thousand-odd carriers needed to support them in the field.

The men of the WIR had been transported from Freetown in considerable discomfort, the 2nd Battalion's luck with ships being no better than that of the old 2nd Regiment:

> It was impossible to find quarters for these four hundred men on an already crowded boat, so they had to make themselves as comfortable as possible with a single blanket on the decks, and down the forehold, which had been cleared for them.

One of the other passengers, whose racial prejudices were all too clearly recorded in the book he wrote after the campaign, became an instant authority on Westindian soldiers as he observed them from his own considerably more comfortable quarters:

> The scene on board was a striking one, with four hundred dusky warriors swarming over the decks, singing, chattering in pigeon English, and laughing as only a plantation nigger knows how. There is something particularly simple and childlike about the sons of our West Indian possessions, and when offended in the slightest degree they show their deeper character of cunning, cowardly brutality. Thus, while they retain their negro simplicity, they are strongly tainted with the curse of slavery that brutalised and crushed out every spark of manliness in their forefathers.

As such views and opinions were not confined to the journalists accompanying the expedition, and were probably not that far removed from those held by Colonel Scott, it is not surprising that when these 'dusky warriors' reached the Gold Coast they were instantly relegated to a support role.

Three companies were sent inland, along the familiar road through places like Dunkwa and Mansu to Prasu, to take over the running of the hutted camps which had been established as staging posts by the Gold Coast Constabulary. The remaining company, saved from such mundane duties, was permitted to join the expeditionary force when it moved out of Cape Coast at the end of December, but only as the rearguard. This proved equally unrewarding; the Asante were not prepared to fight a war which, in their state of disarray, they knew they could not win, and the advance of the force was entirely unopposed. The main body crossed the Pra on 5th January and entered Kumasi twelve days later.. By this time the

WIR rearguard was little more than an escort for the supply column, still one day's march away from the capital.

Scott was joined by the governor of the Gold Coast on 18th January, and two days later Prempeh and his mother made full submission to both men and placed Asante under British protection. The Asantehene, his mother, and a dozen other notables were then made prisoner and taken back to Cape Coast when Scott withdrew on 22nd January. The single WIR company was left behind as part of the Kumasi garrison, while the other companies continued to run the staging posts until after the rest of the expeditionary force had returned to the coast. All four companies returned to Sierra Leone on 9th March, by which time Scott was already in London, where he was a made a knight commander of the Bath and an honorary major-general, and the British troops had returned to their regimental depots. The Asante prisoners were kept in Elmina Fort on the coast for a while and then sent into exile in the Seychelle Islands, where Prempeh was to remain until 1924, twenty-two years after his kingdom had been formally annexed to the Gold Coast.

The last five years of the nineteenth century saw the climax of Anglo-French rivalry in West Africa and Joseph Chamberlain, who became Secretary of State for the Colonies in 1895, was determined to oppose French expansion wherever possible. The boundaries of Sierra Leone and the Gambia had already been defined, but a great deal of the hinterland of both the Gold Coast and the Niger Territories still remained to be grabbed. In June 1897 the governor of the Gold Coast was ordered to seize all the territory to the north of the Asante kingdom not yet occupied by the French. This was carried out by the Gold Coast Constabulary, with the WIR providing two companies to garrison Cape Coast, and later Kumasi, while it was being done. The operation ended with the acquisition of another twenty-five thousand square miles of land, contributing much to the outline of present-day Ghana.

Further to the east the French takeover of the northern part of what is now Benin was seen as an encroachment on the natural hinterland of the Niger Territories. This provided sufficient cause for Chamberlain to propose the formation of a 'West African Force' of a least two thousand locally-raised troops under British officers which, under the direct control of the Colonial Office, would be strong enough to resist this and any similar French moves. In the House of Commons in February 1898, while this force was still being formed, he gave as part of the reason for its creation:

> Whenever an expedition is required it is necessary to go outside for a military force. We have to go to the West Indian Regiments [sic], a most admirable military force, but as they are not natives of the country, they require in the way of transport and other particulars, very much more expense than anything that would be required for a purely native force ... Now if this force ... is established, and if it answers the expectations we have with regard to it, we believe that we shall be able, in carrying out whatever expeditions may be necessary to dispense altogether with the employment of the West Indian Regiments.

The West African Frontier Force came into being shortly afterwards when the first group of British officers and NCOs arrived in Lagos to begin recruiting, and was soon large enough to relieve the WIR of any responsibility for the defence of the Protectorate of Southern Nigeria (as the colony became in 1900) and the Gold Coast. This was just as well as for the next few years the regiment was fully engaged in the other two West African colonies and other parts of the world.

In London in 1897, at much the same time as the creation of the WAFF was being debated, authorisation was given to raise a third battalion of the WIR in order to provide the garrison of St Helena. This island in the South Atlantic had been a British possession since the seventeenth century, and had a history of plantations and slavery very similar to that of the Westindian islands. Until the opening of the Suez Canal in 1869 it had been an important port of call for ships bound for India and the Far East. Since that date the number of ships calling at the island had decreased steadily and the life of the British troops forming the garrison had grown ever more tedious and unrewarding. By 1897 to those busy reforming the army under the new commander-in-chief, Field Marshall Wolseley, and who like him had little time for the WIR, it probably seemed that St Helena and the regiment were made for each other. Events were soon to prove otherwise, but not before the headquarters and two companies of the 3rd Battalion had taken up residence in the island early in 1898. At the same time as this battalion was moving into camp on the exposed and ominously-named Deadwood Plain beyond Jamestown, the capital of St Helena, the 2nd Battalion, which had had its return to Jamaica cancelled 'in consequence of the unsettled state of affairs on the West Coast of Africa', was assisting the WAFF in resisting French encroachment on the territory of what was to become Nigeria; while the 1st Battalion had arrived in Sierra Leone just in time to fight a full-scale war.

The Sierra Leone Protectorate, reaching inland to the boundaries of the modern state, had been declared by Britain in August 1896, much to the resentment of many of the chiefs of the interior. This discontent, brought about by the prohibition of slave ownership and slave-dealing, was turned to anger by the announcement of a hut tax of five shillings a year which was to be levied from 1898. Although intended to pay for the administration and development of the interior of the colony (albeit with the ulterior motive of forcing tribesmen onto the labour market) this was not explained to the chiefs, nor were they consulted about the effect it would have on their people. As a result, attempts to collect the tax at the start of 1898 met with widespread resistance, and outbreaks of violence.

In February an attempt was made to collect the tax in Kasse, the state ruled by Bai Bureh, the chief who had assisted Ellis and the 1st Battalion WIR in the Tambi expedition six years earlier. Under Bai Bureh's instructions the property owners of Kasse refused to pay, and attacked the members of the SLFP sent to escort the tax-gatherers. This rapidly escalated into a general uprising, and

> if Bureh was an unusually smart man, so did the Temne prove to be in the events that followed. Savages they might be, but even in their very fighting they betrayed such admirable qualities as are not always to be found in the troops of the 'civilised' nations. They loved their chief, and remained loyal to him to the very last, whilst they 'understood bush-fighting as well as you and I do our alphabet'.

As a result, before the end of the month the WIR was engaged in a war which was going to involve 'some of the most stubborn fighting that has been seen in West Africa', and which was to drag on for several months as 'no such continuity of opposition had at any previous time been experienced on this part of the coast'.

To begin with, operations were concentrated on establishing and maintaining a permanent garrison at Karene in the middle of the disaffected region, from where Bai Bureh and his followers could be attacked. On 25th February one company of the 1st Battalion under Major Richard Norris, with one seven-pounder and a Maxim machine-gun, together with some five hundred carriers, entered the deserted town from the west, having entered the district from the Great Scarcies river. Martial law was proclaimed and six days later Norris set off with his column to secure a more direct line of communication with Freetown through Port Loko on a branch of the Rokel river. During the forced march of nearly thirty miles the column suffered repeated attacks, and had two officers, eight soldiers and twelve carriers wounded. In retaliation Norris burned nine villages and shelled three others. From Port Loko he sent word to his commanding officer, Lieutenant-Colonel Arthur Bosworth, that reinforcements were required, specifying the need for both Karene and Pork Loko to be held while other troops took to the field to hunt down Bai Bureh. The sad pattern of West African warfare - the picking-off of hot and bothered soldiers by hidden, poorly-armed 'war-boys', being countered by the wholesale destruction of towns and villages during a short, sharp punitive expedition - seemed all set to be repeated once again.

But it was not to be so simple. Learning from his experiences as a British ally in times gone by Bai Bureh had realised that his men could never fight on equal terms with British troops armed with rifles, rockets and machine-guns. His only chance lay in properly directed guerilla warfare, in avoiding direct confrontation, in concentrating his fire-power on the officers leading the troops, and in utilising the Temne skill in rapidly constructing elaborate stockades. The first WIR reinforcements arrived at Port Loko on 5th March, but it was not until 10th April that complete control over the road to Karene was established. During this period yet more troops arrived, and flying columns as well as heavily-escorted files of carriers travelled repeatedly between the two towns in an attempt to secure the line of communication and to provision the Karene garrison. All this marching and countermarching along 'a narrow bush path, never more than three to six feet broad, both sides lined with an invisible foe', and frequently blocked by stockades made from huge logs and boulders placed in groups to provide mutual support and virtually impervious to gunfire, resulted in the steady loss of both officers and men, demoralisation of the carriers, and acute frustration for all concerned.

On 19th March Bosworth, greatly dissatisfied with the slow progress and alarmed by the casualty rate, arrived at Port Loko to take command in the field. A portly, overweight officer who, unlike Norris and several other of his company commanders, had no experience of bush warfare, he was able to do little to improve the situation. Eight days after taking the field, while attempting to clear the road with one hundred 'specially picked men' marching 'with as little impedimenta as possible' and four other officers, he collapsed and died from heat apoplexy.

> The situation in the Kassi country was now grave indeed. The hunted chief was no nearer being caught than he was [at] the commencement of hostilities, while his warriors were in evidence everywhere ... Since February we had been actively engaged against an adversary whom we did not often see, but whom we knew could see us, and who shadowed our every

> movement. The nerves of the officers and men were severely shaken by this, one of the most trying modes of warfare, and the deadly climate, worse even then the enemy's bullets, was eating into the constitutions of Europeans and natives alike, who by this time, owing to the constant strain of sleepless nights, incessant fatigue, bad food, and severe heat, were in anything but a healthy and sound condition.

Fortunately, help in the form of Bosworth's replacement, was soon on hand. Lieutenant-Colonel John Marshall took over the battalion on 1st April, having arrived from England a day or two earlier. He immediately set about securing the Port Loko to Karene road by setting up two intermediate posts and organising regular patrols between them. The stockades were taken one by one and burned in order to prevent reuse of the logs, and any habitation anywhere near the road was ruthlessly destroyed. By 10th April a regular service of convoys of carriers to Karene had been established, and a few days later Marshall was able to begin extending operations into the surrounding district, and to restart the hunt for Bai Bureh.

Assuming personal command of a flying column 'Owing to the paucity of Regimental Officers' he set out from Kagbantama, one of the newly-established posts on the Karene road, on 15th April, and for the next twelve weeks conducted a smaller West African version of Sherman's 'March to the Sea':

> And now commenced a period of the most stubborn fighting that has been experienced in W.A. From this date the fighting was continuous and the opposition constant. Stockades there were everywhere, 20 of these formidable structures being destroyed in one day.

The column was on the road from daybreak until five o'clock in the evening, halting for half an hour during the morning and one and a half hours in the heat of the afternoon:

> These were the only halts. The remainder of the day was occupied in marching and fighting; it was no uncommon thing to have 4 or 5 fights during the day, while a day rarely passed without two or three.

Crossing and re-crossing Kasse and the surrounding region Marshall gradually restored order, not leaving one district for the next until 'the power of the rebel chiefs [was] utterly broken. Their prestige was gone, and most of them were fugitives, uncertain where to seek protection'.

'Rebel' towns were destroyed as a matter of course, but nearly every habitation suffered to some extent, often to the detriment of the troops as much as to the populace. Because of the onset of the rainy season

> the men were constantly soaked to the skin on the marches, and as they had no change of clothes, were obliged to remain in their wet garments; nearly every night the bivouacs were deluged with rain; it was comparatively seldom that the troops were sufficiently fortunate to sleep in towns, for if the last town attacked during the day was not set on fire by shell fire of the attacking party, it was frequently burnt by the enemy on being driven out, so as to leave no shelter for the troops.

In spite of such conditions, and of the problems connected with looking after the wounded, Marshall's pacification process continued day after day until the end of June, when weather conditions made further operations impracticable. Leaving the garrison at Karene with provisions for six months he took the column back to Port Loko and arrived in Freetown on 10th July. Although Bai Bureh's influence and leadership had been much in evidence during the previous weeks, he had been sighted by no-one on the British side, nor apparently was he ever in any danger of being captured.

His spirited, disciplined and well-organised resistance to colonial rule had had its effect elsewhere in the colony, and at the end of April some of the Mende chiefs in the Sherbro district had decided to follow his example. Their revolt took a rather different turn, with refusal to pay the hut tax being of less importance than avenging what were seen as the exploitation by local traders, the undue influence of missionaries, and the repressive behaviour of the Frontier Police. Many trading factories were looted and burned, and a number of government officials, traders and missionaries were murdered. News of this uprising reached Freetown on 25th April, complete with rumours of 'a host of armed war-boys' crossing the river Ribi only twenty-five miles away, others 'passing Songo Town and Waterloo' only fifteen miles away, and yet more intending to attack Freetown itself.

With the 1st Battalion WIR fully committed to what was by now called the Karene Expeditionary Force, and the Freetown garrison reduced to little more than one hundred and fifty men, 'the majority of whom were invalids sent down from the Kassi country', the situation was potentially extremely grave. However, just as Lieutenant-Colonel Marshall had arrived in the nick of time to pull the Karene Expeditionary Force into shape, so another officer now appeared to organise and direct the operations needed to suppress this new revolt. On 23rd April the officers and NCOs of a Sierra Leone version of the WAFF, called the West African Regiment, had arrived in Freetown. They had been accompanied by Colonel Edward Woodgate, who had been sent out to take overall charge of operations in the colony.

Woodgate wasted no time once news of the Mende revolt arrived. Two companies of the 3rd Battalion WIR had arrived from St Helena shortly before he himself reached Freetown, and had been sent to Port Loko to provide Marshall with reinforcements. One company was immediately recalled at the same time as an advance party of fifty men of the 1st Battalion out of the Freetown garrison was sent by sea to Sherbro Island. Another fifty of the less halt and maimed among the garrison were stood to and on 3rd May these, together with one hundred and ten men of the 3rd Battalion, all under the command of Lieutenant-Colonel Cunningham of the West African Regiment, joined the advance party at Sherbro and began operations to quell the rising. The Sherbro Expeditionary Force, as it was called, was soon reinforced by men of the Frontier Police and the WAR, as well as a considerable number of locals who did not support the dissidents and were known as 'Friendlies'. On 20th May a company of the 2nd Battalion WIR found its way into the force, having been sent from Lagos where they had been languishing for several months, long overdue for return to the Westindies. Finally, on 12th June, another company of the 3rd Battalion WIR joined, diverted from the passage from Jamaica to St Helena. The entire force remained in the field, with naval support in the rivers, operating in flying columns often only fifty or sixty men strong, until 10th July when it was judged all organised resistance had ended. The poorly-led Mende with their antiquated firearms were no match for trained troops with machine-guns and repeating rifles (the WIR had been issued with the bolt-action, eight-round .303 Lee-Metford in 1894), nor could their artillery match the columns' field-guns:

> The native method of firing their guns is very primitive; the gun, without any carriage, is 'layed' ... and is then loaded with a large charge of powder; the projectile sometimes being a round shot, but, more frequently, large nails, legs of iron cooking-pots, bits of iron rods, etc, are used. Besides these projectiles, piles of stones, gin bottles, etc, are in many cases placed on the ground in front of the muzzle, thus decidedly increasing the fire effect of the piece. The gun is fired by applying a lighted stick to a train of powder, seven or eight feet long, laid up to the vent, and as it sometimes happens that the gunner in his zeal has overcharged the gun, a burst is a frequent occurrence.

An account of all the marching, skirmishing, storming of stockades and burning of villages carried out by the Sherbro Expeditionary Force would serve little purpose. There were no particularly noteworthy actions, nor outstanding acts of heroism, although at the end of the day Major Cecil Morgan and Captain Horatio Russell of the 3rd Battalion did each receive the DSO, and Private J E Grant of the same battalion was awarded the DCM. For the men of the WIR the climate, the nature of the country in which they found themselves, and the lack of amenities, were probably all just as irksome as the enemy - if an incident recorded by Major Morgan on 19th May is anything to go by:

> the camp was roused at 1.30am by the firing of the enemy's *bundooks* ... the night was pitch dark, so that nothing could be seen but the occasional flash of the enemy's fire. Our foe, however, soon began to locate himself by shouting weird war songs, when periodical volleys were fired at him. Judging by the noise, the enemy were in large numbers ... our interpreter informed us ... Their chief was most energetic in his exhortations, and as our shots began to tell, he evidently had some difficulty in getting his followers along, and ordered "the cowards in front, and the brave men behind". His generalship was somewhat of a confiding nature, since he shouted out his intended dispositions and plans in a loud voice, which considerably aided the task of the defenders ...

When the rainy season had ended four large columns of troops were sent 'by different routes through the whole of the Protectorate' in order 'by a show of force to overawe all the discontented elements existing in it'. Lieutenant-Colonel Marshall was given command of one, but all the troops belonged to the WAR, by then almost at full battalion strength, and his own men were not used. The WAR also had the honour of capturing Bai Bureh, who remained at large in the vicinity of Karene until 11th November when he gave himself up, running out of his hiding place as the troops closed in shouting, according to Sierra Leone folklore, 'de war don don'. He was taken to Freetown where, after much legal deliberation, it was decided he should not stand trial but be sent into exile on the Gold Coast. He was allowed to return to his homeland in 1905, where he died three years later, and where his name is now revered as that of a national hero. A total of about eleven hundred officers and men of the WIR, drawn from all three battalions, took part in the 'Hut Tax War', of whom 21 were killed and 108 wounded. Those that survived were issued with the West Africa Medal, and the regiment was awarded the Battle Honour 'Sierra Leone 1898-9'.

The progress of the WAR columns through the colony ended in March 1899, with any lingering signs of unrest having been stamped out, and garrisons left at important points. In Freetown, once Bai Bureh was safely in exile and adoring crowds no longer gathered outside the house where he had been detained prior to his deportation, life soon resumed its usual lethargic tenor. It took rather longer for the rest of Sierra Leone to return to normality, and by the time it had the 1st Battalion WIR had already left West Africa to take up entirely new garrison duties, having been relieved by the 3rd Battalion in November.

In the following year yet another conflict with the Asante took place, but one in which the WIR for the first time since 1823 played no part. This was probably just as well as the British losses, sustained by troops of the WAFF, the WAR and the Central African Regiment, were very high. Although the details are of little concern here it is worth recording that in the end the Asante, in spite of great courage, discipline and fighting ability, were defeated because they had no access to modern weapons like the machine-gun, and no leader clever enough to resort to guerilla warfare. As a result the Asante kingdom, which of course had already lost the Asantehene, was formally annexed as a British possession on 1st January 1902.

The only British West African colony which did not see any military action during the last five years of the nineteenth century was the Gambia. After Fodi Silla had been run out of the country in 1894 a detachment of the WIR remained in Bathurst for a year before being withdrawn. Their place was taken by a body called the Frontier Armed Police, but as these were recruited from among the inhabitants of Sierra Leone and heartily disliked by the Gambia civil police, they were disbanded after a few months. Thereafter all the colony's police and military duties were undertaken by the one hundred or so men of the civil police. These kept the peace reasonably successfully until June 1900, when an incident took place which was quite beyond their capabilities to deal with, and which led to men of the WIR returning to the colony once again.

The governor relied on two travelling commissioners to carry out the detailed administration of the country; reviewing the verdicts handed down by the chiefs' courts, supervising the collection of taxes, curbing any excesses among the chiefs, and arbitrating in land disputes; all of which they did under the protection of a small police escort. On 14th June, at Sankandi on the south side of the river where they had gone to settle a land dispute, a fracas brought about by an attempt by the police escort to arrest a man for showing the commissioners disrespect, suddenly turned into an armed conflict. In the ensuing fight both commissioners, all six of their escort, and a local chief and some of his people were shot dead.

The administration now found itself in the worst of all situations, with an urgent need to take action to restore its authority but with no means of doing so. An appeal to the other colonies for troops could not be met because of the Asante war, and the British government had more than enough trouble in South Africa to deal with than to be able to give much thought to a minor incident in a minor colony. News of the incident spread quickly both inside and outside the Gambia, and one man to take immediate advantage of the impotence of the administration was Fodi Kabba. This was the man who had been largely responsible for the trouble which culminated in the storming of Toniataba in 1892, and who ever since had been living at Medina inside French West Africa, stirring up trouble whenever he could for both the British and French. His rush to encourage other chiefs in the Gambia to resist British rule failed to bring about a general uprising, but his activities caused the stock of the governor and his officials to fall even lower.

No assistance was forthcoming until December, when half a battalion of the Central African Regiment, on their way from British Somaliland to join the rest of the battalion in the Gold Coast, were diverted to Bathurst. At the same time the War Office reluctantly agreed to four companies of the 3rd Battalion WIR being sent from Freetown. The combined force of about eight hundred all ranks, under Lieutenant-Colonel Brake of the CAR, embarked in three small naval vessels on 10th January, and was taken up-river to land at Tendaba and in Bintang Creek the next morning. By midday Sankandi had been taken and destroyed, many of its inhabitants killed, and a number of people identified as ringleaders of a planned uprising were taken as prisoner. The next day Brake crossed the river into Badibu and began a march through the country to 'show the flag', arrest more of the 'ringleaders', and to generally let the population know that the British, regardless of what Fodi Kabba might have said, were still firmly in control.

The march lasted six weeks before it was assumed all its objectives had been achieved, and the force returned to Bathurst on 22nd February. Three companies of the WIR were sent back to Freetown the following day. A month later, at the instigation of the British, a French force attacked Medina and destroyed it, killing Fodi Kabba in the process.

The fourth company of the 3rd Battalion was retained in Bathurst for another year. Their departure for Freetown in 1902, having been relieved by a locally-raised body of troops, marked the end of the regiment's association with the colony. The 1902 campaign in the Gambia was the last military action of any consequence undertaken by the regiment before the outbreak of the First World War. For the next thirteen years, having been relieved of responsibility for the defence of any colony other than Sierra Leone, the resident battalion in Freetown was able to enjoy just as peaceful an existence as its opposite number in Kingston had been experiencing, by this time, for as long as anyone cared to remember.

PART FIVE

FIRST MUST COME THE WHITE MAN

It is always judicious in Africa never to give the black man an idea that you seek his assistance against other white men, no matter to what race they may belong. Even with our soldiers, although we gave them to understand that we would fight if the French attempted to molest us in any way, we always spoke as if all they would have to do would be to fight the other black soldiers and avoided reference to their white commanders; and that the men thoroughly understood the position I am convinced. First must come the white man, to whatever race he may belong ...

Brigadier-General Sir James Willcocks (1904)

CHAPTER 16
KING OF FEMININE JAMAICA

> In Jamaica the Army is mainly considered as a prop to society. Among the whites the officers are in great request as dancing men, players at the game of tennis and possible husbands for fair daughters. Among the blacks the same applies to the coloured Tommy, except that there is no tennis ...
> In the daytime the young West Indian Army officer gets through his early morning work as quickly as possible, and then scrambles, schoolboy fashion, into the playing fields ... After dinner he becomes the social animal, and the messroom and barrack-yard know him no more till midnight. That is the life of the Army officer. It is dull and a little monotonous; but the young men make the most of it and meanwhile pray for leave and England.
> With the Colonial Tommy it is different ... He is the idol of the populace; especially on the afternoon of the Sabbath, when, after Church is over, he is permitted to parade at large in the brilliant full-dress uniform of his regiment ... that of a French Zouave West Indianised: and he is the King of feminine Jamaica.

John Henderson (1906)

When the 2nd Battalion WIR returned to the Caribbean in 1898 it was divided up to form part of the garrisons of three islands - Jamaica, Barbados and St Lucia - just as during its previous tour of duty in the Westindies. After 1891 when the garrisons were withdrawn from British Guiana and the Bahamas (ah, the Bahamas! Many a member of the regiment squelching through the West African bush preparing to storm yet another stockade while bullets flew around his head, must have thought longingly of his days in *that* peaceful colonial backwater ...) these were the only places left in the region in which the WIR was stationed. In Barbados and St Lucia, for each of which two companies were provided, the men shared barrack accommodation with a similar number of white troops. In Jamaica the white troops, who formed about a third of the garrison, were housed at Newcastle in the hills above Kingston, under the sort of conditions noted by the English historian James Anthony Froude in 1888:

> here in this extraordinary place were 400 young Englishmen of the common type of which soldiers are made, with nothing to do and nothing to enjoy - remaining, unless they desert or die of ennui, for one, two, or three years, as their chance may be ... They are not educated enough to find employment for their minds, and of amusement there is none ... Healthy the camp is at any rate.

The WIR barracks on the other hand were in Up Park Camp:

> In the outskirts of Kingston, upon the main road, one passes through a gateway into a great bleak open space of some hundred acres, toward the further end of which lay a double row of hideous, uncouth buildings ... They are the barracks of the negro regiment ...

wrote an American visitor to the island in 1890

> ...As one bowls along the road and out the gate at the further extremity one passes by a quaint square building, the only picturesque object in the whole horrid expanse. It is the guardhouse, and in the shade of the porch are three turbaned soldiers in tight shell jackets and baggy breeches, staring with dull curiosity at the passer-by.

But, regardless of the age and condition of the barracks, being stationed in Kingston did have its compensations. For the officers:

> when the full heat of the sun has smouldered into the early evening glow, the games begin ...A few will take a spin on a fast pony; others, it may be, will sail across Kingston Bay and take a surf bath among the palisadoes. But for the majority it is either polo, cricket, tennis, or golf. Golf for seniors, polo for the young subaltern newly joined, tennis for the older captains, and cricket for full lieutenants.

As for the private soldier:

> If he can get off for the afternoon; then he lounges into Kingston and plumes himself on the side walks to the admiration of the black and yellow girls ... His amusement is similar to that of an English Tommy in any garrison town, except that he does not drink so much ... He is popular among men and

> women alike, since the civilian men are conscious of a reflected grandeur when in company with a soldier in full dress.

Such popularity though was not completely universal, being greatly resented by the Jamaican police force in which 'Every constable seems to imagine that, socially and politically, he is far above the ordinary inhabitant', but whose calling made him generally disliked and whose uniform excited no admiration. This led to a lot of ill-feeling between the regiment and the police, and the 2nd Battalion had left for Sierra Leone at the end of 1894 still under a cloud arising from an incident which had taken place in June of that year.

As might have been expected it began with an argument over a woman, carried out between a constable and a soldier of 'A' company, and ended with an attempt by the former to make an arrest in order to save face. This led to the policeman being attacked by other members of 'A' company, and eventually to all those who took part being arrested and fined. The next day about fifty soldiers retaliated by smashing the windows of two police stations and fighting with groups of policemen, before being hauled away by regimental pickets. The affair was blown up by the local press into an incipient mutiny, and as a result the GOC Jamaica placed Kingston out of bounds to the entire battalion. This restriction was only lifted six months later, a few days before the battalion embarked for its three-year stint in West Africa.

The punishment was out of all proportion to the crime and, as the commanding officer, Lieutenant-Colonel James Caulfeild, later remarked in his history of the battalion, 'if the discipline had not been excellent, serious consequences might have arisen' and

> During this trying time there was an absolute absence of crime, the men taking their punishment, as it really was, cheerfully and without the least sign of discontent or insubordination.

To deprive an entire battalion of the opportunity to visit the relatives and friends they must have had in the city during the last few months before going abroad for three years was a punishment, and one which fell especially hard on some of the married men. Marriage for soldiers was still considered a 'privilege' and, as the number of married quarters at Up Park Camp bore little relation to the actual number of married men, lots of men had wives and children in Kingston.

These wives not 'on the strength' had a rough deal at the best of times, never more so than when their husbands were posted to West

Africa. The scene at Kingston docks when the 1st Battalion embarked in January 1898, as described in a letter written by a young officer, or something very much like it, must have taken place many times before, and there is no reason to believe it had been any different when the 2nd Battalion left at the end of 1894:

> We had a terrible time on the warf [sic] with the indulgence passengers. Only a certain proportion of N.C.Os & men is allowed to be married in a regiment. All *their* wives and children are entitled to passages when the regt. sails, but there is always a lot of men married without leave & their wives & children are not on the strength of the regt. Whenever there is any spare room in a vessel "indulgence passages" are granted to these people at the rate of 1/- a day during the voyage. There were numerous applications for these passages & the names were put on a list on the distinct understanding that the passages would only be granted if there was room on board ... when the "Spartan" came it was found there was none at all. All these people had shipped their luggage with the usual negro cocksureness & lack of foresight & when they heard they could not go there was no end of a row. They swarmed round the wretched embarkation officer, who had to do all his walking about surrounded by a crowd of howling women.

Although more joyful scenes must have occurred when a battalion returned from West Africa, the dockside at Kingston can have held few happy memories for the regiment. In another letter written during 1895 the same young officer of the 1st Battalion described another scene when one English battalion was being relieved by another:

The Leicestershires go in the same ship ... to the Cape & I am down to superintend the loading of their luggage with a fatigue party of 35 men of the W.I.R. It is rather rough on this regt. for they have to do all the fatigues for the white soldiers as according to regulations native labour is always employed when possible in the tropics.

This observation, recorded by an officer who throughout his time with the WIR in Jamaica was planning to leave it, and did so after only three years with the regiment, illustrates perfectly just how the men were viewed by the rest of the army and, it must be said, by the majority of their own officers. In this case, West Indian soldiers stationed in their homeland and quartered, fed, trained, armed and equipped to the same standard, and serving under the same regulations as an English regiment (which, because white soldiers had less stamina and resilience in the tropics it was believed, was cossetted in a hill station) were judged to be little more than 'native labour' - to be supervised by their own officers humping white soldiers' kitbags. Not much, it seems, had changed throughout the nineteenth century: the men of the 1st WIR were pulling and hauling for white soldiers in 1800, and their successors in the 1st Battalion WIR were still at it a hundred years later.

Towards the end of 1899 the policy with regard to the deployment of the regiment was changed once again. The decision to provide one battalion as the garrison of St Helena had been made without much thought being given to the views of the island's inhabitants, and their reception of the nucleus of the 3rd Battalion at the beginning of the previous year had been distinctly cool. For many of the 'Saints' the WIR was too closely associated with the mutinous St Helena Regiment whose officers, when it was disbanded in 1862, had mostly transferred to the old 5th WIR, and the British government was petitioned to rescind the decision. Fortuitously for both the regiment and the islanders, the Hut Tax War intervened and most of the 3rd Battalion went to Sierra Leone and never saw Deadwood Plain again. Once the war ended it was found politic to retain the battalion in Sierra Leone, leaving only a small detachment in St Helena. This released the 1st Battalion for duty elsewhere, and in November 1899 they arrived in the troopship Avoca to take over garrison duties in Bermuda, the small British colony in the North Atlantic.

The battalion's arrival was greeted enthusiastically by the black inhabitants, but with something less than delight by the sizeable white community. Among the latter, someone seeing the WIR full dress uniform for the first time referred to the men wearing it as 'booted roosters'. This derogatory remark circulated quickly, probably causing many a white lip to curl in a snigger, but in true army fashion was soon turned by the troops themselves into 'Bully Roosters', the affectionate nickname by which they are still recalled in Bermuda even today. Once the novelty of the appearance of the men had worn off the battalion soon settled into a routine very little different from that being carried out by the 2nd Battalion in Jamaica or Barbados; with ceremonial duties taking pride of place and all other aspects of garrison life seemingly arranged to avoid any interference with sporting and social activities.

All that ever threatened to disturb this peaceful existence stemmed from the South African War which had begun shortly before the battalion arrived in Bermuda - and that for not very long. In 1901 the British decided that Bermuda was a suitable place in which to incarcerate Boer prisoners of war, and the first contingent of what was to be a total of nearly five thousand arrived in June. They were confined on some small islands in the Great Sound and employed quarrying stone on one of them. As guarding and accounting for such numbers, scattered between so many camps, involved their guards in almost the same amount of discomfort and in endless routine drudgery, one would have thought that in the eyes of the Bermudian authorities this would have been an ideal job for the men of the WIR. But, no! Boers were white and the 'booted roosters' were black. And if black soldiers were only fit to act as baggage-handlers for white soldiers in peacetime, how could they be placed in a position of superiority over white soldiers, even enemy white soldiers, in wartime? The governor, General Sir Digby Barker, would have none of it, and the men of the Royal Warwickshire Regiment, who had brought the first shipload of POWs, were given the job, no doubt much to their chagrin. And undoubtedly much to the relief of the 'Bully Roosters', who were able to pursue their social activities undisturbed. (Boer POWs were also sent to St Helena where of course, from time to time, they came into contact with men of the 3rd Battalion. This caused heartache to the island authorities and furious resentment among the Boers, not used to taking orders from, but only kicking, the 'bleedy Kaffirs').

At the end of 1902, by which time the South African War had ended and all the POWs repatriated, the entire 3rd Battalion relieved the 1st Battalion in Bermuda, and the regiment ceased to have anything to do with St Helena. The 1st Battalion moved to the Caribbean, and once again the 2nd found themselves in Sierra Leone. Two years later the 3rd was disbanded and Bermuda joined the increasingly long list of places which the regiment had once garrisoned. The list was added to in 1905, with the withdrawal of all British troops from Barbados and St Lucia. From then on, until the outbreak of the First World War, Up Park Camp in Kingston and Mount Aureol in Freetown were the regiment's only two permanent homes. This period, a lengthy interregnum between the bloody little wars in West Africa and the immeasurably bloodier times which lay ahead after August 1914, was the longest continuous period of peace the regiment, or any of its numbered predecessors, ever enjoyed.

But, if there were no wars, there were other hazards. The ill-fated 2nd Battalion, apparently free at last of whatever curse followed them on board a ship, were resident in Kingston on 14th January 1907 when the city was struck by a long series of earth tremors leading to a severe earthquake. As well as killing more than a thousand people, starting a fire which burned for five days, and causing two million pounds' worth of damage, it also destroyed most of Up Park Camp. An English Member of

Parliament who happened to be in Kingston recorded:

> the West India Regiment lost two officers killed outright, seventeen wounded, twenty-four Native soldiers burnt to death in their Military Hospital, from which they could not escape, and nearly eighty others wounded, some of whom afterwards died. In spite of that there was not a single bugle call that was not sounded night and day in the regular routine and discipline. The Regiment took up its place and lined the streets, assuaged the panic of the crowd, removed the dead and did everything that any soldiers could do.

Both the city and the battalion recovered surprisingly quickly and life went on much as before. Every three years the two battalions crossed the Atlantic in opposite directions; the feelings of the one heading westward perhaps being the more cheerful. 'And now let us bid farewell to Sierra Leone', wrote an officer of the 2nd Battalion in the December 1911 edition of the battalion's magazine:

> It would be the merest affectation to pretend that we are sorry to be going to Jamaica. One does not regret Sierra Leone, except, perhaps, in the same was as one regrets an aching tooth after a visit to the Dentist. To exchange a country, where to fill one's spare time profitably, calls for the exercise of considerable ingenuity, where one must always be on the lookout for fever, and to which one dare not bring one's wife and family, for a land almost as healthy as one's own, where one can play all the games [ah, those games! where would the Edwardian officer have been without them?] of an English summer, and where one's wife and children can join their Pater familias; is this an exchange one can regret? We cannot think it possible.

The writer went back to enjoy a long, long summer in Jamaica, lasting for over three and a half years. When he returned to Freetown in October 1915 with the rest of the battalion it was to find that although nothing much seemed to have changed, in fact - as the whole world was finding out - nothing after August 1914 would ever be the same again.

CHAPTER 17
BLACK EUROPEANS

> The local natives of East Africa were puzzled by this battalion of negroes, indistinguishable in appearance from themselves, yet treated as white and speaking English. Its men came to be called *Wazungu Waeusi* (black Europeans).
>
> **Lieutenant-Colonel Charles Hordern (1941)**

Compared with other European countries Germany left it very late to start acquiring colonies in Africa, but from 1884 joined in the 'scramble' with a vengeance. By the time the First World War began she had four - Togoland, the Cameroons, German South-West Africa, and German East Africa - with a combined area of well over 900,000 square miles. All four were quickly invaded by Allied troops after 4th August 1914, and campaigns begun for their capture which lasted from as little as three weeks to as long as four years. Togoland (modern Togo) was invaded within a few days of the declaration of war by the Gold Coast Regiment from the Gold Coast which bordered it to the west, and by *Tirailleurs sénégalais* from Dahomey to the east, and was surrendered to these forces before the end of August. The conquest of German South-West Africa, undertaken by South African troops, required more men and took rather longer but was still completed by early July 1915. The campaign for the Cameroons took much longer and involved far more bloodshed, while that for German East Africa was still in progress after the Armistice had been signed in November 1918: the WIR were involved in both.

When news of the declaration of war reached Freetown it was no doubt greeted by the officers and men of the 1st Battalion, who by this time had been in Sierra Leone for over two and a half years, with mixed emotions: torn between the luring prospect of their approaching return to Jamaica and the possibility - given their proximity to two of the German colonies - of getting into action. The feelings of the officers and men of the 2nd Battalion in Kingston would have been equally confused, with the looming prospect of another three years in West Africa tempered by anxiety about not getting across the Atlantic in time to see some action in

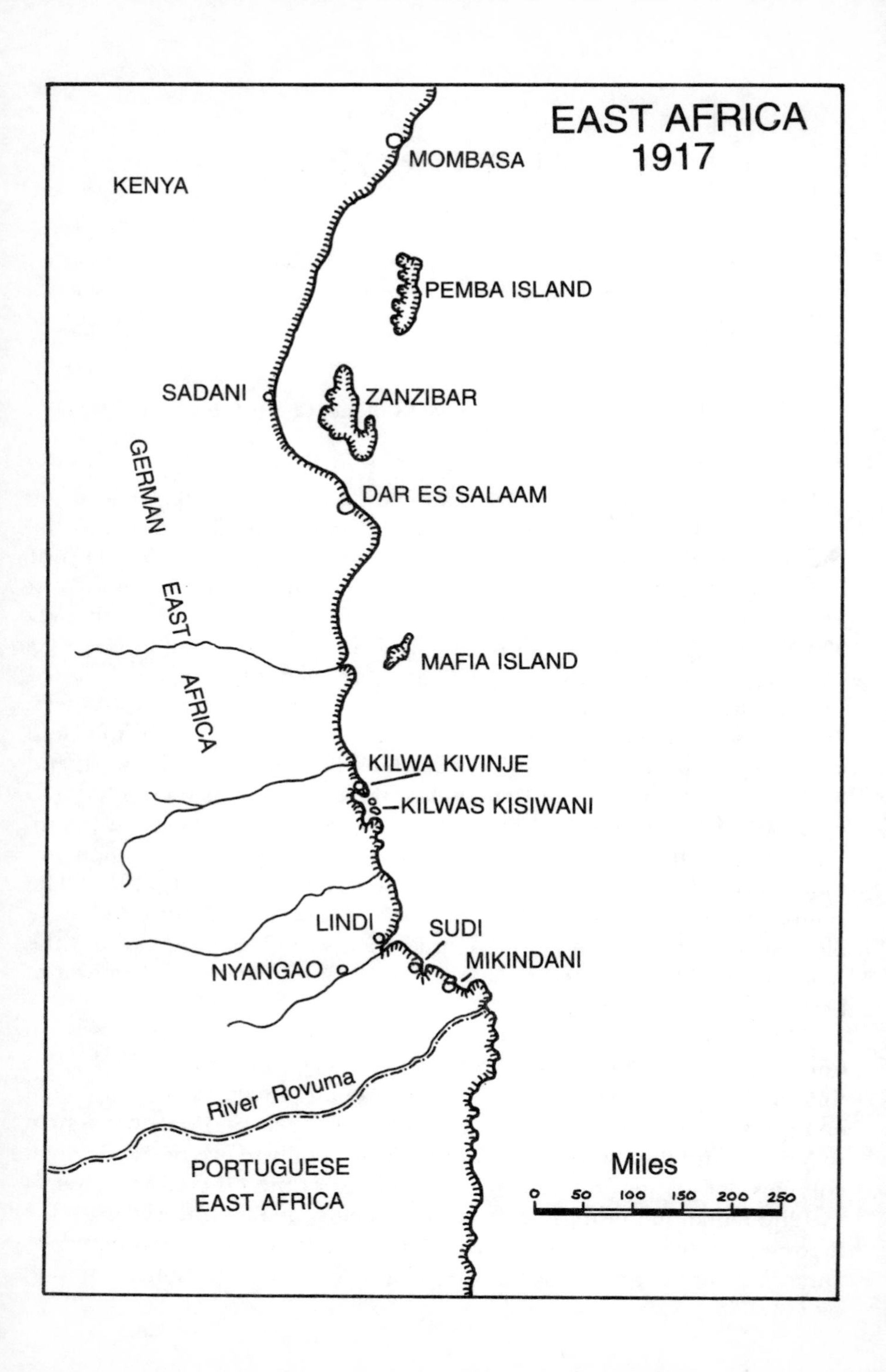
EAST AFRICA
1917
MOMBASA
KENYA
PEMBA ISLAND
SADANI
ZANZIBAR
GERMAN
DAR ES SALAAM
EAST
MAFIA ISLAND
AFRICA
KILWA KIVINJE
KILWAS KISIWANI
LINDI
SUDI
MIKINDANI
NYANGAO
River Rovuma
PORTUGUESE
EAST AFRICA
Miles
0
50
100
150
200
250

a war which, in the earliest days, was widely believed to be one which would be 'over by Christmas'.

Any worries either battalion may have had about there not being time for them to take part in the fighting were soon dispelled. It quickly became apparent that the war would not be over by this Christmas or next, or even the one after that, and that there would be plenty of time for them to take an active part. But ample time was one thing; what no-one could have foreseen was that neither battalion would ever be given much opportunity to fight, and certainly not at battalion strength. By 1914 the WIR had by far the longest experience of any regiment in the army of African bush fighting. In spite of this, and although such fighting was all that was ever going to take place in Africa throughout the next four years, official attitudes towards the WIR were going to prevent Westindian soldiers from ever playing more than minor supporting roles to less experienced and often less well-trained and less disciplined troops.

Things did not start off so badly. The Togoland campaign was over almost before anyone knew it had begun, and the WIR could hardly have expected to have been used, but the conquest of the Cameroons, situated between Nigeria and French Equatorial Africa at the head of the Gulf of Guinea, was a much tougher undertaking. It required the use of far more than the total of seven hundred and fifty men used in Togoland, considerable planning, and close cooperation between British and French troops to ensure success. The colony was attacked from three directions in September. A French force entered the country from the east, a joint Anglo-French force invaded from the north, and a larger combined British and French force landed in the south at the main port of Douala. The 1st Battalion WIR might well have expected to be used in either of the last two, but instead they were given nominal representation only in both. A small detachment of the battalion's signallers served with the northern force for about fifteen months, achieving nothing of any significance, before being sent back to Freetown through Nigeria in February 1916 and returned to the Westindies. An equally small group of signallers landed with the Cameroons Expeditionary Force, under Brigadier Charles Dobell, at Douala at the end of September. These played a slightly more useful role, with Private L Jordan earning a DCM and several other men being mentioned in despatches, before they were relieved by signallers of the 2nd Battalion in December 1915.

Four months earlier Lieutenant W H C Ramsden and the machine-gun section of the 2nd Battalion, sent in advance of the rest of the battalion on their way to relieve the 1st Battalion in Freetown, had landed at Douala. By this time about half the colony had been occupied before operations had been brought to a halt by the onset of the rainy season, and the German authorities and their main forces were concentrated at Yaounde, about one hundred and thirty miles east of Douala. When operations resumed in October the machine-gun section was attached to a column made up of the 5th Indian Light Infantry and part of the Gold Coast Regiment. After some weeks with this column in the field, the 2nd Battalion WIR machine-gunners were transferred to a composite battalion containing troops from Nigeria, the Gold Coast and Sierra Leone for the final push on Yaounde, which was captured on 1st January 1916.

Two companies of the 2nd Battalion, under Major E J Pomeroy, arrived in the Cameroons from Sierra Leone on 13th October, but instead of being allowed to take an active part in the campaign were left on the coast. For six days in November half of one company was sent to assist the Nigerian Regiment capture the town of Nkongsamba, otherwise all Pomeroy's men remained manning the Douala defences until the end of the month, achieving very little except to lose two men 'drowned bathing'. In December both companies were finally moved inland and took part in the final few days of fighting leading up to the fall of Yaounde. A week after this the German authorities with the remains of their army escaped over the border into the Spanish enclave of Rio Muni (modern Equatorial Guinea), and the campaign ended. In March France took over the administration of most of the Cameroons, leaving a narrow strip along the Nigerian border only in British hands. Later, for the part in the campaign played by the two hundred and fifty or so men of the WIR, the regiment was awarded the Battle Honour 'Cameroons 1914-16'.

In April with the whole battalion once again all together in Sierra Leone, the commanding officer, Lieutenant-Colonel C W Long, received orders to prepare the 2nd Battalion for a move to East Africa; to join British, South African, East African and Indian troops in the campaign for the fourth and last of the German colonies. The transport *Heneas* arrived at Freetown at the beginning of July and, after a three and a half week voyage around the Cape of Good Hope, the battalion disembarked at Mombasa in Kenya before the end of the month. On 5th August another transport moved them down the coast to Sadani, a small port in German East Africa opposite the island of Zanzibar where, once they had waded ashore with all their gear and supplies, they were in 'the fighting zone'.

The campaign had already been underway in the northeastern part of the colony for almost two years with the British forces, consisting mostly of Indian troops, attempting to overcome a much smaller enemy force composed almost entirely of the African troops known in this part of the continent as askaris. Very little progress had been made during the first year or more. This was due in part to the incompetence of a succession of British commanders (the first of whom, Major-General Arthur Aitken, had had much time to reflect on his early boast 'the Indian army will make short work of the niggers' as he sailed home in disgrace, having in his first crack at these 'niggers' achieved 'one of the most notable failures in British military history'), but equally to the brilliance of the German commander, Colonel Paul von Lettow-Vorbeck. In February 1916 command of the British forces had been given to the South African, General Jan Smuts, and the number of troops at his disposal greatly increased. When the five hundred and fifteen officers and men of the WIR landed at Sandani they joined at army of around one hundred thousand men. The port had only just been captured and an offensive was underway to seize the railway line which connected the coast with Lake Tanganyika, and to bring Lettow-Vorbeck to battle.

Having been reinforced with fifty men of the Zanzibar Rifles and a similar number of intelligence scouts the battalion joined a column being sent down the coast to secure crossings on the Wami River, a few miles to the south. This was achieved with no opposition and the column continued following the coast to the town of Bagamoyo, about thirty miles from Dar es Salaam, where it arrived on 18th August. Again no opposition was encountered; Lettow-Vorbeck, with rather less than ten thousand troops, had no intention of fighting anything other than a guerilla war, and had concentrated his forces further inland to delay the British seizure of the Central Railway. After two weeks at Bagamoyo the coastal column continued its march south, and Dar es Salaam was taken with no fighting on 4th September.

The ease with which the coastal region to the north of the city had been overrun now led to a decision to capture the rest of the colony's coastline. On 6th September the 2nd Battalion WIR was shipped two hundred miles down the coast to capture the island of Kilwas Kisiwani which guarded one of the finest natural harbours in East Africa. They landed the next day to find it deserted, but met some light resistance a day later when occupying Kilwa Kivinje, a town on the northern side of the harbour. The defenders, such as they were, soon disappeared into the hinterland, and before the end of the month the WIR were joined in Kilwa Kivinje by the 2nd Battalion Loyal North Lancashire Regiment, a battalion of the King's African Rifles, and half a battalion of the 40th Pathans. Together these were more than enough to drive off a German attack mounted on 2nd October, while the WIR moved another eighty miles to the south to take over the port of Lindi, occupied a few days before by the other half battalion of the 40th Pathans. Shortly afterwards the British occupation of the colony's coastline was completed when two companies of the 2nd Battalion WIR occupied the ports of Sudi and Mikindani, which were close to the border with Portuguese East Africa. The WIR then remained undisturbed, garrisoning Lindi, Sudi and Mikindani, until March 1917.

By this time the territory still under German control had been greatly reduced, and Lettow-Vorbeck was only able to operate freely in the southeastern part of the colony where, of course, his presence began to make itself felt on the coastal garrisons. One particular annoyance at Lindi came from the rounds from a 105mm gun which the Germans fired at intervals into the town. The well-concealed gun was one of ten removed from the cruiser *Konigsberg* after it had been sunk in a river much further north two years earlier, and which Lettow-Vorbeck's forces had made much use of ever since. In March, after the garrison at Lindi had been increased to brigade strength, moves began to be made inland in order to locate the gun and to obtain information on the whereabouts and strength of the German forces.

On 10th March a column made up of men from the WIR and the Arab Rifles found an enemy detachment at a farm a few miles inland and attacked it the next day, driving out the askaris and capturing a Hotchkiss gun. Other patrols came upon similar evidence of a buildup of German forces slowly taking place. On 22nd April fifty men of the WIR were used to reinforce a battalion of the King's African Rifles on a longer patrol through the Lindi hinterland. In five days they fought two fierce actions, the second after a long night march, before being forced to return to Lindi when it became evident 'that the young African recruits who now filled the ranks of the [KAR] battalion were none too easy to handle in action without a sufficiency of white leaders, and at this period the proportion of the latter was far too small for effective control'. While this column was in the field the small garrison at Sudi came under heavy attack. Fortunately the WIR were in well-constructed defensive positions and were able to repel the attack, but with the loss of two dead and one man wounded. The next day a naval ship bombarded the German position established just outside the port and forced their complete withdrawal.

In May the officer commanding the troops at Lindi, Brigadier Henry O'Grady, decided on a concerted effort to clear the enemy from around Lindi, using a force made up of a battalion of the KAR, the 5th Light Infantry, the Arab Rifles, the 27th Mountain Battery and the machine-gun section of the 2nd Battalion WIR. After only a single day in the field

O'Grady was forced to return, having been let down by a panic among 'the young soldiers of the reorganised KAR battalions [who] were not yet sufficiently experienced to engage [the enemy] on equal terms'. Three weeks later he tried again, this time with a much larger force and naval support, and with the added intention of capturing the *Konigsberg* gun. Once again the WIR were allowed only nominal representation, providing no more than the handful of men needed to man four machine-guns and two trench mortars. In spite of the great increase in the size of the force the operation was only marginally more successful. The Germans were driven away, but not before securing their gun and taking it further inland, nor before inflicting fifty casualties on O'Grady's troops.

During the next three months Lettow-Vorbeck and his forces, although never being brought to battle, were gradually pushed to the southeast and ever closer to the Rovuma River which formed the boundary of Portuguese East Africa. On 10th September General Louis van Deventer, who had taken over as the army commander in May, moved his headquarters to Kilwa Kivinje and nine days later began what was hoped would be the final offensive.

The only men of the WIR included in the British forces taking part were those making up one section of a Stokes gun battery attached to a column commanded by Brigadier O'Grady. This section performed sterling work, being in action almost daily from 23rd September. At the end of October, by which time their numbers had been increased, O'Grady found time to write to their commanding officer in Lindi:

> I want to write and thank you very much indeed for having helped us so much in the matter of the Stokes Gunners and to try and explain a bit how the situation stands as regards them. Although they are a detachment of your Regiment, they are also a portion of No 2 Stokes Gun Battery, in fact they now form 3 of the 4 sections. They have done jolly well up to date and I am quite sure the honour of the regiment is safe in their hands.

Two weeks before this was written the same gunners had taken part in what was to be the last major engagement of the entire campaign, and also one of the bloodiest. Now known as the Battle of Nyangao, it was fought near a settlement of this name about forty-five miles up the Lukuledi, the river which enters the sea at Lindi. Lasting for two days, the battle consisted of furious charges and countercharges between lines of trenches and dugouts, with all the gore and slaughter of such battles on the Western Front in Europe, but made worse by being conducted in the intense heat of the East African bush. At the end of the second day

Lettow-Vorbeck withdrew, having lost one third of the fifteen hundred men in his force, but it was hardly a British victory. Out of the nearly five thousand British troops who took part, well over half were killed or wounded. The WIR gunners performed exceptionally well; one man, Lance-Corporal Ruben Robertson, who two weeks earlier had already been recommended for an award of the Military Medal, displaying quite outstanding initiative, energy and bravery.

The Battle of Nyangao ended on 18th October. A little over five weeks later Lettow-Vorbeck and his remaining askaris crossed the Rovuma into Portuguese East Africa, where they were then pursued by the British and Portuguese without much success for the remainder of the war. The WIR took no part in this, the entire battalion remaining in or near Lindi until 4th February 1918, when they were shipped to Dar es Salaam.

The battalion arrived in the capital of what was soon to be renamed Tanganyika in extremely bad shape. Out of the more than five hundred officers and men who had arrived in East Africa eighteen months earlier, less than half were still fit to take up the garrison duties to which the WIR was assigned. While a number had been killed or wounded in action, the majority of those missing from the active roll-call were in hospital, had been evacuated, or had died from such causes as those which litter the pages of the battalion's war diary: 'Blackwater Fever', 'Enteric', 'Pneumonia', 'Double Pneumonia', 'Cerebral Malaria' and, of course, the most common, 'Malaria'. All of these ailments, and more, afflicted all the European, Indian and South African troops who took part in the campaign, but not those native to East Africa, nor those from Nigeria, the Gold Coast and the Gambia (these West African troops having been brought to East Africa at much the same time as the 2nd Battalion WIR). As the official history of the war records:

> the African troops on the whole, including the contingents from West Africa, had no undue incidence of sickness. Their European officers, moreover, had not only become acclimatized, but "knew the ropes" and in general had the benefit of the amenities and safeguards to health which experience has shown to be the necessities for the white man in tropical Africa.

In looking for a reason why this same observation did not hold true for the WIR who, to all outward appearances, were of an identical racial character to any of the West African regiments, one is once again - as so often in the history of the West India regiments - forced to consider the effect that reducing or altering the officer structure had on the wellbeing of the rank and file. Dilution of the officer strength, which was not that good to begin with, began soon after the battalion entered the campaign. Those that were wounded or fell sick were either not replaced or their positions were filled by junior officers from other regiments. Others were given appointments outside the regiment; the commanding officer himself returned to Jamaica in the middle of 1917 to take command of a battalion of the British West Indies Regiment (of which more later); and in August of that year the last remaining field officer, Major R R Leader, was sent to take command of a detachment of the BWIR elsewhere in East Africa.

After this matters went from bad to worse. Temporary command of the battalion was given to an officer of the Devonshire Regiment, who within a month had fallen ill and been evacuated to Dar es Salaam, and the majority of company and platoon commanders were young and very inexperienced subalterns from other regiments, none of whom with any understanding of, or rapport with, the men under them. The battalion arrived in Dar es Salaam on 6th February 1918 with only four officers, none of whom belonged to the WIR, and under the command of Temporary Second Lieutenant (Acting Lieutenant-Colonel) F P Cattlin of the Shropshire Light Infantry. The adjutant, the commanding officer's right-hand man and a key figure in the organisation and discipline of any battalion, was Temporary Second Lieutenant (Acting Captain, with pay and allowances as a lieutenant) H P Kettle of the Norfolk Regiment. Such officers, with their wartime only commissions, were far from being 'acclimatized', knew nothing of 'the ropes', and had little of the experience needed to safeguard their own health - let alone that of the unfortunate men for whom they had, at the stroke of some staff officer's pen, now become responsible. Given this situation it is hardly surprising that, as soon as their ship reached Dar es Salaam and Major J P Bliss stepped on board, the reappearance of one of their own officers was 'very heartily cheered by the men'.

Bliss, who had joined the 2nd Battalion WIR in 1895, assumed command as an acting lieutenant-colonel on 7th February and immediately set about pulling his severely reduced battalion into some sort of shape. He found himself beset with administrative difficulties: officers and men continued to fall sick and others died from wounds or illnesses previously contracted; a small group of temporary officers holding acting ranks and appointed from other regiments had to be instructed in the ways of the WIR and the Westindian soldier; and in the middle of April he found himself called upon to preside at a long string of courts martial lasting for five weeks. Things only began to improve at the end of May when Major Pomeroy, who had long been absent in hospital, rejoined as second-in-command. A month later no less than thirteen officers, mostly from Scottish regiments, and of all ranks from second-lieutenant to major, arrived for duty with the battalion. By the end of August, considerably heartened by the award of eight Distinguished Conduct Medals (including one for the indefatigable Corporal Robertson of the Stokes gun section), six Military Medals, and two Meritorious Service Medals for their efforts in East Africa, the battalion was all set to re-enter the fighting war.

It did not quite work out that way. In September the battalion was shipped to Suez, and then put in camp at El Qantara on the canal for a while before being transferred to Lydda in Palestine. Ludd, as it was then called, was by this time a major supply depot for the Egyptian Expeditionary Force, and an important point on the railway linking the Force with its bases in Egypt. The battalion got no closer to the fighting than this, being retained in Ludd on routine line of communication duties until the end of the campaign, which was only a matter of days before the end of the entire war. After this the men of the WIR remained in Palestine, standing guard over a mountain of unwanted stores and equipment while the demobilisation of the rest of the army went ahead, waiting for a ship to be made available to return them to Jamaica. Eight months passed before Bliss received orders to move his men by train to Egypt, where they found a troopship waiting for them at Alexandria, and it was not until 29th July 1919 that they arrived in Kingston.

As it turned out these men of the 2nd Battalion who had taken part in the East African campaign - for which the regiment was awarded the Battle Honour 'East Africa 1914-18' - were the last of the WIR ever to be in action. This was very appropriate in a way: their forerunners in the old 2nd WIR having been the first men of any of the regiments to be in action all those years before in St Vincent. But looking back, and recalling all that the men of the West India regiments did between 1796 and 1917, it seems they deserved better than to end the last war in which they were ever to fight engaged in humdrum guard duties dozens of miles behind the front line. Even the earning of yet another Battle Honour, 'Palestine 1917-18', was small consolation, particularly as the same honour was awarded to two battalions of Westindian troops who not only *did* take part in the fight against the Turkish army, but did so under the command of officers from the West India Regiment.

The return of the 1st Battalion to Jamaica from Sierra Leone in June 1915 had taken place shortly after receipt in the island of news that the British government was prepared to accept volunteers from Jamaica and the other British possessions in the Caribbean, to serve with the army in a unit which, from October of that year, was called the British West Indies Regiment. Jamaica alone supplied over ten thousand volunteers, and by the end of the war the BWIR comprised eleven battalions and two unnumbered detachments, serving in France, Italy, Egypt, Palestine, Mesopotamia and East Africa. Of these no less than seven battalions and the detachment in East Africa were commanded by officers drawn from the WIR. Out of the entire BWIR only two battalions were ever allowed into action, and then only during the last three months of the Palestine campaign. That these took part in any fighting at all was mostly due to the intense lobbying of senior officers carried out by Lieutenant-Colonel Charles Wood-Hill of the 1st Battalion, and to a lesser extent by Lieutenant-Colonel J H L Poe of the 2nd Battalion, both of whom had been transferred from the WIR in 1915.

The two battalions fought well, and recognition of this by the senior officers they served under at least allowed the BWIR to finish the war (and, as it was disbanded in 1919, its existence), if not in a blaze of glory, at least with considerable pride. Wood-Hill and Poe, who both won the DSO, achieved this with men who at the most had only three years in uniform, and who had received only the most basic military training. Who knows what they and the other officers who were transferred might have achieved, had they been allowed to lead the far more experienced and much better trained men of the WIR into action in the same way in East Africa and Palestine?

CHAPTER 18
THE TORN SHRED

> The money saved by disbanding the only battalion existing ... would deprive us of the last of a Regiment so gallant, faithful, and unique - a shred of material that would be torn from the very web, warp and woof of [the] West Indian story. Far better to keep the Regiment's continuity of existence unbroken, than to have to resuscitate it in the day which men of vision see, when there will be an Island Dominion of the British West Indies.
>
> **T H MacDermot (1923)**

The story of the West India Regiment did not end with the return of the 2nd Battalion to Jamaica in 1919, but it may as well have done. The majority of the officers who were serving when the war began, and who survived, never returned to Jamaica. Some had ended the war at or beyond retirement age; others were unwilling to resume a prewar substantive rank and to continue serving out their time in a regiment which had a reputation for notoriously slow promotion; more still had started new careers in the Royal Flying Corps, the Tank Corps or other infantry regiments; all reasons enough for none of them to set foot in Up Park Camp again. It was a similar story with white senior NCOs. Some had died from wounds or disease, others had served out their time, and one or two had been commissioned, so in 1919 there were not too many in either battalion who had been with the regiment before the war.

Then there were the soldiers. Recruitment had virtually ceased during the war, there being no possibility of recruiting outside Jamaica and very little inside, where all efforts were directed towards providing volunteers for the BWIR. When the two battalions were reunited in Kingston at the end of July 1919 the regiment was seriously under strength. By this time, too, the soldier's standing in the community had changed. He was no longer the 'king of feminine Jamaica', and his calling now gave him very little prestige among the male population. Many of the men who hung around the off-duty soldiers in their Zouave uniforms before the war, envying their lives and prospects, had by now had direct experience themselves of the military life. The vast majority of the Jamaicans who had rushed to join the BWIR had spent their time in drab, ill-fitting and uncomfortable khaki uniforms, living under generally appalling conditions, and doing nothing but hump artillery ammunition behind the Western Front. After their return to the island their distinctly jaundiced view of army life soon became that of Jamaican society in general.

In 1920, not as a result of changed attitudes locally, but more because of reductions being made throughout the army, the strength of the WIR was reduced to a single battalion, with Lieutenant-Colonel Bliss in command. He was by then one of the very few officers who could look back upon a career spent in the regiment. The role of the WIR was now little more than that of a Jamaican defence force, although a small detachment was maintained in Belize for fifteen months from July 1920, as a precautionary measure in the long aftermath of a riot which had taken place a year earlier. In the manner of most peacetime garrisons the main effort was soon being put into ceremonial duties. Not the least of these involved arranging the funerals of ex-members of the regiment, and a bandsman who joined in 1917 was proud to recall nearly seventy years later that no old soldier, whatever his circumstances at the time of his death, or however short a time he might have served, was ever denied full military honours at his funeral. In August 1922 what was perhaps the grandest and one of the most moving of such events took place, when Sergeant William Gordon VC died. He had spent his final years in charge of the Up Park Camp firing range, living in an adjacent 'grace and favour' property, and was widely known and respected both inside and outside the regiment.

The regimental band, although obviously much in demand at the grave side, also enjoyed performing in less sombre circumstances. During this postwar period, other than the detachment in Belize, the bandsmen were the only members of the regiment to leave Jamaica. In the same year that Gordon died the band spent three weeks in Toronto, playing at the Canadian National Exhibition. This participation continued a prewar tradition, begun in 1886, when the band of the 1st WIR had been sent to London to perform at the Colonial and Indian Exhibition. The band of the 1st Battalion attended a similar exhibition held at the Crystal Palace in 1905. The Toronto visit was succeeded by the last and longest attendance at such an event when the band went to London for six weeks in 1924, to take part in the British Empire Exhibition at Wembley. Accommodation for the band was provided in the barracks of the Middlesex Regiment at nearby Mill Hill. This was not entirely fortuitous as since February 1923 the WIR had been commanded by Lieutenant-

Colonel W Y Miller DSO, formerly of that regiment.

Miller had been appointed because by 1923 there were no WIR officers of the right rank and seniority still serving to make them eligible for the command. Outsiders had come and gone since wartime days, and by the time Miller took over he had subordinates drawn from seven or eight different regiments. All of them, doubtless, were efficient and conscientious; some, like the commanding officer himself, had served throughout the war and been decorated in the process; few if any, however, had previously been in charge of Westindian soldiers or had dealings with non-white troops. To make things worse, by the time Miller arrived it was already common knowledge in Jamaica that the regiment was under threat of disbandment. He and the rest of the officers would have been only too well aware that they were holding down nothing but short-term appointments which would do little to advance their careers. The situation from the soldiers' point of view could hardly have been less promising. They were now serving under generally antipathetic officers who had only nominal interest in their welfare, and for whom service in the WIR had very little to offer both at the time and in the future.

The voice of the editor of the *Jamaica Times*, Thomas MacDermot (better remembered today as Tom Redcam (his surname reversed), the island's first Poet Laureate), was one of the first to be raised in protest against any thought of disbanding the regiment. The words quoted at the head of this chapter, which appeared in an article he wrote for *United Empire*, the journal of the Royal Colonial Institute, may appear ridiculously quaint and bombastic more than seventy years on, but at the time his sentiments were shared by many in the Westindies. In the case of those in Jamaica who echoed his views, and were equally keen to refer to the regiment's long association with the island, it is ironic that most - like MacDermot himself - were direct descendants of those Jamaicans who had been so vociferous in opposing the admission of black soldiers into the island at the beginning of the nineteenth century. But, regardless of who protested and how, when or where, the future of the regiment was settled in September 1926 when Army Order 317 ordered its disbandment, specifying that this was to be completed by 31st March of the following year.

Within a few days of receipt of the order, Lieutenant-Colonel Miller wrote to the Officer Commanding Troops, Jamaica Command, requesting that 'on the Disbandment of the West India Regiment, His Majesty the King may be graciously pleased to allow the Colours of the Regiment to be deposited in Windsor Castle', something for which there were many precedents. In then going on to justify his request by mentioning events in the past which reflected to the credit of the regiment he may have helped his cause, but he also showed that he had no real grasp of the regiment's history: his assertions that

> the Regiment was raised as part of the Forces of the Crown in 1779 and immediately took part, on behalf of the Crown, in the American War of Independence,

and that 'it has served continuously ever since', both being untrue. He closed the letter by stating

> how very much the honour that I ask would be appreciated by all ranks. It would go very far, I feel sure, to alleviate the sorrow with which the order has been received and which is being loyally carried out.

Colonel Mudge, the OCT, in forwarding the request to the War Office with his endorsement, enlarged on this last point:

> Should the favour sought be granted I feel sure that it will go far to allay the sense of soreness felt by the Regiment and be looked on by all Ranks as a very real honour indeed...

before indulging in a little homespun sociology:

> ... I would also add that, in a way that the more phlegmatic Englishman who does not know the emotional West Indian, both white and coloured, can hardly appreciate, it will enormously strengthen the feeling of personal loyalty to the KING which cannot fail to strike anyone who travels as I do as having such a very live existence in West Indian life.

In London the proposal was taken up by the Secretary of State for War, the Earl of Derby, with the King's Private Secretary, Lord Stamfordham, and in November the Adjutant-General, General Sir Robert Whigham, was instructed to arrange with Lord Stamfordham the details of the handing over of the Colours to the King.

With such panjandrums as these now involved the matter took on an altogether different aspect, and no further mention appears in the correspondence which passed between the War Office and Buckingham Palace of any benefits which the ceremony being planned might have on 'all Ranks', amongst 'emotional West Indians', or on 'West Indian life' in general. By the end of the year any hopes Miller may once have had of the ceremony being something which might help 'alleviate the sorrow' felt in Jamaica about the loss of the regiment had been dispelled. He received orders that the Colours were to travel in the same ship which was due to bring him and the rest of 'European Cadre of the West India Regiment' back to England on completion of the disbandment. A 'short ceremony' would then take place a few days after the ship's arrival, at which the King would 'be pleased to see any of the Officers and Warrant Officers' who had not already 'gone off' on leave.

The disbandment was completed well ahead of time. The West India Regiment paraded for the last time on 31st January 1927 at Up Park Camp, at a ceremony attended by the Governor and Colonel Mudge, and a host of island dignitaries. The appropriate marks of respect were exchanged, the appropriate speeches were made, and the appropriate music was played. The Colours, having been trooped for the last time, were then crated ready to be shipped to England. The next day the *Gleaner*, the island's leading daily newspaper, printed its farewell editorial and rehashed the regimental history. The soldiers turned in their uniforms and arms before starting to look for work or, in a few cases, draw their pensions. Two dozen members of the band were more fortunate; they retained their uniforms and instruments and were transformed into the Jamaica Military Band, as part of the local defence forces. Having completed all the paperwork Lieutenant-Colonel Miller, accompanied by three other officers and three warrant officers, sailed for England in the SS *Patuca*.

The ship docked at Avonmouth in the middle of February, and two of the officers and two of the warrant officers immediately disappeared on leave. This left Miller with Captain R W M Webster and RSM N Morrison to take the Colours to London, where the hand over had now been arranged for the morning of Friday 18th February, and where Miller now had two days in which to scout around to find other officers to make up a reasonably-sized party to attend at the palace.

By Thursday evening he had managed to track down five who, although they all like Captain Webster belonged to other regiments, could claim to have had some connection with the WIR at one time or another. He also found one actual, but now retired, WIR officer who agreed to attend the ceremony, but who in the event failed to turn up on time. At 10.30 the next morning the Colours, which had been kept in the officers' guardroom at St James's Palace overnight, were brought to Buckingham Palace and handed over to King George V (afterwards being transferred to St George's Chapel in Windsor Castle, where they still hang). The King read a short farewell address, shook hands with each of the eight regimental representatives, exchanged a few pleasantries, and then brought the proceedings to an end. The whole 'ceremony' was over in less than twenty minutes.

This then was how, in the words of the King, the West India Regiment's 'nearly 150 years' of 'loyal and devoted services to the Empire' came to an end. A group of eight men wearing on their drab service dress uniforms the badges and buttons of no less than five different regiments, standing in a draughty anteroom of the Palace on a gloomy English February day, listening to a short, bearded man mouthing sententious phrases about 'your achievements during the Great War' being 'handed down to posterity', and 'your Colours' being 'held in reverence as the outward and visible sign of a famous Regiment'. His listeners were all white, and not one of them had spent more than two or three years attached to the regiment the ceremony was supposed to honour. Of the men who had made up the regiment, and whose predecessors had been responsible for 'Dominica', 'Guadeloupe', 'Sierra Leone' and all the rest appearing on the Colours; or of the splendid uniform they had been wearing since 1858; there was no sign whatsoever.

EPILOGUE

The 'Island Dominion of the British West Indies' envisaged by Thomas MacDermot, or something very much like it, came into being in 1958 with the creation of the Federation of the West Indies; comprised of all the British possessions in the region with the exception of British Guiana, British Honduras, the Bahamas, and the British Virgin Islands. Although the question of defence had been under consideration for some years prior to its formation, it was not until the very end of 1958 that the federal legislature got round to passing the necessary Act to bring a federal defence force into existence.

As a result, in Jamaica on 31st December, the 300-strong local defence force was paraded and its members informed in a message from the governor that their services were terminated:

> The West India Regiment will be established tomorrow [and] will absorb the greater part of the Jamaica Regiment ... The Regiment will start with the priceless heritage of regimental tradition and of military efficiency which it will inherit from the former West India Regiment and from the Jamaica Regiment.

The intention was good. The re-raised regiment would inherit the Colours, the cap badge, the regimental march, the trophies, and the officers' mess silver along with the regimental tradition. The plan to increase the numbers to full battalion strength by recruiting in the other member states, given the general enthusiasm for the Federation among ordinary Westindians, also seemed eminently practicable.

Unfortunately (and how often this word makes its appearance in the history of the Westindies), the 'men of vision' cited by MacDermot in connection with his 'Island Dominion' in 1923 were not much in evidence nearly forty years later. The Federation collapsed amid much acrimony in 1961, and the following year both it and the West India Regiment disappeared into history.

BIBLIOGRAPHY

Abbreviations

ASR	African Studies Review
BAR	British Army Review
BIFAN	Bulletin de L'Institut Fondamental D'Afrique Noire
BM	Blackwood's Magazine
CQ	Caribbean Quarterly
CS	Caribbean Studies
ERS	Ethnic and Racial Studies
HNMM	Harper's New Monthly Magazine
JAH	Journal of African History
JCH	Journal of Caribbean History
JHR	Jamaican Historical Review
JHSN	Journal of the Historical Society of Nigeria
JSAHR	Journal of the Society for Army Historical Research
JWAS	Journal of West African Studies
MCH	Military Collector & Historian
MM	Military Modelling
NR	National Review
RCIJ	Royal Colonial Institute Journal
RUSI	Royal United Services Institution
SLS	Sierra Leone Studies
USM	United Services Magazine
USR	United Services Review

Abbott P E *Recipients of the Distinguished Conduct Medal 1855-1900* (London 1975)

Ajayi J F A and Crowder M *History of West Africa Vol 2* (Harlow 1987)

Allen D M *Report of Indian Soldiery* (Belize 1887)

Anon *Proceedings of the General Court Martial in the Trial of Major John Gordon, of the Late 8th West India Regiment* (London 1804)

Anon *Sketches and Recollections of the West Indies by a Resident* (London 1828)

Anon 'The Mutiny of the 8th West India Regiment from the Papers of a Veteran Officer', *USM 275* (1851)

Anon 'A Further Account of the Mutiny of the 8th West India Regiment', *USM 276* (1851)

Anon 'The Sofa Expedition and the West Indian Soldier', *BM* (May 1894)
Anon 'Major Alexander Laing of the 2nd West India Regiment', *SLS* XVII (1932)
Asiegbu J U J *Slavery and the Politics of Liberation 1787-1861* (London 1969)
Aytoun J *Redcoats in the Caribbean* (Blackburn 1984)
Baden-Powell R S S *The Downfall of Prempeh - A Diary of Life with the Native Levy in Ashanti 1895-96* (London 1896)
Baker B G 'The West India Regiment' *USR* (March 1939)
Banbury G A L *Sierra Leone or The White Man's Grave* (London 1888)
Bolland O N *The Formation of a Colonial Society: Belize from Conquest to Crown Colony* (Baltimore 1977)
- *Colonialism and Resistance in Belize* (Belize 1988)
- and Shoman A *Land in Belize* (Kingston 1977)
Boyle F *Through Fanteeland to Coomassie* (London 1874)
Bradley T *The Humble Petition of Thomas Bradley Esq, Formerly Lieutenant-Colonel of His Majesty's 2d West India Regiment to the Hon. the Commons of the United Kingdom of Great Britain* (London 1834)
Brakenbury H *The Ashantee War: A Narrative* (Edinburgh 1874)
Brathwaite E *The Development of Creole Society in Jamaica, 1770-1820* (Oxford 1971)
Brereton B *Race Relations in Colonial Trinidad 1870-1900* (Cambridge 1979)
- *A History of Modern Trinidad 1783-1962* (London 1981)
Brereton J M *The British Soldier: A Social History from 1661 to the Present Day* (London 1986)
Bridges G W *The Annals of Jamaica* (2 vols London 1828)
Buah F K *A History of Ghana* (London 1980)
Buckley R N 'The Destruction of the British Army in the West Indies 1793-1815: A Medical History' *JSAHR* 226 (1978)
- 'Slave or Freedman: The question of the legal status of the British West India Soldier 1795-1807' *CS* 17 (1978)
- *Slaves in Red Coats: The British West India Regiments, 1795-1815* (New Haven & London 1979)
- '"Black Man" - the Mutiny of the 8th (British) West India Regiment' *JHR* XII (1980)
- 'Brigadier-General Thomas Hislop's Remarks on the Establishment of the West India Regiments - 1801' *JSAHR* 236 (1980)
- *The Napoleonic War Journal of Captain Thomas Henry Browne 1807-16* (London 1987)
Burdon J (Ed) *Archives of British Honduras* (3 vols London 1931-35)
Burns A *History of the British West Indies* (London 1954)
- *History of Nigeria* (London 1972)
Burton R G 'The Romance of a West India Regiment' *NR* 89 (1927)
Butt-Thompson F W *Sierra Leone in History and Tradition* (London 1926)

Capadose H *Sixteen Years in the West Indies* (2 vols London 1845)

Carmichael G *The History of the West Indian Islands of Trinidad and Tobago 1498-1900* (London 1961)

Carter S *Blaze of Glory: The Fight for New Orleans 1814-1815* (London 1972)

Caulfeild J E *One Hundred Years' History of the Second Battalion West India Regiment* (London 1899)

Chace R E 'Protest in Post-emancipation Dominica: The 'Guerre Negre' of 1844' *JCH* 23 (1989)

Chan V O 'The Riots of 1856 in British Guiana' *CQ* 16 (1970)

Chartrand R 'The Early Zouave Uniforms of the West India Regiments' *MCH* XXXIII (1981)

Chichester H M and Burges-Short G *The Records and Badges of Every Regiment and Corps in the British Army* (Aldershot 1900)

Claridge W W *A History of the Gold Coast and Ashanti* (2 vols London 1915)

Coke T *A History of the West Indies* (3 vols London 1808-1811)

Cook H *The Battle Honours of the British & Indian Armies 1662-1982* (London 1987)

Creagh O and Humphris E M (Eds) *The VC and DSO* (3 vols London n.d.)

Cribbs W D 'The Royal Africans' *MM* (April 1991)

- 'Campaign Dress of the West India Regiments' *JSAHR* 283 (1992)

Crooks J J *A History of the Colony of Sierra Leone* (Dublin 1903)

- *Records Relating to the Gold Coast Settlements from 1750 to 1874* (Dublin 1923)
- *Historical Records of the Royal African Corps* (Dublin 1925)

Crowder M (Ed) *West African Resistance: The Military Response to Colonial Occupation* (London 1971)

- *Colonial West Africa: Collected Essays* (London 1978)

Cundall F *Jamaica's Part in the Great War 1914-1918* (Kingston 1925)

- (Ed) *Lady Nugent's Journal* (London 1939)

Davies F J 'The Expedition Against the Jebus' *USM* (1892)

Davis R P M *The History of the Sierra Leone Battalion of the Royal West African Frontier Force* (Freetown 1932)

Davy J *The West Indies Before and Since Slave Emancipation* (London 1854)

Day C W *Five Years' Residence in the West Indies* (2 vols London 1852)

Duffy M *Soldiers, Sugar and Seapower (Oxford 1987)*

Ekeko A E 'British Defence Policy in Western Africa 1878-1914' *unpublished PhD Thesis, Aberdeen University* (1976)

Ellis A B *The History of the First West India Regiment* (London 1885)

- *A History of the Gold Coast of West Africa* (London 1893)

Farmer J S *The Regimental Records of the British Army* (London 1901)

Farewell B *The Great War in Africa 1914-1918* (Harmondsworth 1987)

Featherstone D Captain *Carey's Blunder: The Death of the Prince Imperial* (London 1973)

Finlayson W F *The History of the Jamaica Case* (London 1869)
Forrest A S and Henderson J *Jamaica* (London 1906)
Fortescue J W *A History of the British Army* (13 vols London 1899-1930)
Freestone B *The Horsemen from Beyond* (London 1981)
Froude J A *The English in the West Indies* (London 1888)
Fryer P *Staying Power: The History of Black People in Britain* (London 1984)
Fyfe C *A History of Sierra Leone* (London 1962)
Gad H *"The Killing Time": The Morant Bay Rebellion in Jamaica* (Basingstoke 1994)
Gardner W J *A History of Jamaica* (London 1873)
Gibbs A R *British Honduras: An Historical and Descriptive Account of the Colony from its Settlement, 1670* (London 1883)
Gore A A *A Contribution to the Medical History of our West African Campaigns* (London 1876)
Gorges E H *The Great War in West Africa* (London 1930)
Goveia E V *Slave Society in the British Leeward Islands at the end of the Eighteenth Century* (New Haven & London 1965)
Graham J J (Ed) *Memoir of General Graham* (Edinburgh 1862)
Gray J M *A History of the Gambia* (Cambridge 1940)
Hall D *Free Jamaica: 1838-1865: An Economic History* (Aylesbury 1986)
Hallows I S *Regiments and Corps of the British Army* (London 1991)
Hamshere C *The British in the Caribbean* (London 1972)
Harfield A (Ed) *The Life and Times of a Victorian Officer* (Wincanton 1986)
Hayward J (Ed) *Out of Slavery, Abolition and After* (London 1985)
Haywood A and Clarke F A S *The History of the Royal West African Frontier Force* (Aldershot 1964)
Heneker W C G *Bush Warfare* (London 1907)
Henty G A *The March to Coomassie* (London 1874)
Hordern C *History of the Great War: Military Opertions, East Africa, August 1914 - September 1916* (London 1941)
Ijagbemi A 'The Yoni Expedition of 1887: A Study of British Imperial Expansion in Sierra Leone', *JHSN* VII (1974)
Ingham J M *Defence not Defiance: A History of the Bermuda Volunteer Rifle Corps* (Hamilton c. 1992)
Johnson H *The Bahamas in Slavery and Freedom* (Kingston & London 1991)
Joseph E L *A History of Trinidad* (reprint London 1970)
Kiernan V G *European Empires from Conquest to Collapse 1815-1960* (London 1982)
Killingray D 'The Idea of a British Imperial African Army' *JAH* 20 (1979)
- 'Race and Rank in the British Army in the Twentieth Century' *ERS* 10 (1987)
Kingsley C *At Last: A Christmas in the West Indies* (New York 1900)
Laurence K O 'The Settlement of Free Negroes in Trinidad Before

Emancipation' *CQ* 9 (1963)
Leslie N B *The Succession of Colonels of the British Army from 1660 to the Present Day* (London 1974)
Loscombe A R *The 1st West India Regiment: A Brief Historical Sketch* (London c. 1905)
Lotz R and Pegg I (Eds) *Under the Imperial Carpet: Essays in Black History 1780-1950* (Crawley 1986)
Lucas C *The Empire at War* (5 vols London 1921-1926)
MacDermot T H 'A Unique Regiment (West India Regiment)' *RCIJ* 14 (1923)
McInnes I and Fraser M *Ashanti 1895-96: A Roll of British and West Indian Recipients of the Ashanti Star* (Chippenham 1987)
McIntyre W D *The Imperial Frontier in the Tropics 1865-75* (London 1967)
Magor R B *African General Service Medals* (Printed Calcutta n.d.)
Marrion R J 'The West India Regiment' *MM* (June - September 1987)
Mbaeyi P M 'The Barra-British War of 1831: A Reconsideration of its origins and importance' *JHSN* III (1967)
- *British Military and Naval Forces in West African History 1807-1874* (Lagos 1978)
Millette J *Society and Politics in Colonial Trinidad* (Curepe and London 1985)
Moberly F J *History of the Great War: Military Operations in Togoland and the Cameroons 1914-1916* (London 1931)
Morgan C B 'The Rising in Sierra Leone' *USM* (1898)
Musgrave G C *To Kumassi with Scott* (London 1896)
Newbury C W *British Policy Towards West Africa: Select Documents 1786-1874* (Oxford 1965)
Newland C H 'The Sofa Invasion of Sierre Leone' *SLS* XIX (1933)
Norman C B *Battle Honours of the British Army* (London 1911)
O'Connor L S 'On Military Defences and Expenditure of the West Indies' *USM* (1851)
Olivier Lord *The Myth of Governor Eyre* (London 1933)
Orr G M 'The Origin of the West India Regiment' *RUSI* 72 (1927)
Owen P J 'The Defence of Orange Walk' *BAR* 110 (August 1992)
Parliamentary Papers 1812 *Papers relating to a recruiting depot on the coast of Africa for the West India Regiments*
- 1821 *Negroes: copies of the Several Returns Annually made by the Collectors of the Customs, in the Several West Indian Islands*
- 1899 *Report by Her Majesty's Commissioner and correspondence on the subject of Insurrection in the Sierre Leone Protectorate 1898*
Peterson J *Province of Freedom: A History of Sierra Leone 1787-1870* (London 1969)
Pinckard G *Notes on the West Indies; written during the Expedition under the command of the late General Sir Ralph Abercromby* (3 vols London 1806)

Poole T E *Life, Scenery and Customs in Sierra Leone and the Gambia* (2 vols London 1850)
Pyle H 'Jamaica, New and Old' *HNMM* 477 (1890)
Ramsay B D W *Rough Recollections of Military Service and Society* (2 vols Edinburgh 1882)
Rankin F H *The White Man's Grave: A Visit to Sierra Leone in 1834* (2 vols London 1836)
Ricketts [H J] *Narrative of the Ashantee War* (London 1831)
Riviere P *Absent-minded Imperialism* (London 1995)
Shaw A G L *Sir George Arthur, Bart, 1784-1854* (Melbourne 1980)
Shepherd C *An Historical Account of the Island of St Vincent* (London 1831)
Southey T *Chronological History of the West Indies* (3 vols London 1827)
Stanley H M *Coomassie: The Story of the Campaign in Africa 1873-4* (London 1896)
Stephens J L *Incidents of Travel in Central America, Chiapas and Yucatan* (2 vols London 1842)
Stewart J *A View of the past and present State of the Island of Jamaica* (Edinburgh 1823)
Stewart J 'Extracts from a diary written on active service' *SLS* XVII (1932)
Stuart A R *Precis of Information Concerning the Colony and Protectorate of Sierra Leone* (London 1901)
Surtees W *Twenty-Five Years in the Rifle Brigade* (Edinburgh 1833)
Thompson B E and Gero A F 'West India Regiments (Dress Uniforms) circa 1870-1900' *MCH* XXXIII (1981)
Thompson L *An Autobiography* (Crawley 1985)
Tylden G 'The West India Regiments 1795-1927 & from 1958' *JSAHR* XL (1962)
Ukpabi S C 'The Origins of the West African Frontier Force' *JHSN* III (1966)
- 'The Gambia Expedition of 1901' *BIFAN* XXXIII (1971)
- 'West Africa and Europe in Military Confrontation' *JHSN* VI (1971)
- 'West Indian Troops and the Defence of British West Africa in the Nineteenth Century' *ASR* XVII (1974)
- 'Recruiting for the British Colonial Forces in West Africa in the Nineteenth Century' *JWAS* (July 1974)
- *The Origins of the Nigerian Army* (Zaria 1987)
Wade S O D 'The South Carolina Regiment?' *JSAHR* 289 (1994)
Walker R W *Recipients of the Distinguished Conduct Medal 1914-1920* (Birmingham 1981)
Wallis C B *The Advance of our West African Empire* (London 1903)
Ward W E F *A History of Ghana* (London 1958)
- *The Royal Navy and the Slavers* (London 1969)
Warren R A 'Zouave Uniforms of the West India Regiments' *MCH* XXXIV (1982)
Willcocks J *From Kabul to Kumasi: Twenty Four Years of Soldiering and Sport* (London 1904)
Wyvill R A *A Sketch of the Military Life of Richard Augustus Wyvll* (London 1820)

INDEX

Countries are indexed under the name by which they were known at the time, with references to alternative names. Ranks and titles are those held at the date of the main reference, and are not necessarily the highest achieved or awarded.

OTHER TITLES BY HANSIB

ST LUCIA - Simply Beautiful
Voted 'Best Honeymoon Destination' in 1995 and 'Best Wedding Destination' in 1996, St Lucia has become a popular choice for newlyweds throughout the world. With its serene beaches, dramatic waterfalls and lush mountain rainforests, this beautiful Caribbean island is a sight to behold. Illustrated using more than 300 colour photographs, this is the first book to highlight the historic and contemporary aspects of this tropical paradise.
£25.00 Hardback, 320pp, colour
976 8163 07 0
November 1997

BARBADOS - Just Beyond Your Imagination
As one of the world's leading tourist destinations, many visitors consider that Barbados is the Caribbean. Its natural beauty and stunning beaches, coupled with the warmth and friendliness of its people, make it a first class and popular choice throughout the year. Illustrated with more than 280 colour photographs, this book evokes the spirit of the country both past and present.
£25.00 Hardback, 320pp, colour
1 870518 54 3

INDIA - A Wealth of Diversity
It is the same size as Europe and is the world's largest democracy. It is home to 960 million people and more than 1600 languages. It boasts the sixth largest economy in the world and produces more movies every year than any other nation. It experiences every conceivable climate, every type of landscape and is rich in most of the world's natural resources. India. It is rich, it is spectacular, it is diverse.
Using more than 230 colour photographs, this book unlocks the door to a magical nation. Experience the diversity for yourself.
£29.99 Hardback, 352pp, colour
1 870518 61 6

UGANDA - Africa's Secret Paradise
From snow-capped mountains to lush rain forests; vast national parks to spectacular lakes and rivers - including the mystical source of the Nile - Uganda is, truly, one of Africa's best kept secrets. As well as uncovering the historic and cultural treasures of a relatively untapped nation, this book presents a vivid picture of modern Uganda as it moves into the 21st century. Commissioned by the President of the Republic of Uganda, this publication includes over 300 colour photographs which feature many aspects of daily life in addition to the natural splendours of this ancient civilisation.
£25.00 Hardback, 320pp, colour
1 870 518 66 7
Spring 1998

JAMAICA - Absolutely
As the third largest Caribbean island, Jamaica accounts for nearly half of the region's English-speaking population. This book takes a close look at a nation born out of 300 years of colonial rule and highlights its contribution to the rest of the world in areas such as music, religion, cuisine, literature and lifestyle. With the help of more than 300 colour photographs, every aspect of Jamaican life is featured. From the tranquil waters of Montego Bay to the hurly-burly of Spanish Town, this vibrant, island nation should not to be missed.
£25.00 Hardback, 320pp, colour
976 8163 06 02
Spring 1998

GRENADA - Spice Island of the Caribbean
For the first time ever, a comprehensive study of this three-island state (Grenada, Carriacou and Petit Martinique) from past to present. More than 260 colour photographs depict today's Grenada - a flourishing, independent nation born out of French and British colonial rule. Appropriately nicknamed 'Spice Island of the Caribbean', Grenada produces one third of the world's nutmeg.
£25.00 Hardback, 304pp, colour
1 870518 29 2

ANTIGUA AND BARBUDA - A Little Bit of Paradise
A spectacular book - with more than 650 colour photographs - capturing the essence of this renowned twin-island nation. Highlighting the past and present of one of the world's most exclusive tourist destinations, this publication is a must for historian and hedonist alike.
£25.00 Hardback, 304pp, colour
1 870518 53 5

DOMINICA - Nature Island of the Caribbean
From rugged volcanic peaks to stunning rainforests, Dominica's natural beauty and wildlife is unrivalled anywhere in the Caribbean. With more than 350 colour

photographs, this book reveals the unique splendour of this emerald isle.
£19.95 Hardback, 320pp, colour
1 870518 17 9

NAOROJI: The First Asian MP
A biography of Dadabhai Naoroji - Indian Patriot and British Liberal
Omar Ralph
Known as the 'Grand Old Man of India', Dadabhai Naoroji became Britain's first non-European Member of Parliament. Berated by the then Prime Minister, Lord Salisbury, as unelectable on account of his being a 'black man', Naoroji proved his foremost critic wrong by being elected to the London seat of Central Finsbury in 1892.
£11.95 Paperback, 208pp, illustrated
976 8163 05 4

THE GREAT MARCUS GARVEY
Liz Mackie
One of the towering figures of the 20th Century, Marcus Garvey devoted his entire life to the political and economic emancipation of Africans throughout the world. This colossal undertaking laid the foundations of black consciousness, black power and the evolution of Pan-Africanism on a global scale.
£5.95 Paperback, 160pp
1 870518 50 0

WOMEN OF SUBSTANCE
Profiles of Asian women in the UK
Pushpinder Chowdhry
More than 200 entries are included in this celebration of the achievements of Asian women in the UK. From trades union activists to business women, the sciences to the arts, this publication reveals the ever-changing roles of Asian women.
£10.95 Paperback, 168pp, illustrated
1 870518 56 X
Published in association with Asian Women in Publishing

PRIDE OF BLACK BRITISH WOMEN
Deborah King
A collection of individual profiles featuring successful black women in Britain. Entries include the famous and the not-so-famous.
£5.95 Paperback, 80pp, illustrated
1 870518 34 9

A NEW SYSTEM OF SLAVERY
The Export of Indian Labour Overseas 1830-1920
Hugh Tinker
Originally published in 1974, this book was the first comprehensive study of a hitherto neglected migration - the export of Indians to supply labour needs on sugar, coffee, tea and rubber plantations in Mauritius, South and East Africa, the Caribbean, Guyana, Sri Lanka, Malaysia and Fiji. This practice followed the legal ending of slavery, but Professor Tinker shows how the two systems had much in common.
£11.99 Paperback, 448pp
1 870518 18 7

THE OTHER MIDDLE PASSAGE
Journal of a Voyage from Calcutta to Trinidad, 1858
Extracts from the journal of Captain and Mrs Swinton of the 'Salsette', a ship bound for the Caribbean and carrying Indian indentured labourers. The diary of this horrific, 108-day journey, evokes the stark terror that overshadowed the entire voyage. Although not slavery by name, the effect of the indentured labour movement on the lives of these migrants was the same.
£3.95 Paperback, 64pp, illustrated
1 870518 28 4

LEST WE FORGET
The Experiences of World War II Westindian Ex-Service Personnel
Robert N Murray
Few people know of the significant participation of Westindian men and women during the Second World War. Their stories are told - largely through oral histories and personal recollections - from arrival during the war effort, to subsequent settlement of a substantial number after the war.
£11.95 Paperback, 192pp, 8pp photographs
1 870518 52 7

RASTA AND RESISTANCE
From Marcus Garvey to Walter Rodney
Horace Campbell
Rastafarianism is not, as some of its detractors say, a fad of intellectual dilettantes, but a well thought out and coherent philosophy of ideas and actions to bring about fundamental changes in the condition of the oppressed. This book is both a record of the resistance to tyranny and a refreshing critique and analysis of the imperialist conspiracy to perpetuate its dominance by any and all means necessary.
£9.95 Paperback, 252pp
0 9506664 7 5

PROSPERO'S RETURN?
Historical Essays on Race, Culture and British Society
Paul B Rich
In this wide-ranging collection of essays, Rich

explores the nature and meaning of race and racism in British society and the nature of British and English national identity. Using political, social and cultural sources, he shows that many of the contemporary issues surrounding the position of black minorities in British society have a long and complex history.
£8.95 Paperback, 216pp
1 870518 40 3

A READER'S GUIDE TO WESTINDIAN AND BLACK BRITISH LITERATURE
David Dabydeen and
Nana Wilson-Tagoe
Two experts in this specialist area, chart the highly productive and very rewarding literary terrain of the Westindies and black Britain. This title provides an excellent introduction to an important part of world literature, its history and development, and recommendations of suitable texts for further reading.
£8.95 Paperback, 192pp
1 870518 35 7
Published in association with the University of Warwick Centre for Caribbean Studies

INDIA IN THE CARIBBEAN
Edited by David Dabydeen and Brinsley Samaroo
A collection of enlightening essays, poems and political and historical analysis celebrating the Indian presence in the Caribbean. Some of the leading Indo-Caribbean scholars and writers provide an insight into the cultural, social and economic impact since the Indian arrival in the early 19th century.
£8.95 Paperback, 328pp
1 870518 00 4
£11.95 Hardback, 328pp
1 870518 05 5

THE WEB OF TRADITION
Uses of Allusion in V S Naipaul's Fiction
John Thieme
Few will deny that V S Naipaul is one of the most stylish, elegant and thought-provoking essayists of the 20th century, and a novelist of world class. Thieme explores classics such as 'In a Free State' and 'A House for Mr Biswas' in the context of the Western literary canon, while at the same time revealing their 'essential Indianness'.
£6.95 Paperback, 224pp
1 870518 30 6

THE IDEOLOGY OF RACISM
Samuel Kennedy Yeboah
A masterly study of the peoples of the African Diaspora with a long overdue reminder of their gigantic, but unrecognised, contribution to art, science and technology. This is a searing analytical account of the ideology of Western racism and its horrific consequences for Africa and the Diaspora.
£9.95 Paperback, 320pp
1 870518 07 1

THE WEST ON TRIAL
My Fight for Guyana's Freedom
Cheddi Jagan
First published in 1966, this re-printed title is a moving, personal account of the struggle against imperialism by one of the leading political figures in the Caribbean. The late Dr Jagan passionately weaves together his own life-story with that of his people's battle for independence and freedom in an environment dictated by race and class factors, and colonial attitudes.
£9.95 Paperback, 496pp
976 8163 08 9

FORBIDDEN FREEDOM
The Story of British Guiana
Cheddi Jagan
The name of Cheddi Jagan was synonymous with anti-imperialist struggle. But his work did not end with the expulsion of the British Occupation, it was the beginning of another struggle against the most vicious neo-colonialism the Third World has ever seen. This noble statesman became his country's first ever genuinely patriotic President in a world asphyxiated by corruption, greed and sleaze.
£4.95 Paperback, 128pp (Second edition)
1 870518 23 3
£5.95 Paperback, 144pp (Third Edition)
1 870518 37 3

CHEDDI JAGAN Selected Speeches
1992-1994
One of the world's most outstanding leaders, the words of Guyana's President, Dr Cheddi Jagan, bears witness to his vision, integrity and concern for the potential as well as the plight of the Guyanese people.
£6.95 Paperback, 144pp
1 870518 49 7

PASSION AND EXILE
Frank Birbalsingh
The English-speaking Caribbean has produced a quantity and quality of literature that is renowned throughout the world. Birbalsingh gets to the heart of the literary Caribbean in an accomplished and riveting work.
£7.95 Paperback, 192pp
1 870518 16 0

INSEPARABLE HUMANITY
An Anthology of Reflections of Shridath S Ramphal
Former Commonwealth Secretary-General, Shridath Ramphal reflects on his own world view with eloquence and rationality. A man of action, his deeply moral approach to world politics made him an influential player in the field of human rights on the international stage.
£14.95 Hardback, 424pp, 16pp photographs
1 870518 14 4

BENEVOLENT NEUTRALITY
Indian Government Policy and Labour Migration to British Guiana 1854-1884
Basdeo Mangru
This ground-breaking study examines the issue of indentured labour from India and how the new arrivals adapted to life in a strange and sometimes hostile environment.
£12.95 Hardback, 272pp
1 870518 10 1

SPEECHES BY ERROL BARROW
Edited by Yussuff Haniff
The late Errol Barrow was one of the most revered statesman of the Caribbean. He was a remarkable Caribbean patriot, whose speeches not only gave an insight into the evolution of modern Barbados under his prime ministership, but also his vision of a united and politically and economically sovereign Caribbean.
£10.95 Hardback, 200pp
1 870518 70 5

THE NORMAN MANLEY MEMORIAL LECTURES 1984 - 1995
Caribbean and world issues are addressed in this collection of lectures presented by such noted world figures as Sir Shridath Ramphal, The Rt Hon Tony Benn MP and The Rt Hon Michael Manley.
£6.99 Paperback, 96pp
976 8163 00 3

CORNERED TIGERS A History of Pakistan's Test Cricket
Adam Licudi with Wasim Raja
The first comprehensive account of the history of Pakistani Test Cricket from its beginnings in 1952 up to the 1996 season. This unparalleled collection of profiles includes every Test player, including the first Test captain, Abdul Hafeez Kardar, in addition to the giants of the nineties, Wasim Akram and Waqar Younis. It pays tribute to other 'Tigers' such as Imran Khan and Javed Miandad, in a meticulous chronicle of one of the great cricketing nations.
Includes full scorecards from every Pakistan Test Match up to August 1996, and all Test and One-Day Averages for every player.
£16.95 Paperback, 304pp, 16pp colour
1 870518 31 4

THE RISE OF WESTINDIAN CRICKET
From Colony to Nation
Frank Birbalsingh
Historical reflection and reminiscence of the events, issues, and personalities that were central to the evolution of Westindian cricket from the 1920s to the 1960s. This rich blend of match descriptions, biographies, book reviews, commentary and analysis of the cricket administration and public response to the game pays fitting tribute to the Westindies' dominance on the world stage.
£12.95 Paperback, 288pp, illustrated
1 870518 47 0

100 GREAT WESTINDIAN TEST CRICKETERS
Bridgette Lawrence with Reg Scarlett
Foreword by Viv Richards
Westindian Test cricket is traced from its 1928 debut at Lords to the unmatched triumphs of the 1980s. This unique publication is more than a record of cricket supremacy, it is also a human document, vividly recapturing some of the great moments both on and off the field. Illustrated with many rare and dramatic photographs, this superb book is a must for all cricket-lovers.
£14.95 Hardback, 232pp, illustrated
1 870518 65 9

INDO-WESTINDIAN CRICKET
Frank Birbalsingh and Clem Shiwcharan
Much is written about the massive achievements of Westindian cricketers of African background, but the availability of literature on some of the equally powerful cricketers of Indian origin is somewhat thin on the ground.
This book serves to redress the balance by featuring the genius of such Titans as Kallicharan, Kanhai and Ramadhin, and places the Indo-Caribbean role in Westindian cricket in the political and cultural context.
£7.95 Hardback, 136pp
1 870518 20 9